My Backyard Jungle

My
Backyard

James Barilla

Jungle

The Adventures of an

Urban Wildlife Lover

Who Turned His Yard into

Habitat and Learned to

Live with It

Yale UNIVERSITY PRESS
New Haven & London

Published with assistance from the foundation established in memory of
Philip Hamilton McMillan of the Class of 1894, Yale College.

Yale University Press books may be purchased in quantity for
educational, business, or promotional use. For information, please e-mail
sales.press@yale.edu (US office) or sales@yaleup.co.uk (UK office).

Designed by James J. Johnson.
Set in type by Integrated Publishing Solutions.
Line woodcut art courtesy of The Florida Center for
Instructional Technology; http://etc.usf.edu/clipart.
Printed in the United States of America.

The Library of Congress has cataloged the hardcover edition as follows:

Barilla, James, 1967–
My backyard jungle : the adventures of an urban wildlife lover who turned
his yard into habitat and learned to live with it / James Barilla.
pages cm
Includes bibliographical references and index.
ISBN 978-0-300-18401-3 (clothbound : alk. paper) 1. Urban ecology
(Biology) 2. Habitat (Ecology) 3. Animals and civilization. I. Title.
QH541.5.C6B37 2013
577.5'6—dc23   2012040298

ISBN 978-0-300-20566-4 (pbk.)

A catalogue record for this book is available from the British Library.

10 9 8 7 6 5 4 3 2 1

To Nicola, Brook, and Beatrice,
my fellow backyard enthusiasts

Contents

Acknowledgments

This book could not have been written without the generosity, indulgence, knowledge, and inspiration of many people, only some of whom appear in the book. I am deeply grateful to all who shared their time and stories with me. In a select instance or two, the exact circumstances and identity of some sources have been altered to preserve anonymity. The Provost's Office at the University of South Carolina provided essential support for completing much of the requisite travel. I am also grateful for the support of my colleagues at the University of South Carolina, who listened patiently to my incessant chattering about squirrels and monkeys and contributed many stories of their own. In Delhi, Ashwani Bazaz provided a welcome sanctuary from the urban bustle at the aptly named *Tree of Life* and helped immensely with the logistics of my explorations. J. P. Sharma at *Wild Frontiers* was also instrumental in helping me find my way through the city. In Brazil, Jeri Pollack, Yara

Acknowledgments

Castro Roberts, and Esther Ribeiro made tracking down Niteroi's tamarins possible, while Vinicius Goulart, Aryanne Clyvia, Leonardo Oliveira, and Luis Paulo Ferraz all helped shape my understanding of the complexity of Brazil's environment. At Yale University Press, Jean Thomson Black's enthusiasm for the project was indispensable. Early on, she helped clarify my thinking about the structure of the book and how these different strands of narrative could all fit together. I truly appreciated the help of Laura Jones Dooley, who skillfully polished my prose and suggested ways to tame some of the more convoluted passages. My sincerest appreciation goes to my agent, Wendy Strothman, and her assistant, Lauren MacLeod, who served as expert guides from the earliest stages of the publication process. And finally, my enormous thanks to my family, who with great good humor, curiosity, and forbearance allowed this experiment to take place in their backyard.

My Backyard Jungle

1

Certified

FACT: Twenty-two percent of endangered plant species are found in large metropolitan areas in the United States. Sixty-seven federally listed species are found in the San Francisco Bay area, fifteen around New York City.

This story starts with a move. Actually, yet another move, from the woodsy shores of Lake Michigan to the capital city of South Carolina. This after a sizable sojourn in the redwood country of Northern California and, before that, a stint of several winters in Vermont. My wife, Nicola, is English, and we began our connubial life as renters in a damp Yorkshire city. We've always been renters. Our new place, a brick house in a leafy neighborhood of Columbia, South Carolina, is the first place with our names on the deed, a fact that has a certain heft to it, as if this document comes not with strings attached but with roots, the delicate white tendrils that sprout from a cutting in a windowsill jar, waiting to take hold.

Rentals always have a temporary air about them, a sense that there's no point in planting anything out back because you won't be around to see it bloom. This house feels different. We could create something here. And I have a long list of things I want to create. I want to taste the fruit of a garden I had tended—that's one fantasy, creating a little patch of pastoral bliss back there. I dream of creating habitat for wildlife out there, too, a miniature wilderness in our own backyard. I want our yard to be the kind of place where my kids can catch grasshoppers by day and fireflies at night, where they can dig up potatoes and pick strawberries. The yard I imagine will be interesting and alive.

What I really want, I suppose, is to feel as if I have some small way of pushing back the tide of bad news that seems to arrive every day: the menace of a changing climate, bats dropping dead in their caves, frogs dying, coral reefs disappearing. I've got two little kids—I'm not interested in apocalypse. I want a different story. I want to learn how to coexist with other species, to be able to look out the window and see at least the glimmer of an alternative to extinction. In the parlance of those who study this kind of thing, I have become a stakeholder.[1]

After the moving truck departs from the curb, leaving us with two children under the age of three and boxes stacked to the ceiling in every room, the extent of our dislocation begins to sink in. You can imagine the scene: two brand-new homeowners standing in the front lawn with the kids clamped tight, looking around as if for the first time. They take in the sidewalk that looks like pita bread baking in the noonday sun. They see a palm tree slouching in the distance, hear the cicada trill rising to a fiendish crescendo overhead. You can see them thinking, *Where on earth are we? What on earth have we done?*

Maybe that's what inspires me to certify our backyard as wildlife habitat: the idea that creating habitat can help us feel at home, as if we belong in this ecological community about which we know so little. Creating habitat in the backyard means learning where wildlife likes to live and forage, which in turn means understanding the climate, the soil, the interplay of sun and shade. I'm thinking there will be books to read and stones to turn over and holes to dig, plants to nurture and uproot, a mix of field research, grunt work, and serendipity. It sounds like the kind of project I've been hankering after for years.

There's more to the appeal of *certifying* the yard than learning alone, however. You can create all the habitat you want in your yard, but only certification comes with a laminated aluminum sign. It's about a foot tall—big enough to be seen and read from the sidewalk. And it looks official, like the kind you'd find at the gates of a nature preserve. As the National Wildlife Federation's website describes it, "This easy-to-read sign will help neighbors (and wildlife!) easily recognize your yard as wildlife-friendly."[2] That's exactly what we want: recognition. We want to be recognized as friendly folk. And we certainly don't want people to mistakenly identify us as the new people from out of town who never mow the lawn. It's wildlife habitat, not laziness! The sign will let everyone know we want to be good neighbors—not just with the people next door but with the local fauna, too.

Okay, so as a new homeowner maybe I'm a tad naive. It comes with the territory.

To get the sign, you have to have some knowledge about what's going on outside your house, but unlike some of the other environmental certification processes you might undertake for your dwelling, like trying to achieve a gold or platinum rating according to the LEED (Leadership in Energy and Environmental Design) ratings system, the bar isn't *that* high. To certify your house according to LEED requirements, you need a professional to inspect it and take you through multiple multilayered checklists. Backyard certification, on the other hand, is designed to encourage do-it-yourself newbies like me. You answer questions online, checking a minimum number of items off a list. It's a bit like filling out a census form, only easier. Do you have at least two kinds of food sources out back? Check. Do you have at least one water source, like a birdbath? Check. Places to find cover? Check. Places to raise young? Check. Over a hundred and fifty thousand people have passed the test since the National Wildlife Federation (NWF) began offering it in the mid-1970s, and their numbers have accelerated since the checklist went online in 2005, according to David

Mizejewski, who ran the program for seven years and hosted a backyard habitat show on *Animal Planet* from 2005 to 2008.

Then comes a series of questions about sustainable gardening practices, which I find more challenging to answer. The first asks which techniques I use to help conserve resources—do I have a "riparian buffer" near a waterway, for example, or a rain garden? No, and no. I have a wide swath of dried-up dead grass, which probably doesn't make the grade as "xeriscaping." Fortunately, "Limit water use" and "Use mulch" are two of the possible responses here, so I scrape by.

One of my other options here isn't so much technically challenging as it is unsettling. If I don't have enough soil and water conservation going on, and I'm not doing enough in the composting department, I can still opt to certify my wildlife habitat by "Controlling Invasive Species." I might use native plants or reduce the size of my lawn. Or I can pass the test by removing nonnative plants and animals—killing things off, essentially.

I leave that part blank.

Unlike the LEED certification process or the certification process for an organic farm, nobody is coming to inspect the quality of your habitat. Pay up and you're done—it could take less than ten minutes to complete the process. But for a backyard greenhorn like me, living in an unfamiliar landscape, the questions about my yard are at first unanswerable and then profound. Do we actually make habitat or just put away the tools and leave the yard alone? Should we restrict the guest list to native species or try to optimize diversity by bringing in as many species as we can? What if the new residents don't behave like model citizens? What if they sting or bite?

It could take months or even years to answer these questions. The backyard, it turns out, is a microcosm of all our fantasies and fears, all the rewards and tribulations of life with other species.

Let me begin with an inventory. That's where I begin as summer turns to fall, by thinking about what the before photo is going to look like in the before-and-after comparison of our yard. When it comes to faces, the before photo is supposed to look lumpy and haggard, pockmarked, worse-for-wear. That's a pretty good approximation of the appearance of our yard. After all, the previous owners appear to have used it as a parking lot for extra cars, boats, and rolling garbage bins. Rather than mow the encroaching weeds, they blasted the edges of the lawn with herbicide, leaving a broad swath of shriveled ivy tendrils around the perimeter of the property. Our tenure here begins with last year's exfoliated leaves, big blotches of bare dirt, and the wispy stubble of unwatered grass, an ugly portrait indeed.

But wildlife, as it turns out, doesn't give a hoot about our aesthetics. They're not going to turn up their noses because the lawn isn't manicured or the bushes haven't been clipped or the leaves haven't been blown into a tidy pile. In fact, they like it when things are unkempt and neglected—that's *habitat* as far as they're concerned.[3] Once I start looking closely at the ugliness, what I see is all kinds of life.

We have lots of what are known as urban adapters, creatures that can live with us but can also live in the woods outside of town. We have barred owls ululating in pairs outside the bedroom window at night; they like to perch in the boughs of a hackberry snag in our front yard and startle us with their eerie cries. We have Cooper's hawks discarding their mockingbird drumsticks on the driveway under a trio of tall pines. We have skinks, both the adults whose orange heads look like smashed pumpkins and the youngsters with glowing blue ribbons of tail, and skinny-as-a-twig anoles and nocturnal toads and even legless lizards, which I discovered when I inadvertently dug one up by the side of the house while making space for a vegetable garden. We have shrews and cottontails, and I've seen a single small bat fluttering through the canopy at dusk.

We have wrens, hummingbirds, cardinals, mockingbirds, juncos, titmice, chickadees, brown thrashers, and the occasional sudden seething mob of waxwings. Warblers and flycatchers glean the boughs on their southern migration. Mourning doves tiptoe across the brick patio. We have several kinds of woodpecker and the occasional nuthatch and creeper. We have blue jays. Turkey vultures vector overhead, and a clan of Mississippi kites likes to perch on the highest treetops after a thunderstorm and stretch out their platinum wings to dry—they look like the hood ornaments of expensive sedans. We've seen a red-tailed hawk pluck a squirrel from a branch in the park.

We have monarchs and sulfurs and swallowtails and gulf fritillaries and sphinx moths and azalea caterpillar moths, which are really just a few pretty faces in the invertebrate crowd. We have multitudes of "palmetto bugs," also known as cockroaches, which are gigantic but fortunately seem to prefer the outdoors. At night, if you shine a headlamp across the yard, a galaxy of tiny stars glitters back—the eyes of wolf spiders on the prowl.

And we have squirrels. Lots and lots of squirrels.

We do not have deer or coyotes as far as I know, and I have not had visual confirmation of a rat or a raccoon or a skunk or a possum. We've seen no venomous snakes, although the big-box home improvement store does stock an impressive array of snake repellents. Strangely enough, I have yet to see a mouse or a vole, never found their dot matrix signature on the stovetop in the morning. We do have termites that will perforate the soil under a log. No chiggers, no ticks, but swarms of tiny mosquitoes that breed in "keyholes," fetid pools of rainwater high up in the trees. We do not have gray foxes, although I saw one trotting into a yard on the other side of a busy road one evening. There's a seven-acre arboretum over there, which is where the fox was headed. I'm told she died, along with her litter of kits, of distemper. I haven't seen any more foxes.

I know there are more critters out there, especially when it comes to invertebrates. There's more coming and going and sprouting and buzzing around our plot than I'd ever be able to name. To be honest, as this list accumulates over the first few months of our occupancy it becomes a little intimidating, and surprising, too, given that I'd been expecting something about as rich in biodiversity as the inside of a volcano. Reading journal articles about urbanization is like watching a bulldozer belch smoke: most warn that cities are basically wastelands where the life of the planet has been sawed down, plowed up, and hauled away in a dumpster, leaving only a handful of unsavory survivors behind. "Urbanization is one of the leading causes of species extinction," declares the first line of an oft-cited article by Michael McKinney, professor of evolutionary biology and environmental science at the University of Tennessee, which may be true of new development but seems to run contrary to the richness I discover everywhere I look.[4] I find myself wondering how cities can be engines of death and despair, and yet be such rich and diverse habitat at the same time. Are we talking about the same cities? Are we talking about urbanization as it currently exists or as it could be? Might we find a different version of this story in the untapped potential of our own backyards?

In our neck of the woods, the damage was done at least

a generation ago. Our neighborhood has had eighty years to develop into an urban forest, and the habitat has come back vertically, rising up in colonnades and then sprawling out over our dwellings in a dense canopy of evergreen hardwoods and lofty pines. Our yard is bounded by a trio of massive oaks that qualify as "grand trees" under the city landscape ordinance, which protects all trees whose girth is greater than twenty-four inches at breast height. I'm no expert on southern oaks, but two of the surrounding giants appear to have the jagged leaves of red oak, and there's also what I'd guess is a sizable laurel oak. A live oak sprawls its almost horizontal limbs across the street, and what appears to be a water oak is pushing for daylight in the shadow of these giants. There's an understory, too, cherry laurel and privet and what is called cedar even though it looks like juniper to me, and even a variety of palm trees, a tropical flourish. Arboreal life moves through this system with electric speed, like a signal through the dendritic matter of the mind.

The laminated metal sign arrives in what would be the dead of winter up north. It's tidy and attractive, unlike the yard, which has suffered under the double whammy of extreme drought and my ignorance. How was I to know you had to water the grass every day down here? Why would you plant grass that needs constant watering in a hot zone like this? What's left looks like long-dead road kill, dried-up chunks of hide and gristle sitting in the sand of the borrow pit.

"This property provides the four basic habitat elements needed for wildlife to thrive," the sign proclaims, "food, water, cover and places to raise young." There's a decorative and yet somehow still authoritative emblem of a child facing a deer with a mountain silhouetted in the background, the official seal of the NWF. The white lettering at the top is big enough to provide a status update from the windows across the street. Seventy-five percent of people who certify order the sign, and the organization has recently added an array of custom options, including brass plaques.

I'm hesitant about putting mine up. When I was filling out the questions, it all seemed hypothetical. But putting up a sign is indeed a proclamation for other people. What am I trying to tell my neighbors? Am I saying, *Yes, my yard looks like crap, but so what? The birds like it that way?* Is this a statement about me or a not so subtle critique of what the neighbors are doing? In essence, by putting up the sign, I'm inviting people to look at the yard. I'm inviting their reaction and judgment.

Many of the people on our street are friendly and welcoming, but they have a different vision when it comes to yard care. We have ants in our yard, for example. They're not fire ants. They won't sting, even when I put them on my hand, but in late winter their small, sandy mounds erupt like pustules from cracks in the driveway. My neighbors hate that. They spread ant killer all over their yard. They sprinkle granules of preemergent weed killer on the lawn, too, and hit the survivors with liquid sprays. We won't be winning any neighborhood garden awards any time soon.

Part of me can't help but agree that a nice yard is a tidy extension of the house, an outdoor room that should be cleaned and decorated. I don't want unkempt weeds and slovenly shrubs out there any more than I want dirty dishes or balled-up socks on the living room floor.

The city of Columbia has rules about the height of your grass. If somebody complains, you'll get a knock on the door from a city inspector. First comes a warning—city code stipulates that your grass and "weeds" cannot exceed twelve inches in height. If you're not home when they knock, they'll stick a little day-glo green notice on your door, something to the effect of *Cut your grass . . . or else.* Failure to comply will result in a fine. The thing about dead grass, of course, is that it doesn't get any taller. In fact, with every passing month there's less of it to worry about. Can you get a ticket for dead grass and scabby patches of dirt? I don't really want to find out.

Give me some time, I want to tell everybody. *I'm just getting going here.* I said I was naive; I'm also impatient. Once I unwrap that sign it's as if someone has fired a starting gun. I'm dying to get going, to start planting, digging, chopping, raking, pruning—whatever it is, I want to get the job done and see results. More than anything I want to see results, and that's the fundamental problem with the desire to create habitat: human time frames and environmental time frames aren't really in sync. As soon as you start thinking about planting trees, you come to the melancholy realization that humans don't live very long. It's taken an entire human life span for the trees in our yard to become as big and complex as they are now. The people who planted them are probably no longer alive.

The first thing I learn: when it comes to creating habitat for wildlife, you have to take certain parameters as given. Even in the city we are stewards of the land, of the investment others made, the landscape they imagined for us. We couldn't duplicate the twin rows of majestic trees that line our street—not in our lifetimes. To lose them would be devastating. One of the first major decisions I have to make is about the dead hackberry looming over our roof. If I don't have it taken out, at some point one of the major branches is going to come down on top of our bedroom. But cutting it down alters the canvas dramatically—we have more sunshine in front now, more sun-stroked grass and fewer visits from the owls. I'm not sure I'd do the same again.

Even though we have to live with the habitat we inherited, however, the urban backyard also offers us a sizable measure of freedom. Our rows of grand trees are works of imagination that bear little resemblance to prehuman history. What was this place like before the developers came eighty years ago? You can find a clue in the undulating sandy soil to the northeast of us, in the "Sandhills" that used to be dunes along the shore of the prehistoric ocean. Once, when fires burned through regularly, old-growth longleaf pines dominated the canopy, although the understory was very diverse.[5] What you see growing there now, long after the big trees were cut and the fires suppressed, is a rolling shag carpet of stunted pines and oak scrub—nothing like the stately size and girth of our specimens, which benefit from the watering and fertilizing of our lawns and the way we limit competition around them. It's rich habitat up there in our canopy, but it's not a remnant or replica of the original landscape. It's unique to the urban environment.

Feel free to experiment. That's what this landscape says to me. Try to optimize the richness of what you already have here. Mix things up. Make the yard as diverse and interesting as possible. And try not to make it look so messy that the neighbors complain.

An unseasonable hint of spring is in the air when I pound a bamboo stake into the ground in our front yard and proclaim to all the joggers and dog walkers and neighborhood kids that this patch of ground is certified wildlife habitat. The experiment is under way.

Not long after I plant the sign, I'm riding my bike past the arboretum one warm sunny morning, and there in the middle of the road is something that looks a bit like a speed bump in need of a fresh coat of yellow paint. I slow down. Even from a distance, something about the shape says this is something unusual, not your typical urban citizen. When I get close I see that the dome is patterned in a kind of brown and ochre plaid, like an old wool scarf. A box turtle. I fear the worst—this street runs parallel to a four-lane route to campus, and students who are late for class sometimes use it as a shortcut around the stoplights. But miracle of miracles: the turtle is unscathed, and as I pick it up it hisses softly at me and raises the drawbridge of its front scute, which is angled like one of those ramps that moving trucks use to unload. I set down my book bag and stand there on the edge of someone's yard with the surprisingly hefty dome in my palm.

I don't know what to do with it. If I had to offer an example of an "urbanophobe," a creature that cannot abide urban life, the box turtle would come to mind. Because of suburban sprawl, they have disappeared from places where they were once common, and yet apparently a remnant population of at least one is holding on right here in the city.

They don't reach maturity until they're ten years old, and they can live for twenty-five years or more in the wild.[6] How old is this creature? Is it roaming in search of a mate? A place to lay eggs? It's early in the year for it to be out and about, I think. My first instinct is to take it home—this would make a fine addition to the backyard, a real showstopper. Anybody questions the validity of my sign and I'll just point to the turtle.

At the same time, I certainly don't want to get in the way of making more urban box turtles if that's where this creature was headed. These plodding reptiles may not look like migrants, but in fact they're known to follow set routes between the nooks and crevices where they hibernate and the sandy places where they breed. Take them out of their customary terrain, and they may never breed again. Of course, this one was pointed in the direction of the Piggly Wiggly parking lot, beyond which lies not procreation but almost certain death. The logic of roads is move fast or die. Turtles are built according to entirely different specifications: you can't carry a fortress around on your back and scuttle out of the way when you hear a car coming.

I began by painting a portrait of an urban idyll, but of course our neighborhood is full of threats, particularly for creatures that live on the ground and move slowly, the turtles and toads and snakes of the world that don't do well around spinning tires. Our street is essentially a dead end, but there's plenty of traffic in the vicinity. All of the greenery I've been rhapsodizing about is within a couple blocks of a four-lane road. It's a five-minute walk to the Piggly Wiggly in one direction and Bi-Lo in the other. There's a major intersection with an oil change place and a dry cleaner and a gas station and tattoo parlors and payday cash places, which you could probably see from our front yard if it wasn't for the trees. It's never dark down there. We hear sirens at all hours.

"Location, location, location" is as true of habitat as it is of commerce—nobody wants to live in a dangerous neighborhood, and many species are not going to live in my backyard no matter how enticing I make the relocation package. Which to some degree is fine with me. Do I really want to invite hungry deer into the vegetable garden or step outside with the kids to find a canid the size of a small wolf munching a cat in the driveway or, worse, hear the snuffling of a black bear getting cozy under the planks of the back deck? When I'm lying in bed with my eyes closed, watching my dream garden grow ever more wild, sure. Why not have a mini-Yellowstone back there? But when I'm outside in the actual yard . . . probably not.

I wind up placing the turtle between the bars of the arboretum's iron fence, nose facing away from the road. As I wait for it to poke out its head and make a move toward safety, two cars rumble past. The drivers see me with my bike on its side and my hands in my pockets. They slow down and look at me quizzically as they pass, wondering what this strangely stationary behavior is all about. Roads are for moving, not for sitting tight or basking in the sun. What's wrong with me? Am I hurt? It's a small dose of what it's like to be a turtle in the city.

2

Zoos Without Bars

FACT: The Christmas Bird Count has used citizen scientists to gather data on wintering bird populations for more than a century. Last year, sixty thousand volunteers participated in counts that spanned the continent. Volunteers also conduct the Breeding Bird Survey every spring, covering three thousand routes across the country.

Since the sign went in the ground, I've been spending a lot of time in the backyard, mostly with a shovel in hand as I try to turn a patch of turf into a vegetable patch. As a break from turning the soil, I've also been prying and pickaxing away the asphalt, trimming the parking for two cars down to one, gaining ground for habitat. But habitat for what kind of wildlife? Getting rid of tar is actually the easy part. The hard part is thinking about what comes next. Depending on the species I hope to attract, I could create a xeriscape with drought-loving nonnative cacti and leathery yucca baking in the sunshine or a rain garden where runoff puddles around water-loving iris.

But none of these alternatives have really sparked my imagination like the day my family and I spent at the Riverbanks Zoo in Columbia. We were sitting in one of the outdoor eating areas, listening to the booming voices of the siamangs, long-limbed gibbons from Indonesia that look a bit like shaggy trolls. The children were just getting started with their pizza when we spotted a black ribbon of something winding its way along the edge of the bamboo hedge. A long, long, scaly ribbon, with glittering black eyes and a darting tongue, making its way toward us.

No bars. No Plexiglas. No viewing area. In the middle of the zoo, outside the cage: the wild.

We stood up, rather abruptly, and backed away. The kids were exhilarated, wriggling into our arms and screeching. The snake, which I guessed was a black rat snake, although the possibility of venomous alternatives did cross my mind, slipped through the legs of our table and kept going, aware of us, it seemed, but unperturbed. It had its own business. And so did the rats, waiting to feast on the choice morsels my youngsters were scattering over the bricks. Our lives separate yet intertwined.

It occurred to me then that the categories of zoo animal and wild animal are somewhat arbitrary, imposed by us. It's possible that I could walk over to the reptile exhibit and see a rat snake coiled up on a branch under a heat lamp, waiting for someone to feed it a rat. Or I could see one living by its wits outside the cage, hunting rats on its own. Many zoos today manage their acres for the wild animals that inhabit them, and they also allow a surprising variety of creatures to "free-range" across the grounds, from peacocks to geese and even, at a handful of zoos, the small, endangered primates known as golden lion tamarins.[1]

These are very different experiences, for the animals certainly, and also for us. Cages, fences, and bars are all meant to protect us from one another, to preserve the idea that urban wildlife habitat is parks and yards and vacant lots while human habitat is something—and someplace—else. There are plenty of valid reasons for that separation, some obvious, like the incompatibility of top carnivores to the backyard lifestyle, and others less so, like the transmission of disease between wild animals and humans. Fewer deer in the neighborhood, for example, might mean fewer deer ticks carrying Lyme disease and a reduction in the twenty thousand cases of the illness reported each year. And yet, the more you immerse yourself in the landscape and try to imagine areas for wildlife to live, the more you begin to see the human world as other species might see it, as habitat. You start to fantasize about the possibilities.

Why a squirrel and not a squirrel monkey, I've wondered while wielding the pickax, particularly if that monkey is threatened with habitat loss in its original home? What are the limits of citizen-based conservation? By 2050, according to United Nations estimates, over 70 percent of the human population will live in cities, as over half the world does now. Our experience of wildlife will be primarily virtual unless we do something about the nature of the urban environment. I wonder how people in other corners of the world are dealing with this challenge. What can we learn from each other? How can we imagine these spaces so that we maximize their potential as habitat in an urban future?[2]

The longer I ponder these questions, the more I realize I'm going to have to get out of my own backyard. Thinking deeply about my own patch of habitat is one way to understand the challenge of coexistence, but staying home doesn't feel like I'm doing enough to understand what's really happening out there. There are cities whose inhabitants are decades, even centuries, ahead of me in the quest to find ways to coexist, and I suspect they have a lot to teach me about what's possible in my yard.

It's midwinter when I embark on my first voyage, driving sixteen hours on the freeway south to the city of Dania Beach, Florida, just down the coast from Fort Lauderdale. Monkeys inhabit the urban wild here. I've read the online messages; I've viewed the blurry cell phone footage. I've seen these simian figures loping along the top of a chain-link fence and bounding between parked cars, and I've spoken with a documentary filmmaker, Dale Minnich, who shot most of his footage of the monkeys in a motel parking lot. The city's human residents have come to accept these free-ranging primates in their midst. In fact, they've even passed laws intended to protect them.

My visit to the Sunshine State happens to coincide with a dip in the Gulf Stream. Normally this band of air currents undulates across the midriff of the continent, keeping arctic and tropic apart. But the current seems to have stalled and sagged south, which means that the icy breath of the Canadian prairie is funneling down the I-95 corridor and buffeting my rental car from behind, and frigid temperatures are settling all the way down to Key West. Not just a cold snap, but day after day of record-breaking temperatures. Below freezing in Miami at night, the forecasters are predicting, and mid-thirties during the day. On the news, the anchor teases us into the commercials: "Coming up after the break, rare snow in the forecast for Florida!"

This extended cold spells doom for the various industries that raise tropical species as crops. The citrus industry is bracing for heavy losses—workers are out spraying the fruit with water to create a protective coating of ice over the rind. Millions of tropical fish, stranded in outdoor raceways and pools, are dying. For wildlife, and in particular for the tropical stowaways and escapees that have been calling Florida home, it's also life or death, a test of their acclimatization. Iguanas, some of them six feet long, have been falling out of trees and landing belly up on suburban lawns, still alive but stiff with cold. How long can they survive in this torpor? Can the monkeys survive?

It's ten at night when I arrive at my hotel. I can see my breath. The coconut palms hang limp on their skinny necks; the bananas look like they're shuddering in the floodlights. Traffic lights blink through their palette, although headlights are few. Everything is hushed, expectant. I fall asleep to the adumbration of a cold rain pelting the window, thinking about how miserable it would be to wait for dawn out there.

When it comes to surviving extreme weather, the green monkey is one of the best prepared of all primates. Taken together, the six similar-looking *Chlorocebus* species have evolved to deal with just about anything the climate can throw at them. They can be found in bone-dry savannahs and swampy tropical forests, at elevation in the mountains and at sea level along the coast. The species commonly referred to as the "grivet," for example, inhabits the mix of grassland and gallery forest of southern Africa, while the "green monkey" can be found in the coastal scrub of Senegal, four thousand miles to the north. Not surprisingly, these species also possess a wide-ranging palate: one study documented their consumption of 190 plant species. Although they prefer flowers and fruit, they're omnivores and will consume whatever else they can catch, such as shellfish and insects. Their fundamental requirements for making a home are quite simple: they need access to fresh water, and they need trees for sleeping in at night. They share our propensity to adapt to life in very different landscapes, to make a home of wherever they find themselves.[3]

For nearly four hundred years, they've made themselves at home in the Americas, where they were first brought to entertain sugarcane planters on the islands of Barbados, St. Kitts, and Nevis at the end of the seventeenth century.[4] There are now about ten thousand green monkeys and 275,000 humans all living on Barbados, whose total area is about two and a half times the size of Washington, DC. Living in such close quarters has not been without conflict, particularly since the Caribbean monkeys have always relied on agricultural crops as their main food source.

Ironically, when agriculture was Barbados's primary economy, the crop damage was spread out over most of the island. As farming on the island has waned in favor of tourism, however, the monkeys have concentrated their foraging on the remaining fields, to such an extent that in 1979 the government resumed the practice of offering a bounty, to be collected with three inches from the dead primate's tail. According to a study in the *International Journal of Primatology*, farmers reported ten thousand monkeys either trapped or killed between 1980 and 1994.[5] Yet the monkey population proved surprisingly resilient: when researchers conducted surveys at the end of this period, they found the monkeys were just as numerous as before the bounty was offered.

Like their Caribbean counterparts, vervets came to Florida as something of an afterthought, riding the coattails of a larger-than-life, publicity-savvy pair of adventurers who arrived in Dania in 1940 to found the Denis Roosevelt Anthropoid Ape Foundation, which was also known as the "Chimpanzee Farm."[6] Newspaper photos show Armand Denis standing before a painted white sign while a giant King Kong figure towers overhead, welcoming visitors with a display of its massive white fangs. Denis was a pioneer of the commercial wildlife film industry, one of the first to take the motion picture camera into the field to record encounters with exotic wildlife. When he wasn't directing the stars of the time in feature films like *Dark Rapture* and *Wild Cargo,* he was filming his own exploits in Africa and Asia.

His wife, Leila Roosevelt, was an extreme sports enthusiast in her own right. She was a first cousin of Teddy Roosevelt, to whom she attributed her adventuresome spirit, and a second cousin of Franklin Delano Roosevelt. In 1934, while Denis was off on an expedition of his own, she and a female friend drove a truck from Europe to Singapore, traveling over ten thousand miles. A year later, Denis and Roosevelt embarked on a trek by automobile from Spain down the length of the African continent, searching out exotica along the way. The trip was sponsored by Dodge, and in the resulting film Denis can be heard extolling the virtues of hydraulic brakes as the couple navigates a steep and winding track in Morocco.[7]

At the height of World War II, the couple began amassing a collection of African primates, gathering what now seems like a stunning trove of rare wildlife for shipment across the Atlantic. An account of this enterprise in a 1946 spread in the Sunday edition of the *Miami Daily News* suggests that their first attempted shipment included fifty gorillas, all of which died of an epidemic while they waited on shore for a ship to navigate the wartorn seas. After another stint in the bush, they managed to load a boat with a similar number of wild primates. This voyage ended with a torpedo from a German U-boat, killing all the animals on board, although the crew escaped.

Not long after the war ended, Armand Denis left the Chimpanzee Farm. He'd met Michaela Holdsworth, who looked a bit like Grace Kelly and was seventeen years his junior. Together, they went on to make a series of BBC documentaries whose mix of glamour and authoritative intellect became the standard format for wildlife programming. Watching the couple and their cohorts wrangle a baby elephant or join in the frenzy of a tribal dance, I'm reminded of all the wildlife shows I used to watch as a child, like the one in which Marlon Perkins wrestles a giant python on Mutual of Omaha's *Wild*

Kingdom, or my other favorite, *The Undersea World of Jacques Cousteau,* in which Jacques and company swim with the sharks in the great watery unknown. In a sense, by coming to Dania in search of the monkeys, I've uncovered the origins of my own early fascination with wildlife.

By the time Florida Power and Light took the property by eminent domain in 1958, the green monkeys had been on the loose for years. According to an interview with one of the farm's workers who appeared in Minnich's documentary, they escaped from a large, aviary-like enclosure in 1947.[8] The cages at that time were secured with simple hook-and-eye latches, and not long after Denis brought a troop of about fifty monkeys to the farm, someone either forgot to latch the door or the monkeys figured out how to unhook it. They all escaped. About half were eventually recaptured, but the rest remained outside the cage.

In the morning, I eat breakfast with a throng of pale and disgruntled seniors, many dressed in Iowa Hawkeyes yellow, or in tie-dyed electric green T-shirts emblazoned with their dashed hopes, things like "Spring Party 2010" or "Margaritaville." They're in transit, on their way to the cruise ships parked at Port Everglades, a major shipping point that sits next to the airport. Some are playing cards, but most are just standing around, looking stunned. Trapped inside a small and not very luxurious hotel while a "wintry mix" howls outside? This wasn't in the brochure.

The wind has picked up, driving horizontal sheets of rain against the tarmac and ripping through the palm fronds. It looks like hurricane weather, except it's 37 degrees outside. Waiting for my waffle to cook, I watch a feature about elephants enjoying the novelty of snow in their zoo enclosure. They push the white stuff around with their trunks, mixing it with hay and stuffing it into their mouths like a straw-flavored slushy. The reporter goes on to reassure us that zoos bring all animals inside when it gets below 40 degrees.

Unlike those lucky zoo animals, I'm going to be spending most of the day outside. Sean Brown, the city fire marshal, has agreed to spend one of his days off taking me on a monkey search, and rain or shine, I want to make the most of his knowledge of the city's hidden nooks and crannies. Sean grew up near Dania, and he's a self-described "nature freak" whose job includes inspecting the various commercial enterprises around the city. He's even sent me a Google satellite map with points marked to indicate the places the monkeys are known to frequent.

He's waiting for me in his minivan outside some city offices, a compact figure with wafer-thin glasses and close-cropped, salt-and-pepper hair. He doesn't look like a nature freak at first. It's a Saturday morning, and in his crisp jeans and unsullied gray sweatshirt he looks more like a suburban dad who's shuttling the kids around between soccer practice and the mall. But then I'm not looking much like "Crocodile" Dundee myself—I haven't even brought a raincoat.

After a brief and sodden greeting, I climb in the front seat. The defroster is roaring, and rain-laden gusts are making a snare drum of the roof. Sean's eight-year-old daughter is in the far back, playing with the game console she got for Christmas. Sean says she likes this kind of adventure, loud enough for her to look up and nod indulgently. His coworker Jeri is in the next row, huddled down in her coat. She's kind of a nature freak, too. You'd have to be, under these circumstances.

On the way to the port, Sean and Jeri tell me about some of the other creatures affected by the cold. The iguanas, for example. They're everywhere. Jeri points to a median as we sit at a stoplight. She's seen them stretched out in the grass right there after a cold night, like monster zucchini. Sean's daughter pipes up from the back—remember the time you tried to get rid of one from the yard? It was a big one, nearly six feet long, and when he seized it from behind, the lizard responded by raking him across the arm and legs with its powerful, spike-fringed tail. It left an impressive weal. "There's too many of them around these days," Sean says, looking slightly chagrined. "They're kind of out of control."

At the security checkpoint, Sean waves a pass, and the

guard in the booth motions us through. Homeland Security has tightened access to the place, and the general public wouldn't be able to get in here. Which means the monkeys are living in the city, but they also have a refuge in which to some degree they don't have to accommodate people, and people don't have to accommodate them.

We're headed for the backside of the port, not the part where the cruise ship passengers congregate but the area where the industrial warehouses, storage bins, and fuel tanks mushroom up from the marsh that serves as an approach for the runway. Planes are thundering down overhead, close enough that we can hear the wing panels whine as they adjust to the wind. The entire place is ringed with eight-foot-high chain-link topped with strands of barbed wire, and security cameras are everywhere. "They're watching us right now," Sean says, as we turn down a dirt road and pull around the barrels that are meant to serve as a roadblock.

On one side of the road is the marsh, and on the other is a strip of mangrove swamp following a drainage canal, fringed with what Sean and Jeri call "holly" but is actually Brazilian pepper tree, a shrubby invasive with yellowish, glossy leaves and clusters of red berries. "You'd be amazed by how small this area actually is," Sean says. As we drive, I peer into the shadows beneath the leaves, marveling at the mangrove's impenetrability. The ground is glossy muck, and the mangrove branches grow almost horizontally, seemingly impenetrable.

I'm trying to imagine what this place would have looked like in the early 1980s, before the airport drained and paved 322 acres for a runway expansion, including 132 acres of mangrove swamp. Workers clearing the vegetation complained that this "Amazon" was "infested" with monkeys, particularly rhesus macaques that responded violently to having their habitat removed. Fifteen were shot during some initial tree clearance, and the remaining thirty were trapped after public outcry over their fate swayed the Broward County Board of Commissioners to seek a nonlethal solution. Before the expansion the area was also inhabited by a troop of squirrel monkeys, which roosted in an area of higher ground with taller trees, according to a Fish and Game officer interviewed in Minnich's film. When those trees were cut, the squirrel monkeys retreated to a stand of ficus trees to the north, where there were also a number of fruit tree nurseries.[9] Development soon claimed that habitat too, and most residents believe the squirrel monkeys are now gone from Dania Beach. Only the green monkeys have survived, in tiny fragments like this.

"If you honk the horn they come right out," Sean tells me as we approach the end of the airport access road. I laugh incredulously. Seriously? What kind of wild animal responds to the call of a minivan? Although I knew these were urban monkeys, I'd been envisioning a different kind of encounter. I'd imagined us wandering down a trail of some kind, peering up into the branches to catch a glimpse of an elusive, furtive figure, as if monkey watching was going to be like watching a warbler flit through the canopy. A walk in the park—that's what I imagined.

Now I see that if the monkeys are back in those mangroves, we aren't going to see them. Not without waders and a machete. Honk the horn and out they come—I'd better hope that's true.

Still, I'm not expecting anything when Sean bips the horn in a long, trilling salute and leans over to peer into the undergrowth.

"There they are!" he exclaims, jerking the gearshift into park. What I see at first is trash. So many Styrofoam clamshells are trapped under the mangroves, it looks like an oyster bed. Then, it's as if the moss and leaf litter are taking shape, sprouting limbs and slender bodies and springing between the boughs.

There are seven of them. The adults are about the size of a long-limbed cat, with angular black features tapering to a pointed chin, like some pensive Modigliani figure. They have large black ears that look crumpled around the rim and a fringe of greenish fur surrounding their faces. Their tails manage to appear powerful and delicate at once, arched back, prodding the sky. One of the biggest adults is sporting only a stump, a thick tuft where a tail should be. There are several youngsters, one an infant cradled to its mother's chest, the others bounding forward into the grass, testing the limits. Their faces are pink and almost hairless. It makes them look more human.

I've seen monkeys in their enclosures at the zoo. This is not like that. The containment of an animal in a cage does something to us, makes us complacent, keeps us from being fully present. The caged animal, confronted with a daily stream of faces, isn't fully present in the encounter either. Without the bars, however, the etiquette, the boundaries of behavior, have to be negotiated.

The troop watches intently from the bare lower branches as we all get out. "God, it's cold!" Jeri complains, tugging her coat tight between her arms. The Floridians are shivering, but there's too much adrenaline coursing through my veins for me to feel it. Sean has brought a fruititarian's feast: ripe bananas, bunches of red grapes, oranges and kiwis cut into wedges. When Sean bends down with a piece of banana, a small monkey dashes forward, reaches out with the full extent of its surprisingly long arms and plucks the food away with its fingertips. Then it retreats to a branch to gobble it. Each time Sean bends down with a piece of fruit, a different monkey dashes forward. Soon, they're all taking turns grabbing chunks of banana and yanking grapes off the clusters he holds out. Some look like they are developing jowls—vervets have pouches in their cheeks they can stuff with food.

Jeri is surprised there aren't more of them. The last time she was here, the monkeys emerged in an eager swarm of nearly thirty. "I was scared, there were so many of them," she says. The others may be hiding from the rain. Or they may be gone. Both Sean and Jeri suspect someone has been trapping these animals recently—someone they know found a trap in this very spot. They destroyed that one, but that probably didn't deter the trappers.

"You want to give it a try?" Sean asks. I've been holding back, hiding behind the journalist's need to observe and take notes, because I'm not sure where I stand on the feeding of wild animals. First and foremost, I have to confess that I'm afraid. To feed an animal, you have to make yourself vulnerable. You have to trust that the thing isn't going to sink its fangs into your hand, and the animal has to trust you, too, trust that you aren't going to pounce and haul it away in a cage. Clearly, the monkeys don't entirely trust me, and I don't entirely trust them. We're right on the edge of interspecies contact.

Even though I've seen them take fruit from Sean and his daughter without incident, I've been reading recently about rhesus macaques on Puerto Rico that have established wild populations after escaping from a medical research facility. A number of them are infected with a strain of the herpes virus that is fatal in humans, for which there is no vaccine.[10]

I know these are an entirely different species and we are hundreds of miles of ocean away from those other monkeys, but still: one bite from a monkey that happens to be shedding the virus, and that's the end. I think of Timothy Treadwell, face to face with an Alaskan brown bear, pushing ever closer to the line that separates species. I think of Steve Irwin, the "Crocodile Hunter," gleefully picking up poisonous snakes. Both of them eventually got too close. The penalty for crossing the line is potentially severe, as both men repeatedly pointed out in their films. And ultimately we can't know where that boundary lies, will never know exactly what is running through an animal's mind as we approach.

Still, I can feel the draw of it. Am I supposed to remain objective? To observe from a distance, not just physically but emotionally? Science teaches us that—objectivity toward subjects of research, toward subjects of management. Our relationship to the individual only gets in the way of more important objectives. And yet, the desire to offer this gift, to use food as the means to transcend the boundaries between species, feels like an instinctual gesture, even if it's also the very thing we've been warned repeatedly against.

Habituating wild animals to humans used to be common—it wasn't that long ago that going to Yellowstone National Park meant sitting in a car while a grizzly ambled along begging for handouts. When I worked in Yellowstone, one of my primary responsibilities was to warn the tourists that these were indeed wild animals, that elk did not want to be petted, that bison would not want to give children a ride on their back, that a bear given human food is probably a dead bear. Habituation is both salvation and curse for wild animals, especially when the food comes from a culture whose altruism isn't always benign. How do monkeys get fooled into entering traps? By what seem like generous offerings of food.

In the end, I decide to do as the locals do and worry about the implications later. I peel down a piece of banana and crouch down. Sean is videotaping me, as if I'm some modern protégé of Armand Denis. One of the younger monkeys, a slender, almost gangly adolescent, drops from its bough and pauses, its head tilting so quickly through a repertoire of expressions that it suggests the relativity of time, so much happening, so much experience to be processed, so much living to do in what feels to me like a second, a span of time too brief to do more than hold my breath.

It bounds forward, reaches out, extending both arms. I feel its fingertips brush my index finger and thumb. It feels like a moth taking flight from my palm, swift but precise, a pickpocket's touch.

What do I feel? Guilt? Ambivalence? No. What I feel immediately is closer to elation, the kind of thing you find when nature writers encounter the sublime, that potent mix of fear and awe. What's happened is different than simply observing the monkeys as they forage, and it doesn't really compare to filling a dog's bowl with kibble. If there are boundaries between the domestic and the wild, between nature and culture, then reaching across that line with an offering of food—and having it accepted—is akin to Henry David Thoreau standing on the windswept flank of Mount Katadhin or John Muir riding out a Sierra windstorm in a swaying tree. It's a transcendent experience. But it's more than that, since these are not entirely wild animals; they're animals that live on the margins of the city and rely on humans to some degree for food, existing somewhere between the domestic and the wild, more like squirrels in the yard than grizzlies in the Alaskan bush. And there's the undeniably anthropogenic quality of their gestures and relations with each other. They're alien and familiar, us but not us. They make us consider the nature of humanness.

Primates, it seems to me, offer the greatest test of the limits and possibilities of community and citizenship, because in the mirror of their behavior, their physiognomy and culture, we see some measure of ourselves. In chimpanzee culture, as Frans de Waals notes, the struggle for dominance among males plays a central role. But there are also the bonobos, whose matriarchal society is marked by pacifism. "If chimpanzees are from Mars," de Waal argues, "bonobos must be from Venus." We can find clues to our own nature, he writes, in both species.[11]

It's the recognition of the darker side of human society that keeps me from romanticizing the moment further. Although most of the troop seems to be eating amiably together, we've noticed one of the adults seems to be an outcast, a scapegoat enduring the others' consistent abuse. Vervets live in matrilineal groups; they organize hierarchically around a primary breeding female. Every echelon of vervet society is defined by birthright—the closer you are to the breeding female, the higher your status in the group. Males have their own pecking order, which they enforce by raising their tails to display their scarlet and turquoise genitalia. There's been no flashing so far, however. It's a bit cold for that.

These monkeys do have a mechanism for keeping their clan from becoming insular to the point of inbreeding. Females tend to stay with the troop, but adolescent males, often brothers, leave to seek out new groups. Could the outcast be a lowborn female? Could it be a scion of another troop, a subadult male trying to win acceptance through an excessive display of humility? The outcast sits on a branch, watching the others eat but unwilling to come down. The apparent injustice is upsetting to those of us on the human side. We all seem to be trying to redress it, trying to coax the outcast along. Every time it makes a move, however, one of the other adults notices and warns it away with a menacing shriek. If that doesn't work, the others attack, and the outcast winds up sitting disconsolately in the tree once more.

The wind begins to pick up, driving rain into our faces. We've been bracing ourselves against it for some time—my fleece is already soaking through at the shoulders. The monkeys seem to be getting full, squatting on the lower limbs under the canopy where the wind can't reach, occasionally tugging down clusters of ripe holly berries and nibbling them out of their palms. Once we get back into the van and slide the doors shut and crank up the defroster, they, too, retreat, clambering slowly through the branches until they're invisible. The monkey with the stump is the last to leave, clutching a cluster of grapes to its chest.

Section 5-10 of the Dania Beach Code of Ordinances, entitled *"Feeding, molesting monkeys or other wild animals,"* reads: *"The feeding or molestation of monkeys or other wild animals (ferae naturae), including alligators, is to be unlawful and prohibited within the corporate limits of the city."*

The simplicity of this statement belies the complexity of its history and the visionary nature of its intentions. That it exists at all is due primarily to the efforts of people who lived in the community and shared habitat with the monkeys, who spearheaded a campaign to keep the monkeys in the community at a time when they were in danger of eradication.

Dania's vervets first came into the public eye in 1993, when a driver hit one crossing the road near the Motel 6. When he got out to see if he could help the dying monkey, the rest of the troop mobbed him. The resulting story caught the attention of various news outlets, and as the city tried to figure out what to do with its primate residents, even NPR's *All Things Considered* arrived to cover the controversy. When Dale Minnich saw some of this coverage on the evening news, his reaction was a mix of astonishment and curiosity. "There are *monkeys* there?" he said to himself. "I never knew, and I've lived here all my life. I've got to go over and investigate this!"

He wasn't alone. In the aftermath of this media circus, people who wished the monkeys well came to town just for the chance to get close to them, even if it meant tramping across somebody's yard. And more insidiously, the news reports revealed the monkeys' location to people who didn't wish them well at all, who wanted to trap them and sell them as pets or biological research subjects, maybe even eat them, if the more extreme conspiracy theories can be believed.

Most of the players in the subsequent drama have feature roles in Minnich's documentary. Minnich arrived just as things were coming to a head: the owners of the neighboring parcels, which included a trailer park, had gotten fed up with the crowds trespassing across their property and had hired a pest removal outfit to capture and ship the monkeys to a breeding facility in Illinois, where their offspring would be destined for a life as research subjects.

Some of the residents confronted the fatigue-clad trappers one evening as they were heading into the mangroves with a collection of blowguns, nets, and tranquilizer darts. With the help of a state Fish and Wildlife officer, the group managed to convince the trappers that they had to have maps showing ownership boundaries so they could be sure they weren't trespassing on adjoining property. The trappers left that evening without their quarry, and the effort to get laws on the books to protect the monkeys began.[12]

The problem, all parties agreed, wasn't the monkeys. They'd been there for decades, and there wasn't a single recorded incident of them biting anyone. They ravaged some people's tomato plants and demonstrated a fondness for hibiscus flowers, but other than that, they didn't seem to be affecting the local flora and fauna. Some residents claimed them as "natives," and even the property owners admitted that the monkeys had been in Dania long enough to have "squatters' rights."

Instead, the trouble came from people, mostly tourists, who didn't view the monkeys as wild animals and wanted to get as close as they might to a friendly dog. The trailer park owner claimed to have seen a grown man lying in the grass, placing bananas on his stomach for the monkeys to grab.

The idea that took shape was to protect both monkeys and property owners by making it illegal to feed or "molest" them and then enforcing the ban with public outreach, including warning signs and neighborhood patrols. The hope was that once people stopped feeding them, the vervets would eventually stop associating humans with food and return to foraging in the mangroves. They would still be part of the community, in other words, but the boundaries between human and monkey would be more clearly defined.

The city soon passed its rule designed to allow humans and monkeys to inhabit the same urban space. "Monkey Xing" signs were posted along the city's busiest thoroughfares. Other signs warned that feeding monkeys was a violation of city ordinance.

It sounds simple enough. Leave the monkeys alone and nobody gets hurt. And to a certain extent, the law was a success. Seventeen years have passed since the monkeys hit the airwaves, and Dania still has its monkeys. Nobody has been bitten. There have been no lawsuits. But the monkeys still come out to be fed at the motel, and the threat of fines hasn't done much to deter people from feeding them. Or trapping them.

"I don't know how much it's helped," Minnich said of the law he helped pass.

"They're gone."

The problem is not just the scope of the local laws or even a lack of enforcement. Cities exist within the larger landscape of politics and commerce. And the climate for nonnative species is increasingly hostile at both the state and federal levels. According to Minnich, at the time the code was passed the activists tried to get the state to provide feeding stations deep within the mangroves of West Lake State Park. The park is the largest undeveloped mangrove ecosystem along this urban stretch of coast, and it also happens to sit right across the road from the Motel 6. They envisioned something like a zoo without bars—the monkeys could be fed by trained staff, visitors could observe them from a safe distance, and the monkeys wouldn't need to come into heavily trafficked areas for handouts.

Standing in their way, however, was a complex and contradictory tangle of jurisdictions and laws. Wildlife are managed at the state level according to different categories and statutes, with some species, like the endangered manatee, receiving particular attention under one category, game animals like deer managed under another category, and domestic animals like horses under still another category. Invasive species have their own special statutes. And that's just at the state level. Nonnative species—those that are not considered invasive—live precariously in a kind of gray area, with limited legal protection. On the one hand, most states have animal welfare laws designed to protect domestic animals (most of which are nonnative) from abuse or inhumane conditions, but they also have laws that allow people to catch and destroy "nuisance" animals, which could be a raccoon or a monkey.

The motel troop Minnich followed for his film has dwindled from thirty individuals to just a pair. Even if I can't legally sell a monkey I've trapped in the wild, I can sell its offspring that I've raised in captivity. A quick Google search turned up baby squirrel monkeys for sale for $6,500 each. Infant green monkeys can be had for $5,500. With prices like this, it's no surprise that wild monkeys disappear quickly once their whereabouts are known.

We check the motel. No monkeys. We check the picnic area near the harbor, where the food trucks park on warmer days. No monkeys. It looks like they should be everywhere: the holly berries are abundant, the mangroves are dense with shadows. Yet there's no sign of them. Back at the airport, we curve down a taxis-only lane, headed for the cabbie waiting area. The cab drivers honk at us, waving us back and gesturing wildly—to them we look like just another wayward minivan meant to be picking up our relatives at arrivals, not a field crew of intrepid monkey researchers.

The booth guard waves us through. What lies beyond is an unsettling tableau. Planes thunder overhead, and the dispatcher's summons roar from tinny overhead speakers in heavily accented taxi-speak, creating an aural maelstrom so loud that the only way to communicate is by shouting. The thickets surrounding the perimeter fence are carpeted with fast food trash—the undergrowth is literally white with napkins and Styrofoam drink cups and clamshells, and the trash is also blowing around the parking lot, where iridescent grackles are parading around and squawking inaudibly. Mourning doves and pigeons peck at french fries while a single white ibis stalks across the tarmac, pausing to consider the edibility of a ketchup packet. Nearby, a young raccoon ambles between the tires of parked cabs. It takes no notice of us or of the gulls wheeling and hovering overhead.

"You don't have to guess what the monkeys are doing here," Sean yells over to me.

It occurs to me that when we have nightmares about globalization, this is what they look like. This is the world without categories, the cosmopolitan landscape we all fear: a vast parking lot heaped with trash, faceless people barking commands at each other in unintelligible languages, habituated animals plying their trade between cars, chain-link fences everywhere.

There's a tin-roofed picnic area on one side, and two very thin, very dark-skinned men are eating their lunch standing up, dressed in layers of shirts and sweaters against the cold. We ask if they've seen the monkeys. They look at us like we're crazy. *No, no monkeys,* they reply in their heavily inflected English. *No monkeys here.*

In 1890, a New Yorker named Eugene Schieffelin stood in Central Park. With him were sixty caged birds from Europe, which he soon released into the surrounding trees, reputedly to bring the birds of Shakespeare to the shores of a continent that lacked such refinements. Those birds were European starlings, and thanks to the actions of Schieffelin and a group known as the American Acclimatization Society, we now have hundreds of millions of these little literary references roosting in the eaves of downtown buildings and poking around in the grass for grubs.[13]

Zoos and acclimatization societies both emerged during the same frenzied period of global exploration and colonization, but in terms of purpose they were almost mirror opposites. The zoo brought unfamiliar animals to the city for display. The acclimatization society, in contrast, brought *familiar* animals to homesick colonists. You can almost imagine the same ship loading up kangaroos and cockatiels at an Australian port for the voyage to London, then filling the same cages with nightingales and bullfinches for the trip back. These societies were especially busy in Australia, where they released all kinds of comforting creatures from the English countryside, such as rabbits and foxes and house sparrows, to help the newcomers feel at home in a disconcerting landscape. Some of these introductions didn't take. But the rabbit did. By 1890, even as Schieffelin was releasing the Shakespearean starlings, Australians were stringing fences across hundreds of miles of open country in a vain attempt to contain the bunny horde.[14]

Be careful what you wish for might be the moral of these stories. I'm mindful that releasing animals from their cages comes with risks and that in imagining greater diversity in the city I'm getting uncomfortably close to the acclimatization dreams of another era. What their members wanted most was to feel at home, and they looked to the company of other creatures for help — not so far from what I'm trying to do in my own backyard.

Yet I'm also wary of dismissing this impulse too quickly. I worry that if we relegate the city to the dustbin of biodiversity, we may very well wind up seeing all but a handful of creatures on the wildlife channel and in doing so miss the opportunity to learn how to coexist. How are we ever going to learn to live with other species if we never actually encounter them in the flesh?

We have to be careful. I think of chestnut blight and sudden oak death and Dutch elm disease. I think of Étienne Trouvelot in Boston in the 1860s, accidentally releasing gypsy moths into his neighborhood trees during a failed experiment with silk production. More than a century later, gypsy moth caterpillars would devour the woods of western Massachusetts, stripping the shade from my childhood summers. One study puts the annual US cost of dealing with invasive species at $123 billion.[15] It's enough to make me think that wild animals and humans should never go anywhere near one another.

But I also think of the small primates I once saw "off exhibit" at a zoo, all living in a row of cages not much bigger than what you'd see holding birds in a pet store. They seemed healthy enough down in the basement, and it was a warm place to be on a blustery afternoon. But there were no windows in there.[16]

I'd like to think there's a path between these two

possibilities, for the sake of the animals, and for our sake, too.

On the last morning, the clouds have lifted and the sky to the east looks like a lemon meringue, aluminum and primrose, the breast of a waxwing. The puddles in the parking lot are sparkling, but the temperature has dropped. It's 31 degrees out there, and the Canadian front is still gusting through the tropical foliage. I've been in Dania Beach for three days, and I haven't had even a glimpse of their eponymous beach, an oversight that at this point seems almost peculiar. Who drives all the way down here just to poke around the garbage-strewn swamps outside the port? I should at least *see* the beach, especially since it was probably beach traffic that brought the Chimpanzee Farm with its curios and caged monkeys to town. The monkeys may not go to the beach, but indirectly, they're here because of it.

I'm expecting the usual concrete barricade of condo towers and hotels along the waterfront, so I'm surprised when I cross the canal and find the beach hidden behind a tangle of sea grape and Brazilian pepper. Head left and there's the entrance to a state park and campground. Go right and it's secluded small parking areas all the way to the adjacent city of Hollywood. Or at least they seem secluded on a frigid morning like this. The road is deserted, and the lot where I park is empty except for a white van with the back door ajar. I notice that several scruffy tom-cats are preening at the edge of the lot. And then I see a woman coming along the line of brush. Her face is hidden by a sweatshirt hood, and she's encased in several layers of jackets and sweaters that make her arms stick out, like stubby penguin wings. I can tell that she's watching me furtively, hoping I won't be able to figure out what she's doing. As if I don't already know.

I pretend not to be interested and walk across the lot to the beach. She gets back to work, half a dozen cats gathered around her shins. Looking back, I see that her hands are cupped with sea grape leaves, cradling lumps of wet food to the bushes. My immediate reaction is that she shouldn't be feeding these cats—they're killers, and their population grows constantly, especially if you feed them. Think of all the songbirds, I want to say to her. Stop caring for these animals. But are monkeys any different? She's bending down with her offering when I reach the boardwalk, where I have to look away because the planks are slick with a thin coating of ice.

I step down into the sand beneath a pair of swaying coconut palms, completely alone. The beach is exquisite, a fantasy of white sand and pink pearly sky and cresting turquoise waves. I start for the water's edge, then turn abruptly. My face and ears feel as if they're about to go permanently numb. I feel as if I'm trudging through a frozen Midwestern cornfield—somewhere this wind chill makes sense, where I'd be bundled up appropriately.

Back in the lot, the woman sees me coming and moves surreptitiously away from the cats. I nod to her, acknowledging our kinship.

I'm packing the car to leave when I spot a small lizard on the sidewalk under the palms. It's sprawled on its back, belly up, completely vulnerable to whatever fate the world has in store for it. Its tail is snapped into a crook, as if something has tried to drag it into a tree.

I recognize the type from the small lizards that inhabit our backyard, an anole of some kind. Is it an exotic? I'm assuming the native anoles know what to do when it gets cold—the ones in my own yard like to hibernate under sun-warmed stacks of empty clay pots. But I can't be sure. I know it's not a Knight anole, which is supposedly quite a bit larger and blotched with white, or a Cuban anole, which is small and brown. But it seems marginally bigger than the Carolina anoles we have in our backyard. Could it be a Jamaican anole? Could the native anoles down here be bigger than the ones farther north?

I'm not a herpetologist. I wouldn't know whether to measure the crest along its spine or examine the extent of the dewlap under its chin. I don't even know if the thing is dead or alive.

This is my chance to make sure there's one less stranger in paradise. I could stomp on this lizard. A single footstep would "euthanize" it. Or I could just leave it there on the concrete. If it isn't dead now, it soon will be. Things will get even colder when night falls. Nature will take its course.

On impulse, I pick it up and stretch it out in my palm. Its eyes are pinched in the line of death, its head a half-split edamame pod. I think of the cat lady with her leaves full of food. I think of the vervets snatching grapes from our hands. I think of those starry-eyed believers in the exotic who unleashed the scourge of the gypsy moth and the starling on our shores. Here it is, the moment of decision, time to choose between emotional attachment and scientific detachment, compassion for the individual versus consideration for the welfare of other species. Which side am I on?

I go inside and get a Styrofoam coffee cup from the breakfast bar. I scoop the lizard into it. An hour later, I'm on the freeway with the heater blasting. I pry open the lid. The lizard's eyes are open. It tilts its head, fixing me with an incomprehensible look.

We head north.

3

Little Eden

FACT: United States fruit, vegetable, and nut growers lose $146 million worth of crops to wildlife damage each year. The primary culprits are deer, squirrels, and starlings.

In my estimation, the Chilean peach has made great strides in recent years. Most of the time, it no longer tastes like a ball of sawdust soaked in corn syrup; it actually tastes a bit like a peach. Actual juice may in fact emerge from a bite; actual tree-ripened hues may be detected on the surface. It's not terrible, not for early February, when most of us are looking at a foot of snow on the ground and praying Punxsutawny Phil or whatever they're calling this year's groundhog isn't going to see his shadow.

But no matter what the little sticker says on the fruit flown in from the Southern Hemisphere, whatever you're getting in the supermarket in the middle of winter isn't really a peach. If you've had the pleasure of an encounter with an actual peach, one left on the tree until the Brix measurement of its sweetness is off the charts and a single bite makes the whole thing melt like ice cream toward your elbow, you know what a real peach is. You also know that finding such a fruit isn't easy. Taste and travel are for the most part mutually exclusive in the world of fresh produce, and peaches are probably the least amenable to making the trip to market. A peach purchased at the grocery store, it's safe to say, is usually a disappointment.[1]

Imagine, on the other hand, that those delicate fruits never sit in a packing warehouse or the cargo hold of a jet, never get jostled in a crate in a pickup bed, never get crushed in a heap at the supermarket. Imagine if you, the farmer, walked out one fine warm morning to find that perfect peach for your breakfast—right there on your own tree. How simple, how rapturously flavorful, how carbon-friendly that piece of fruit would be. Take one for you, and one each for your little ones, too. After all, the commercial peach is often drenched in systemic insecticides and fungicides, enough to put it near the top of every list of contaminated produce.

Sound a bit like catalog copy? That's probably because I've been under their spell for years. I love leafing through gardening catalogs, love the photos of abundance on the bough, the hyperbolic descriptions of the flavors, the way the horticulturalists distinguish the acid balance of the pippin from the delectable aroma of the sheepnose. As a renter, however, I've had to admire these tantalizing fruits from afar. With the exception of a potted lemon and a scattering of ill-conceived saplings left behind in various yards, this is the first chance I've had to indulge the fantasy of a backyard orchard.

Not surprisingly, I go a bit crazy. There are over seven thousand known varieties of apple, and peach varieties can be numbered in the thousands, too.[2] I'm tempted to grow all of them, and the multitude of mirabelles and gages, plumcots and pomegranates, too. Here in South Carolina, where the temperate meets the tropical, you can grow just about anything if you know what you're doing.

Just to get started, I order a pineapple pear, a seckel pear, a "20th century" Asian pear, a "Blanc d'Hiver" apple, a "William's Pride," and a "Whitney" crab. That's from one catalog. Then I get a "Jiro" persimmon, a "Wonderful" pomegranate, and figs by the name of "Violette de Bordeaux," "Italian Black," and "Peter's Honey." Still not enough. Seven different blueberries of the "rabbiteye" and "Southern highbush" types, some raspberries, some strawberries. Oh, and some muscadines and scuppernongs. And why not a pair of kiwis? And pawpaws, too. It's madness! And it's not over. When it comes to the peaches and nectarines, I don't want an unbranched whip, some stripling that will take years to produce. I want the unpruned eight footers I've seen on display at the DIY superstore. I drive home with three kinds of peach and nectarine jutting out the passenger window like spears, all of them already stippled with pink buds.

In these parts, what I'm doing is unorthodox, probably even eccentric. If I look up and down my street, I'm the only one growing so much as a tomato for as far as I can see. In fact, I've never seen anyone growing food anywhere in the entire neighborhood. What we grow here, for the most part, is centipede grass. And we also grow ornamental vegetation; hybrid magnolias and dogwoods and azaleas burst like fireworks across otherwise nondescript lawns in early spring. Later, when the streets are simmering in the afternoons, the yards will be neon with crepe myrtle. We water heavily for this experience of color and beauty. In the evenings the sprinklers sway their plumes across the grass. Mowers drone through the afternoons, and the leaf blowers grumble every weekend—leaves and needles drop year-round here. We put a lot of work, in other words, into creating an aesthetic experience, but the edible potential of the yard is at best an afterthought.[3]

I like to think of two moments in history, the first being the commissioning of the landscape architect Frederick Law Olmsted to create what at first was termed a *greensward* in the heart of New York City. We can see his work in the wilder corners of Central Park, the idea that a long, narrow rectangle of turf in the heart of the city should nevertheless have a "Ramble," a counterpoint to the regular geometry of numbered streets and rectangular buildings surrounding it.[4] Bringing wildlife into the city has its roots in this aesthetic idea, that the urban park should be a contrast to urban life rather than an extension of it. The wild belongs in the city but does not partake of it.

I also like to think of the campaign that Londoners undertook in the dark days of World War II, when backyards and urban deer parks were tilled up and planted with "Dig for Victory" gardens. The culture of the "allotment," the block or two of urban ground divvied up among the neighbors for growing sprouts and turnips and marrows, persists in England today.[5]

As I'm excavating holes for all my purchases and backfilling them with humus and cow manure and crumbled pine bark and coffee grounds and just about any other organic matter I can get my shovel on to counteract the extreme sandiness of our loam, I start to realize I have company: squirrels. They're doing pretty much what I'm doing—scrabbling furiously at holes in the yard. I'm just about eye level with them, especially when I'm on my knees scooping the last loose sand out of the holes with my hands.

It's a timely reminder. The sign out front says this is wildlife habitat, too. What does that mean for the urban farmer? Without realizing it, I've been working my way into one of the great challenges of coexistence: how to keep the wild things from harvesting the food we want to eat ourselves.

I do want to create a little patch of untamed habitat for the wild things, but I also want to till and sow and reap. Most of all, reap. Maybe it goes back to my grandfather and the vegetable garden he planted every summer in the backyard, the pride he'd take in the tomatoes he'd harvest, each wrapped in paper to keep through the early frosts. Maybe it's the feeling that putting down roots means literally embedding seeds in the soil you've amended, watching as the plants absorb nutrients and finally swell into something you can harvest without harming anything, a fruit that was intended to entice you, that was intended to be eaten. Somehow, even if we tend to deny the certainty of our own eventual return to the black crumbly matter of leaf mold and sediment, there remains a sense of ritual about eating the food we've grown, a sense that our bodies are being nourished by our own soil. At the level of nutrients, home and the body merge.

This earthy transubstantiation can only take place, however, if you can actually get something into your mouth before somebody else gets it first. Whether you're leading your sheep to an allotment on the edge of a Montana wilderness or trying to coax a crop out of your backyard trees, you're going to be dealing with all the other denizens of that habitat. I said the fruits of your labor are meant to be enticing, but that doesn't mean they were intended to entice you. In fact, despite all the years of breeding and selection that have transformed apples and blueberries into bigger and sweeter versions of their wild ancestors, they still seem to be designed to be eaten by creatures other than humans.

Berries, for example, are designed to travel through the gut of an animal and come out in a nice pile of fertilizer, ready to sprout somewhere far away from their parent. Birds are great for berries. Berries are great for birds. Keeping the two apart in your backyard wildlife habitat seems almost unfair, like telling children they can look inside the toy store, but they can't touch anything. The backyard, I'm already beginning to suspect, is the canvas for incompatible fantasies, like having the regimented quadrangles of Versailles and the tousled romantic heath of Central Park in the same quarter acre of turf.

What are the "right" creatures for the backyard habitat? Ideally, they'd be partners in the landscape. We'd enjoy a symbiotic relationship; they'd scratch my back and I'd scratch theirs, that is, if they had a back and would let me get near enough to scratch it. The warblers and the tufted titmice and the flycatchers coming through on the leading edge of spring are great friends; they eat bugs. I like things that eat bugs. But maybe something more prosaic and permanent should be the backyard gardener's mascot, something like the earthworm. The lowly worm may not be pretty or even visible under normal circumstances, but it's a pretty good partner for the backyard farm. All my hard work has been basically replicating what worms do all the time: mixing rotting plant material from the surface down into the deeper layers of the soil. They live underground in space I don't need, help out around the place by enriching the soil, and ask for nothing in return but dead leaves and maybe a bit of rotting produce from the kitchen. Perfect.

Or maybe not so perfect. It should be noted that the ubiquitous and useful earthworm is often a nonnative species, and the welcome role it plays in the garden is not so welcome in the wilderness. Worms fertilize the soil, which is great if you're trying to coax food out of sand. But in the wilderness, that nutrient mixing gradually changes the plant community, as plants designed to live in poor soil give way to plants that like more fertility. Invisibly, and perhaps insidiously, the lowly worm changes the wilderness.[6]

As a farmer, I don't care. I want as much nitrogen and micronutrients as possible, and I can use all the help I can get. But what about the backyard wilderness? If it's a mini-wilderness I'm after, then the worm is not a model citizen.

If I could divvy up the yard into distinct areas with clear boundaries, then the worm could be the friend of the garden, and some other creature, something like the box turtle, could be the icon of the wilderness area. But then, where is the wilderness boundary, exactly? Is it the hedge and the lawn but not the vegetable patch? Is it the whole yard, excluding all plants that bear fruit for human consumption? Historically, hedges have always been the habitat for wildlife on the farm. In England, when I worked for a native plant nursery, most of our work involved restoring hedges to the edges of farm fields, making habitat for hedgehogs and dormice, badgers and foxes and hares. But there was a lot more room between the house and the hedge and the pastures on those sheep farms than there is in my backyard. If the National Park Service can't keep bison from wandering out of Yellowstone's million-plus acres every winter to browse neighboring cattle pasture, what hope do I have of restricting cardinals to the azalea hedge?

It's the first really warm day, 75 degrees and sunny, the kind of day the stone fruits and their pollinators have been longing to see. All the tight buds on the nectarine tree seem to burst open on cue, transforming this stick-figure mannequin into something hot pink and dazzling. Giant bumblebees and many smaller bumblebees, and even the occasional honeybee, are all paying court. They're joined by an insect that's as golden and fuzzy as a pipe cleaner, which hovers at the entrance of the blossom, probing with a needle-like snout. A hoverfly? The giant bumblebees spar with each other in midair, and the flowers break their fall.

I have no idea what to call these creatures. I've never

bothered to look at bees this closely. Aldo Leopold once predicted that our love of wildlife will eventually move us toward looking rather than harvesting. For his own part, Leopold focused on reading animals tracks in the mud and extolling the beauty of the tiny flowers we tend to overlook. Paying attention to the small and quotidian, to what can't be harvested for the dinner table—that's what Leopold wanted us to do.[7]

For a long time, I found his interest in these particulars quaint but not terribly interesting. Working at the urban wildlife garden in England, I used to secretly sneer at the idea of creating "mini-beast" habitat. I'd just come from Montana, where I'd been surveying birds in forests that stretched for hundreds of miles in almost every direction. Having grown accustomed to worrying about bumping into bear and moose, the scale of things in the wildlife garden left me feeling incredulous. Was I really being asked to stack up some logs and label them on a map as a snail and centipede hotel? It took a long time to get used to the idea that looking closely was not a diminishment of experience, that a scene without epic grandeur could still be worthy of attention.

Now that I have a "farm" of my own, however, I need mini-beasts. They're my vessels of procreation. In fact, over the winter I put my limited carpentry skills to work on bee blocks, homes for the kind of small, innocuous creatures I've never really noticed before. They're known as orchard bees, and they're supposedly metallic blue, like the hood of a muscle car. They normally nest in holes that some other creature has punched into tree trunks and stumps, but I've mimicked their dwellings with a drill; all you need, supposedly, is to drill lots of holes deep into the surface of a six-inch-thick block of wood and smooth out the splinters. Put this bee block up high in a sunny spot, and the bees that pollinate your fruit trees will flock to your place . . . supposedly.

Once the blocks are up on the south side of the house near the eaves, I have a reason to pay attention to the details of invertebrate life, and what I discover out there is diversity and richness, as if the focus of the lens I use to view the world has been sharpened. I've had a similar experience hunting for mushrooms in the duff of the forest floor—nothing, nothing at all, until all at once the perception expands, and the invisible details of the world are everywhere in sight. Suddenly, the morels are right there, underfoot and all around.

The good news about the various little black bees I've never noticed before: many of them don't sting, or if they do, they sting reluctantly. There are leafcutter bees that stuff their nests with swatches of foliage. There are miner bees that excavate galleries in the soil. There are iridescent green bees and yellow frowzy-headed bees, thin and graceful types and chunky, bombastic types, though you probably need some degree of magnification to see the difference. The orchard bee is also known as a "mason" bee, because it walls off the entrance to its nest with little bricks of mud and saliva. There are more than four hundred species of orchard bees, but I can't tell from the various range maps whether any are common in the Midlands. They certainly don't come rushing to fill the new homes I've built for them.[8]

There's bad news, too. Buzzing the World Wide Web for ways to promote my wild bee colony, I soon come across a number of references to carpenter bees. *Carpenter bees?* the novice homeowner and backyard enthusiast asks. *What are carpenter bees?* It sounds intriguing at first; maybe these guys are special because they hammer together their own nests, giving new meaning to the term stick construction. Soon enough, however, I find out the truth: these members of this *Xylocopa* clan don't build things out of wood. They tunnel into it instead, creating galleries for their young to grow during the winter. And the wood they like best is already in use—it's holding up your house.[9]

On the ride home from my office through the warm, pollen-scented air that seems to be almost vibrating with the ecstasy of flowers and their ardent visitors, it occurs to me that many of the "bumblebees" I've watched with pride at the trio of peaches might very well be carpenter bees. The males are big and shiny black—to the untrained eye, they look like bumblebees. They're known to be extremely territorial; they will often hover in front of people right at eye level, trying to get the human to flinch first.

Sure enough, when I get home I'm confronted at the back porch steps by a black, hovering, jumbo-sized bee. It gets right up in my grill and stays there, buzzing menacingly. Eye contact: in the annals of interspecies communication, looking into the eyes of an animal is usually not the way to create good vibes. There are lots of ways to express a desire to get along—roll over on your belly, wag your tail, stick your butt in the air, bow and scrape—but looking a grizzly in the eye or raising your eyebrows and staring at a macaque is likely to evoke a savage response.

Having a bee try to stare me down does not make me feel warm and fuzzy or help me to acknowledge its subjectivity.[10] It makes the hackles rise on the back of my neck, even if I've just finished reading about *Xylocopa* impotence: male carpenter bees are big, but they do not have stingers. It's all just a macho pose.

Now that my eyes are opened to the truth that not all bumblebees are bumblebees, I see more of them jousting around the eaves, especially the seams where the asphalt shingles lift to expose what's behind the painted fascia trim. Under those seams isn't plywood, which these bees might not find so easy to chew their way through. This old house has actual inch-thick pine boards as underlayment. Just right for drilling.

What am I supposed to do? I don't want these guys turning my house into their own little love nests.

The advice of the pest control people is to locate the invaders' entry holes and blow insecticidal dust into them. But wait! Before I pull the trigger, I have to consider their role in the garden. Unlike termites, carpenter bees don't eat the wood they turn to sawdust with their jaws. Instead, they stuff their tunnels with the pollen they gather from spring-blooming plants. Take them out of the yard, and the number of bees flying around the peaches would be pitifully few. It's a predicament growers are facing all across the country—as honeybee colonies have collapsed due to a mysterious combination of disease and parasites and insecticidal assault, farmers have been forced to scramble for replacements like these.

So, do I find their half-inch holes tucked under the eaves and puff poison into them with a makeshift blowgun? Do I allow that toxic dust to filter down through the multitude of gaps and crevices in the old walls and into my kids' breakfast cereal? Am I really planning to provide a block of wood full of holes for one set of pollinators to nest while poisoning their pollinating cousins at the same time?

What, exactly, am I doing here?

I wind up on a ladder, looking to discourage the bees with a fresh coat of white paint, which doesn't feel like tending Eden at all.

One afternoon, after the pollinators have done their job and the peaches have blushed scarlet and butterscotch under their creamy blanket of fuzz, I notice that some of the smaller branches are broken, the leaves tattered and wilted in the heat. They're also devoid of fruit. The culprit is sitting on the arm of our teak lounge chair, spitting fragments of green peach into a pile so he can get at the pit—a squirrel, who springs into the trees with what looks like guilty speed to me, as if expecting retribution.

The gray squirrel is one of those native species, like brown-headed cowbirds and red-winged blackbirds, whose populations have boomed along with our own. As we built neighborhoods for ourselves and shaded them with rows of graceful trees, we gave squirrels a chance at the good life. They're doing quite well abroad, too. After being introduced to England in the early 1800s, more than half a century before European starlings first fluttered out of their cages into New York, the gray squirrel population has reached two million. Meanwhile, England's native red squirrel, once a common sight, has almost disappeared from most of the country.[11]

They're easy to anthropomorphize.[12] Like us, they're omnivores, and a backyard like ours is a veritable buffet of nuts, rosehips, and songbird eggs. Of course, there are certain seasons like the fall, when cars grind sack loads of acorn flour into the tarmac, when the feast is more ample than others. Chestnut oaks in particular are almost hazardous in the sheer quantity of autumn nuts they shed onto the streets, and indeed, many a squirrel seems to meet its fate trying to retrieve them.

Around here, however, between the late spring, when

the squirrels shred green pinecones and drop the remains on top of our car, and the early fall, when the acorns ripen, there's a lull in the food supply. This shortage seems to coincide with the time when the first litters of pups leave the nest and start scrounging for food. Just when the green pinecone supply has been gnawed down to the cob, the peaches and nectarines begin to blush. Very tempting, indeed.

I'm actually okay with the male squirrel's pilfering at first—I couldn't bring myself to thin my first-ever crop, so the squirrel is actually doing the young tree a favor by relieving its sagging branches. By the next evening, however, things get serious. This large male (you can sex a squirrel when they stand up on their hind legs and squint at you) has stripped every peach from all but the tips of the branches. He's not like the others. The other squirrels—and there are plenty of them, probably at least half a dozen living in our little patch alone—are busy digging in the lawn for last year's acorns. Maybe they know that the pit's bitter almond fragrance comes from cyanide.

If you invest enough of yourself into this microcosmos, it seems, the conflicts and satisfactions of actual farming reveal themselves in full. But there's one key difference between my backyard orchard and the real thing: my livelihood doesn't depend on the harvest. Although I've invested a lot of time and water in this fantasy of self-sufficiency, it's not as if this critter's appetite is putting my mortgage at risk. My kids won't go hungry if they can't eat a backyard peach. They may have to eat fruit that isn't as healthy or as tasty or as carbon-friendly, but they won't starve. As long as this guy leaves us a few, we'll still get to taste the fruits of our efforts, and that's what really matters. We have the luxury, here in the backyard, of sharing the bounty.

Sharing, however, is apparently an alien concept in squirrel society. These are territorial animals, and they're hoarders, too. The whole point of their fall madness is to keep as much of the bounty for themselves alone. They'd rather let an acorn rot in the dirt than see somebody else pop it into their mouth. And for some reason, something that has to do with expecting just a hint, just a tiny shred of interspecies appreciation and respect, I can't let the squirrel have his way.

I come home, and the deed is done. The peach tree, once loaded with too many fruit, is now barren. Half-gnawed fruit litter the ground at the base of the tree, fruit he could've left for us, wasted.

And now the scoundrel has started on the nectarines.

I can see where he lives, in a clot of dead leaves between the branches of an oak on the other side of my neighbor's garage. That's where he goes to hide when I appear in the yard. He's sneaky. He skulks. He perches in our crepe myrtle and watches as we load kids into car seats, and once he sees the car roll backwards into the street, he hops purposefully across the grass and bounds into the fruit trees.

I know this because I've spied on him, too. There's a small window near the hot water heater in an alcove of our house, and there, if you happened by our backyard, you might see a face pinched with consternation, the look of a backyard farmer whose harvest is being ransacked right before his eyes. Somehow I don't think this is what Aldo Leopold had in mind when he extolled the virtues of watching rather than shooting wildlife as a pastime.

I buy black mesh and wind it in a shroud around the nectarine. When I'm done, the tree that once was so frilly and elegant looks like it might detonate if touched. *There's no way he's getting in there now,* I think, having spent half an hour just trying to untangle one of my shirt buttons from the strands.

The strawberries are ripening, and the cardinals are taking more than their share, slashing Zorro-like marks across the fruit. They watch the fruit's progress even more jealously than I do: as soon as a blueberry shows a tinge of pigment, they snatch it. There's a single plumcot turning a deep sapphire on the bough, a handful of raspberries are coming along, and the smattering of early figs are beginning to swell. If I want to taste any of this, it seems, I'm going to have to drape half the yard in mesh.

Either I'm providing food for wildlife, as I said I was

going to do, or I'm trying to feed myself. Which is it? Being the first certified property in the neighborhood isn't making things easier. As it stands, the trees in my yard are the only fruit-bearers around, and the scale of my yard is too small to provide some trees for humans and others for wildlife. Maybe if we began to think in terms of planting fruit trees for wildlife on a citywide basis, if "summer-ripening food source" was added to the list of criteria that makes for a good urban tree, then maybe our yard wouldn't be the only pick-your-own place in town. It's not hard to imagine, actually, a street in which the towering oaks with their plenitude of acorns alternate with stretches of plum and peach, cherry and apple. It's not hard to imagine an understory planted with fruit-bearing bushes, like the rabbiteye blueberries, native to the South, that the birds are plundering in my backyard. With more options, maybe we frugivores could all get along.

And then there was one. One last nectarine tucked under a canopy of drooping leaves. Not the biggest or prettiest of the bunch, but still hanging in there. I inspect this fruit before we head to a birthday party, feeling its weight through the multiple layers of nylon strands. Not ripe enough to pick yet. I drape a few more layers over it, until it looks like a grenade. I feel as if I'm being watched.

As we back out of the driveway I deliver an ultimatum: if I come back and that fruit is gone, I swear there will be consequences. Under my breath, of course, so I don't look too much like the characters we won't let the kids watch on television.

When we get back in the evening, the tree is stripped bare. Some of the branches are snapped, and there are tufts of wilting leaves festooning the mesh, as though it had been a real struggle to finagle that final fruit.

I'm feeling murderous. Not one? Not one left for us, for the people who planted and watered this tree? I've already had slingshot fantasies, even imagined myself smashing the guilty party with a broom and then clubbing him to a pulp.

In the woods, squirrels are fair game for hunters, who still harvest quite a few for the stew pot, especially in the South. In the city, however, nobody I know eats squirrel. Or rabbit. Or possum. Or pigeon. In England, gray squirrels have been poisoned and trapped to clear space for the reintroduction of red squirrels. Some of my home-owner friends have confessed their anti-squirrel strategies to me, like filling a garbage pail a third of the way with water, with a board as a ramp and a sprinkling of floating bird seed as an incentive to take the fatal plunge. Or just a good dog—one friend tells me that from time to time she'll find her otherwise benign golden retriever sitting out in the yard with a long bushy tail hanging out of its grinning lips like the end of a furry hookah.

Is this what the dream of coexistence is going to wind up looking like, bloodlust and vengeance swaddled in the backyard version of concertina wire? There has to be another way, but I don't know what it is, or at least, I don't know of a technique that sounds feasible. When I speak with Cindy Machado, director of animal services with the Marin Humane Society in California, she suggests ringing each tree in a cylinder of steel flashing. The steel would need to be at least four feet high, so that the squirrels couldn't take a flying leap over the top. But my trees split into branches at two feet—if I wanted to enclose them in steel, they'd look like missile silos.

I'm actually standing in the produce aisle of the supermarket when it hits me with a jolt of applied anthropomorphism: this is what it's really like to be part of nature.[13] Not the fantasy of symbiosis and mutual aid, not the backyard Eden where lions lie down with lambs, but something far closer to actual participation in the local ecology, far closer to the food chain. To participate in the natural world is to find yourself jostled and threatened, your belongings usurped, your blood turned into food. You get a taste of this reality and it's astringent, not soporifically sweet. You begin to recognize that this participation ends with your body being devoured—there's a reason for the urgency of spring. To be part of it means looking over your shoulder for competitors, not tending and musing like some detached, beneficent god. There are friends and enemies, victims and victors, various hierarchies of dominance and strategies of subversion, all in addition to the symbiotic and sympatric, the nurturing, the gift exchange. It's a lot more dramatic and complex and interesting, as well as infuriating and spiritually unsatisfying. I crave harmony, a vision of an ideal world. I get irony and drama instead.

I'm actually glad the battle's over, at least for this season. Yes, I'm going to have to eat those balls of West Coast sawdust, and they're going to taste even less like nectar because of the ones I never tasted. But there's always next year.

4

The "Monkey Menace"

FACT: In India, ten primate species and subspecies live in proximity to human settlements. Of these, four are relatively abundant. The other six, however, are listed as Near Threatened, Vulnerable, or Endangered by the International Union for Conservation of Nature.

D read.

That's what I feel as I report to the airport for my seventeen-hour flight. I'm bound for one of the world's great twenty-first-century megacities, and I really don't want to leave my own backyard.

If you're exploring the limits of coexistence, Delhi is the logical place to go. It's a sprawling megalopolis of twenty-two million human inhabitants and growing, a place where the traditional meets the transnational, where the car shares the road with the cow. It's also the habitat for tens of thousands of rhesus monkeys that are both revered and maligned by the people who live with them.

And yet, every description of the place gives me pause.
They all seem to begin with the word "overwhelming."
The *overwhelming* crush of humanity. The *overwhelming* noise and pollution. The *overwhelming* traffic. The *overwhelming* horde of touts and pickpockets descending on hapless travelers as soon as they exit the airport.

This isn't what I had in mind when I planted my certified wildlife habitat sign—I'm a homebody. I saw myself poking around in my yard, which I'd transformed into a quiet and harmonious refuge from the fretful roar of urban existence. Everything I've read about Delhi suggests there is no refuge on the streets, which is where these "urbanophiles" spend their time.[1] They live in the chaos, and they know how to live there. I have no idea.

It doesn't help matters when one of the first authorities I consult, a noted primatologist, calls me on my cell phone. This is twenty minutes after I emailed him.

I haven't given him my cell phone number.

"My advice to you is: *Don't Go*," he says ominously, after a brief initial chat. I'll be harassed by Hindu fundamentalists. They don't like people trailing around after the beings they hold sacred. And if the fundamentalists don't get me, the police will. The guards will see me loitering around the government buildings in Connaught Place, and they will arrest me as a CIA spy. After an interrogation, they'll stick me on the first plane out of there.

As I listen, my head feels like a bag of microwave popcorn filling up with steam and noise. Now I can add fear of arrest and religious persecution to the list of things I'm already dreading. Maybe I can even manage to contract dengue fever, get bit by a rabid dog, and crushed by an auto rickshaw before they put me in handcuffs.

I try explaining that I wasn't really intending to follow the monkeys around. What I had in mind was more of a journalistic approach; you know, talking to all kinds of people, seeing the monkeys interact with people, that kind of thing. Would that be better?

"CIA agents *all* claim they're journalists," he replies. I should go to Gibraltar instead. The monkeys on Gibraltar are an interesting story, and I won't have all these problems.[2]

I agree. I'm sure Gibraltar would be fascinating. As the planet urbanizes, the list of city-dwelling primates is growing longer, and there are many stories of people and primates living in close quarters all over the world. Long-tailed macaques hustle tourists for snacks in Kuala Lumpur, Malaysia. Rufus-naped tamarins dwell in the parks and yards of Panama City, Panama, while hamadryas baboons inhabit Riyadh, Saudi Arabia. One of the world's most endangered primates, the western purple-faced langur, clings to life in suburban patches of Sri Lanka.[3]

The thing about Delhi, however, is that the struggle to find ways to coexist is written in high relief there. Perhaps more than anywhere else, the city is wrestling with the conflict between its ambitions and its beliefs, and the monkeys are at the center of this conflict. The reasons I don't want to go there are the very reasons I should go.

The first thing I notice when I limp toward immigration is the tang of something familiar in the air. But what is it? The airport is brand-new; even the carpet still feels pristine. The city just finished hosting the Commonwealth Games, an event whose athletic significance was overshadowed by the magnitude of its political and economic connotations. This gleaming terminal was meant to convey a first impression of the *New* New Delhi, the prosperous, cutting-edge capital of an emerging world power.

A place like this should smell of solvents and paint fumes. But instead something musky pervades the place. I can't quite place it at first—it smells almost like sweat, like a stadium full of fans lifting their arms in a wave on a sunny afternoon, but there's a sharp metallic finish to it. Something must be burning, but the fire alarms aren't going off. Which is amazing really, because by the time I'm standing in line at immigration and looking beyond into the bejeweled and hyper-lit temptations of the duty-free shops, the haze is so thick that the perfume bottles and frosted vodka bottles and backlit Bulgari signage look like they're floating in a nebulous gray soup.

What's on fire? I don't find out until I've passed the irascible functionary at the desk, a middle-aged man with a thick black mustache who has just finished barking at a

gaggle of Tibetan monks who failed to follow his commands, since they spoke barely a word of English. He
pounds a stamp into my passport without making eye
contact or offering a word of greeting, as if the task is far
beneath him. I think back the primatologist's warning—
if this is what the authorities are like, I'm in trouble.

The airport is familiar territory, in spite of the smell.
It's only when you leave the parking garage and head for
the gates that it hits you, the feeling that this place is unsettling, nerve-wracking, overwhelming. The cab sits in a
bottleneck—hundreds of vehicles are squeezing into
lanes with young men dashing between bumpers and
grabbing tickets and waving their arms, and each and
every driver is revving his engine and trilling his horn
like a giant cicada.

I haven't slept in nearly two days. I took off at midnight, watched the sun begin to rise over the wheat fields
of a former Soviet republic and watched it disappear back
into night again. My ankle, which I sprained playing
pick-up basketball a week before departure, has swollen
into a cantaloupe. The rest of my body has lost all sense
of its rhythms, and my mind is struggling to make sense.
I'm coming unhinged, and that's before I look out the
window.

The landscape around the airport resembles the surface
of the Moon. It's chalky rubble, clods of dried gumbo
and broken bricks smoothed in layers of fresh dust, all
illuminated by the orange glare of new streetlights. Plas-

tic bags roll and drift and accumulate in shredded clumps everywhere. They look like jellyfish, but there's no sign of water here, and the only plants capable of surviving seem to be daturas, desert plants whose white trumpet blooms and prickly seedpods are pallid with dust. I see a spark of light in the hazy darkness. It's a campfire. That's what I've been smelling, thousands of tiny fires keeping people warm on a chilly night. It's the smell of a forest fire, the kind of haze that blows into cities in California when the summer wind is coming from the wrong direction. But here it's laced with the heavy tang of burning coal, which I always associate with ribbons of smoke rising from chimneys in the English countryside.

A trio of figures crouches around the tiny glowing pit, warming their hands. Just beyond them there's a structure, a habitation. It's made from sheet metal and mud bricks. No lights. We pass more of these places where people sleep and eat dinner and raise kids—thousands of villagers move to Delhi every day, and finding ways to keep a roof over your head isn't easy.

The first animal I see is standing in this expanse of cratered earth. A bony white cow with humped shoulders and a long, slender muzzle; it's itching its curved horns against a leafless sapling with an imperturbable look on its face.

All of this is an eye-opener certainly, but I've read about these scenes, and to a degree I've steeled myself for them. Not overwhelmed, yet. Not until we get on the highway. Suddenly, as we plunge into a darker stream of nocturnal life, I feel it. Adrenaline and nausea, fight or flight.

There are people in the dark. Some of them are on the side of the road, walking. And some of them are in the middle of the road, between the lanes of oncoming traffic. They dash in front of my cab, and the driver rushes up to their shins, blaring his horn, refusing to swerve. Men on bikes ramble along beside us, auto rickshaws scoot past us into gaps—*somebody is going to get killed here* is what I'm thinking. We're going to kill somebody. That truck with the painted circus flourishes and the sign inviting us to honk and let the driver know we're there— that truck is going to crush us, because we're going fifty miles an hour and we're about a foot from the median where the faces are flashing past and the truck is going to come at us to get around that guy who's facing down the traffic with a matador sweep of his arm . . . we're honking, we're laying on the horn and braking to a complete halt . . . .

We arrive at a stoplight. A family is weaving between the cars, father and mother and a sleeping infant swaddled in blankets. The father sees me and puts his doe-eyed face to the window, tilting the infant so I can see the child's thick, beautiful eyelashes and rapping with the bottom of an empty milk bottle. *Hungry,* he says, from what I can make out. *Hungry.* He's imploring me. Do I roll down the window and hand out rupees? Do I look at my hands? What? Somebody help me here.

The light flashes to green. The father rubs his sparse beard with the bottle and edges down the row. I see him standing still with the traffic speeding past on either side. By the time we reach Saket, the neighborhood where I've booked a room at a small bed and breakfast, I've encountered hollow-faced young mothers with infants in their arms and men on crutches, lifting their robes to waggle the wrapped stump of a missing leg. People pressing their faces to the glass, rapping with a knuckle, begging me to do something.

I'm overwhelmed.

This story, I realize somewhere in the twilight that precedes sunrise, is as much about what we mean by a city as it is about the monkeys that live there. I've been thinking of coexistence as an equation with the city as a constant and animal species as a variable. But of course urban life is not a constant; it varies depending on where you are on the map and where you are in time. The gulf between where I live and where I am now makes this plain. Just two years ago, before preparations for the Commonwealth Games reached a fever pitch, Delhi was not the city it is now. Because of the new airport and the new metro lines and the compulsory shift to compressed natural gas for all the auto rickshaws darting like minnows in the streaming traffic, the air itself is different. It may be full of wood smoke, but it isn't full of diesel fumes any more. Everything has changed so fast that the guidebooks feel outdated—they can't turn their material around as fast as the city is changing.

I'm awake at dawn because someone outside is singing. The voice is haunting and ethereal, and it seems to be building toward something, a fit of ecstasy, a revelation. The only way to find out is to heed the call, haul yourself out of bed and find your way in the dark to the mosque.

Soon the wildlife is awake, too. Over the roar of huge jets sinking toward the airport, I hear the metal-rake-against-concrete shriek of what can only be parrots, and the squawks of something that sounds like crows, and the chatter of what I soon recognize as mynahs. I crack the drapes and see rooftops and cisterns and balconies, rectangles of whitewashed concrete and stucco all begrimed with soot. Crows and parakeets and pigeons are on the wing, and the air outside is damp and cool.

I watch the morning unfold from the balcony, half-hidden behind the fringe of a frangipani tree that's full of plum-headed parakeets and gray-shouldered crows, none of whom seem to mind that I'm only a few feet away. A small striped squirrel, not much larger than a chipmunk, emerges from a cleft in the trunk and edges down toward some potted plants. "Boys" emerge with buckets of soapy water and begin washing the night's chalky dust off the sedans their employers will drive to work. On the corner, beneath a tarp, is a stall for pressing clothes, where an older man greets the customers, a woman wields the iron, and a young man crouches to tend the small charcoal pit fire they use to heat the iron.

There are no yards. Not a single blade of centipede grass. Dogs, however, are everywhere in the street, lying in the sun. None are on a leash. Nobody seems to own them, and they never seem to bark, not even when gaunt figures rattle through the neighborhood on battered black bicycles, calling in a singsong voice for newspaper and cardboard and wire, or when fruit sellers push through wooden barrows piled with green guavas. I try to imagine what would happen if someone like this came rolling through my neighborhood — you wouldn't be able to hear their chanting over the racket of the dogs trying to get at them. Instead, we have the stillness that settles over houses when everybody is at work, interrupted only occasionally by a white truck coming to spray for bugs or tweak the wiring on somebody's cable package.

It's all very comfortable up on the balcony. But I didn't sit on a plane for fifteen hours to watch sleeping dogs lie in the sun. I'm here to find monkeys, and that means going downstairs, out the gate, and into the street.

Sounds simple enough, right? Imagine, however, that you decided against getting the rabies shots — would you feel entirely at ease tiptoeing through a gauntlet of unleashed street dogs? And then, when you reached the corner and found the traffic coming at you according to the British system, which is the opposite direction from where your instinct tells you to look, would you be ready to make your move across? Delhi has the highest level of pedestrian fatalities in all of India—more than five hundred people died trying to cross the street in 2008.[4] There are more pedestrian deaths than murders in this city. And unlike me, most of those people know what they're doing.

I make it to the verge of a four-lane road just above a stoplight. Auto rickshaws, bicycles, ox-drawn carts, cars, and trucks—it's all coming through at top speed. Talk about overstimulation: horns are designed to demand your attention, but where am I supposed to look when there are horns blaring in every direction? Were I to do what the locals do, I would stand at the edge with the tires brushing my toes and when I saw a gap coming in the closest lane I would scoot across, ignoring the complaints hammered out in horn noise. Then I would be standing in the middle of the onrushing traffic with cars and carts and bikes whizzing past both my back and my toes. My self-preservation instincts would be screaming at me. Death! Death! Death and Danger! But I wouldn't be paying any attention to that. I'd have to be focusing on the next gap so that I could scamper to the median. Same thing with the other two lanes, and then I'd be across—unless I looked the wrong way and got flattened into naan bread.

This is what I'd do at the corner, if I had the nerve. Forget about my swollen foot and go for it, hobble my way through a real-life version of *Frogger*. Instead, I stand on the sidewalk. White-haired old ladies in saris are crossing. Children are crossing. Dogs are trotting across. I flinch as if I'm going to jump into their wake, willing myself to get off the curb, but I can't do it. I can't bring myself to jump in front of oncoming traffic. I cannot cross.

Back at the hotel, I make calls. I need somebody to help me navigate the experience of this city. The next morning, a car and driver are waiting for me at the door of the hotel. We nudge our way through the stoplight I could not cross, honking liberally at the little old ladies dashing for the median. Our first stop: a corner not far from the Saket metro station, to pick up my guide, Surya. Suddenly, I've gone from solo budget traveler to VIP complete with my own entourage. It feels really strange. And I have absolutely no regrets.

Suryaveer Singh is tall and thin, with a thick black moustache and dark, almost reddish skin. He has the kind of posture most of us are told we should have but don't, back perfectly straight, no slouching, chin up. It gives him an air of dignified detachment, as if he is calmly surveying the world from on high. He comes from a small village in Rajasthan, where his family owns a farm.

"I am Rajput," he says soon after we shake hands, as if this explains a great deal. From what I recall reading in the guidebooks, the Rajputs are a warrior caste who at one time ruled much of the north. They are renowned for their bravery in battle.

We haven't traveled far when we put Surya's demeanor to the test. As our taxi tries to scoot around the median and pull a U-turn, there's a thump against one of the rear fenders.

We've hit a pedestrian.

The driver is flustered. I'm flustered and trying to fumble off my seat belt so I can turn around and see the victim. Surya raises an eyebrow. He's in the middle of telling me an abbreviated version of the Ramayana, but he pauses while the driver sticks his head out the door and calls out to the victim, something like, *Hey, you okay buddy?* Whoever it is has disappeared into the crowd of bystanders on the sidewalk, apparently unharmed. The driver waves and shouts something. Off we go into the chaos.

Buddha Jayanti is a city "nature park" of relatively recent vintage. It has no sites of historic interest, which means it's off the beaten track as far as tourists go. Surya has never been here; neither has the driver. Hence the U-turn and the pedestrian collision. My guide's normal job is to usher a small group around the city for a day, taking them to the Red Fort and Old Delhi before they board a private coach for the Taj Mahal. My driver's normal job is to shuttle these tourist groups around.

"I am specializing in sights of historical interest," Surya explains, trying to dampen my expectations. "Not so much nature and animals." He will do his best, he says, while the driver grunts something in Hindi that is definitely not meant to convey excitement.

I actually have to sell the place to get Surya out of the car. There are hundreds of acres of open space here. It's supposedly some of the best-preserved forest in Delhi. Let's check it out. Surya looks at me like I'm five minutes from one of the wonders of the world and all I want to do is wander around a rest stop instead.

"But there will be no monkeys here," he protests, searching for words. "This is not where you find monkeys. This place is known for lovers. The lovers come here for private times."

I explain that I'm not just chasing monkeys, I'm trying to get a look at the big picture. Like habitat. Degraded and lost habitat. One of the reasons people claim there are problems with monkeys now is loss of urban forest—the monkeys, they say, used to live in what is known as the Delhi Ridge, a constellation of ancient hills surrounding the city. As the city has exploded in size, even these steep slopes have given way to new construction, and the monkeys have been forced to make their living in the streets.[5] If the monkeys are indeed absent from this preserved fragment of "Central Ridge" forest, then why would that be? There are plenty of trees and shrubs and even a parched sward of grass here—it looks like promising wildlife habitat to me.

Surya isn't buying it.

"You want monkeys, you look for garbage," he says as we walk across the lawn toward the trees.

"Where there is garbage, there is monkeys."

He's right about one thing: it's early morning, but couples are already clasped in various secluded corners, sprawled out on benches and blankets. Otherwise, the place is deserted. We're the only two people walking around.

We pass lots of tree saplings stubbed into the grass. They don't look like they've prospered in the dry, chalky soil. A new addition to my life list is prodding the lawn with its needle beak: a hoopoe, something like a pale peach robin with a spotted crest.

Surya marches past.

Small orange butterflies with horizontal lobes for wings, the kind you see in butterfly farms or preserved in clear epoxy at the mall, are looping and fluttering over the foliage.

He pays them no heed.

He stops beside a green metal garbage bin. It has no lid, and all the trash has been yanked out of it and the wrappers and plastic bags are strewn all over the ground. In fact, every garbage bin in the vicinity looks as if it has been hit—they're all surrounded by wide circles of trash. There's garbage everywhere, once you start looking, paper cups sagging like old mushrooms under the trees, candy bar wrappers caught like ragged flowers in the branches, plastic bags everywhere.

"Now you see the reason for the monkey problem."

In the past twenty years, he says, more and more people have been coming to Delhi. They make more and more garbage, and the city can't keep up. The trash gets left on the streets, and the monkeys do what you see here—they tear it open and eat it. As a consequence, there are more and more monkeys.

"Also, this is not *macaca* habitat," he says, waving toward the dense stand of trees beyond a bench where a pair of lovers is midtryst. *Macaca* is the Latin name for the species, *Macaca mulatta*.

"This is langur habitat."

He says macaca migrated here from the Himalayan foothills as humans deforested that landscape, following the line of the ancient Aravalli Hills to their termination point here, in the Delhi Ridge. Meanwhile, the langurs, tall, slender monkeys with whiplike tails and charcoal faces, retreated into Rajasthan, where you find them today.

"South of here—langurs. Here, macaca."

He offers the Asiatic lion as an analogy, warming to the task now that we are talking about history. We know that lions existed in the Aravalli Hills, he says, because they appear there in an episode of the Ramayana. Then tigers migrated down to India and pushed the lions back. Lions were pushed into the desert, and today the Forest of Gir is the only place left to see Asiatic lions. All the epics have lots of lions, but they are silent on tigers because there were no tigers here in ancient times. The monkeys, he says, followed the same process.

I have no idea if this is true for big cats, or for monkeys. In fact, the evidence suggests that langurs and macaques today not only have overlapping ranges but in some areas travel together in mixed groups. There's even a documented case of a langur female nursing a macaque infant in the wild. But reading history for clues on ecology—that's a pretty sophisticated approach for someone who professes no knowledge of the natural world. This may work out better than either of us thought.

The first monkey I see on the street is not real. He's probably a hundred feet tall, and he's towering over a frenetic traffic circle: Lord Hanuman, the revered hero of the Ramayana. His powerful hands are joined at the fingertips across his bare chest, accentuating the bulge of his triceps and making him look like a weightlifter striking a pose. He's hairless, his skin is the carroty shade of a fake tan, and from the tip of his nose up to his golden crown, he looks decidedly human. But then there's his upper lip, which juts out, incongruously meaty and brown, into what amounts to an animal's snout. He appears to be both human and animal, and what's striking to me, coming from the land of Bigfoot and werewolves, is that he's ennobled by this blurring of the line rather than degraded into something savage. He's a demigod, not a menacing beast.

Surya had attempted to recount some of Hanuman's

famous deeds as we lurched along through the city streets. The stories mostly seemed to involve service to Lord Rama, an exiled prince and divine incarnation who spends most of his time in the forest battling "demons" from what is now Sri Lanka. At one point, Rama's wife is kidnapped by the evil king Ravana, who absconds with her to Lanka. Rama calls on the animal kingdom to help him get her back—the king of the bears comes to help, and so does the vulture king. The king of the monkeys, Sugriva, sends his prime minister, Hanuman, to help the cause. Hanuman rescues the princess and becomes the devoted servant of Rama, fighting fearlessly against the demons from the south while exhibiting an almost egoless devotion to the needs of his master. All of these stories are collected in the Ramayana, one of the two great epics of Hinduism.[6]

The animal kings were probably based on tribal people, Surya managed to communicate to me between horn-blaring, brake-squealing, near-death experiences. The tradition of these forest dwellers was to wear animal masks into battle. The chieftains would wear the mask of a bear or a lion, and they would lead an army of men all wearing the same mask. Over time, as the details of history were amplified into legend, these warriors took on the character of their animal masks.

"What made the monkeys so special," I managed to ask. "Why not bears or vultures?"

Because those kings were old men, Surya said. They

are always depicted as old men, while Hanuman is always shown as virile and young, the perfect sidekick for Lord Rama.

"You can do Wikipedia and find all these things," he declared, settling back into his seat belt after we came to a particularly violent halt.

There are many Hanuman temples, or *mandir*, in Delhi, one in just about every neighborhood. There's one in Columbia, too, although it doesn't have a figure of this stature to mark its location. This statue towers over the broad tree-lined boulevards and roundabouts of New Delhi, the part of town the British designed as their capital, installing a graceful mix of greenery and imperial architecture.

"You see the tail? It is long, you see?"

Surya points to where Hanuman's tail curls up in a lengthy crescent behind his head. I nod, catching my breath after dashing across a roundabout, not sure why this matters.

"Hanuman always has a long tail," Surya explains. "Never a short tail. This is why the langurs are called Hanuman langurs, because they have the long tail that we see in all the depictions of Hanuman, not the stubby tail of these macacas."

Everybody I encounter seems to like langurs; they're noble and gentle-natured, they say, the kind of creature you could build an incarnation of a deity around, a model of coexistence. Rhesus macaques, on the other hand, are often derided as uncouth ruffians. Farmers hold a particularly deep grudge against them for raiding their crops. Surya won't come right out and say it, but his tone suggests that rhesus monkeys don't deserve the reverence they receive. They're impostors.

Outside the steps of the temple we hand our shoes to a kid, who places them in a rack. Then we pad in our socks along the sidewalk to the marble stairs. The temple is cool and dark but noisy. Devotees are clanging a chain of brass bells as they pass through the entrance, and a priest is sitting cross-legged near the exit, chanting passages from a well-worn tome in a nasal monotone. We pause in front of a diorama in which the characters from the Ramayana are traveling across the sea. Surya is explaining something about the syncretism of the blue and black figures of Rama and other deities, something about the Aryans and Dravidians merging into one faith, but I can't pay attention because a wispy throng of mosquitoes is hovering around my swollen foot as if they can sense there's a motherlode under that sock. They must be breeding in that stagnant puddle that's meant to represent the ocean at the bottom of the display.

Dengue? The "break-bone fever" for which there is no vaccine? I grope in my pockets for a bug repellent wipe and frantically wipe myself down. Surya eyes me impassively.

Karma, he'd been explaining to me in the car, is what allows some castes to eat meat. Two castes, the Brahmins and the merchants, do not eat any meat. Then there are castes whose karma is to eat meat. He himself belongs to one of these castes. Rajputs were known as warriors and hunters, and they were allowed to eat meat in order to survive. Like the lion: the lion must eat meat to live. It is his karma.

But even the carnivorous castes don't kill holy animals. The bond between people and animals is called *shanti*, symbolized by the animals that serve as vehicles for the gods. In temples you will see lions and tigers and elephants all carrying gods, but you won't see any hunting scenes. Those came much later. *Shanti* means that people see the spiritual side of every animal. They see Hanuman in every monkey.

What would happen if I swatted a mosquito in here? That's what I'm wondering. Are we talking about a holy animal born and raised inside a temple of worship or a blood-sucking disease vector?

To exit the temple, you duck through the gaping mouth of a witch, dodging her polished white fangs, and descend the stairs that have been chiseled into her tongue. Looking back, you can see her blue eyes bulging with outrage at your escape. You have just reenacted one of the Ramayana's episodes, in which Hanuman, flying over the ocean to Lanka, confronts a sea witch who tries to devour him. Hanuman strikes a deal with her—if he agrees to enter her mouth one time and then escapes before she can swallow him, she will have to let him go. She agrees. Once he's inside her mouth, he shrinks himself to the size of a fly. Before she can stop him he buzzes right out of her mouth, and she is forced to let him go.

I'm glad I didn't swat any bugs in there.

As we're leaving, a guard barks at me to get my shoe-clad foot off the marble plaza, shooing me off with the back of his hand. My first thought is to protest—I was just backing out of the way of the crowd marching down the sidewalk, not intentionally treading on the temple's landing. And what's the big deal, anyway? Look at the pigeon crap over there, and the grime between the tiles. Then it hits me: the guard is reminding me that the spiritual landscape is all around us. It hasn't been restricted to the diorama inside the temple—it's out here in the living and breathing, dirty and crowded city, the kind of place where you see a tiny clay figure of the elephant-headed deity Ganesh sitting on the concrete pillar of an overpass with traffic roaring overhead. The monkeys inhabit this spiritual landscape, even when they're rummaging through garbage. That's why they've managed to survive in the city for so long.

The North Ridge is a steep fragment of forest jutting up from the ancient heart of the old city. According to news reports, this is where the monkeys have been caus-ing the most mayhem, stealing into the rooms of luxury hotels, tearing through piles of important documents in government offices, and terrifying the bedridden patients of the Hindu Rao Hospital.

The street scenes get older and dirtier and more crowded as we leave New Delhi behind. The air sizzles with urine and burning leaves, and the hazy sky is full of black kites, raptors about the size of a red-tailed hawk. They have taken over scavenging duties for the sacred vultures, which were once abundant in the city but have now been nearly poisoned out of existence by a compound used to treat sick cows. Everywhere I look, the New seems to be eradicating the Old: entire neighborhoods of the old city are coming down. Ironically, the destruction comes not with a crane swinging a wrecking ball but the old-fashioned way, with workers swarming the rooftops of decrepit apartment blocks, pounding at the brick walls with sledgehammers. We sit at a stoplight and watch a crew work—they swing in a continuous rhythm, one after the other. The concrete pylons of an overpass are already in place above the ruins, like talons reaching for the sky. Everything colorful—all the banners and signs—has been stripped away, and what's left has the character of newsprint, gray tones smudged with dust.

There are kids at the stoplights. Some of the boys have a thick black moustache painted on their cheeks, and they pound drums while their sisters do cartwheels or push carnations at the window. After their brief performance, before the light begins flashing, they rap at the

glass, show me their stomachs. Some are younger than
my own kids. I ask Surya what I'm supposed to do. He
says the company he works for discourages giving alms
to children. These kids could go to school and get fed
there, but the parents keep them out to beg instead. It's
easier to have them beg. I ask him where the parents are,
and he says they're nearby, watching. They sit where we
can't see them.

From the old city we climb a winding, narrow road
into the tree cover. This is the smallest and most fragmented part of the Aravalli Hills, the place where the
habitat has been degraded the most by humans. The vegetation is green and relatively lush behind the chain-link
fences and stone walls that run alongside the road, but
there's trash everywhere, fresh garbage layered on top
of old garbage. We have the driver drop us at the Hindu
Rao Hospital and walk in past the armed guards at the
gate. The buildings are the color of bile and coated with
the usual black grime, and the grounds are thronged with
people, sprawled in the grass, pacing anxiously, having
lunch on the ground. Some look very ill. There's an en-
campment in the courtyard, a cluster of blue tarps and
cooking pits where in all likelihood the families of some
of the people who cook and clean and maintain the
buildings live.

According to the news reports, monkeys were once a
common sight here, too. Surya says a place like this produces lots of garbage, which attracts the monkeys. But

where are they now? They're not in the trees. Not in the dumpsters heaped with trash and hospital waste. Not down on the grass trying to steal food from unsuspecting humans or up on the roof jeering at the people down below.

Surya stops a guard. "Where are the monkeys?" he inquires. Or maybe, "Hey, I've got this crazy American who wants to see macacas—help me out here." They converse in Hindi for a while, the guard shaking his head and waving a baton toward the trees.

Surya translates as the guy continues his patrol.

"No monkeys. They are gone."

"Is it langurs?"

Many businesses have started paying for the services of a trained langur, which a guard leads around on a leash. When a rhesus monkey dares to show its face, the guard lets the leash go, and the langur bounds into the treetops in pursuit, chasing the macaques onto somebody else's property. Rhesus monkeys fear this simian equivalent of a K-9 unit with good reason: not only are langurs bigger, but they can crack their whiplike tails with enough force to break the skin. Supposedly, the langur is a docile creature around people, although I'd just been reading about a neighborhood association on the other side of the Yamuna River that had hired a langur to deal with marauding macaques, only to have the hired monkey go berserk and start biting people.[7]

"No langurs," Surya reports. Trained langurs are in

hot demand throughout the city, and the guards who keep them tend to make the rounds, chasing macaques from one neighborhood to the next. Instead, the guard told him they had dealt with the monkeys themselves, pushing them out the gates to the other side of the road, where they could still be seen sometimes.

"There's maybe some garbage there," Surya says, motioning for me to follow him across the road to the top of what I'd describe as a dead man's curve. A big chunk of the stone wall has been demolished, maybe by a bus losing control, which seems about to happen again with every passing vehicle.

Surya motions for me to stop and abruptly turns his back to the wall. The traffic scolds us. There's no sidewalk, just trash and weeds and dried dung from what could be humans or animals.

He motions with his chin toward something behind him.

"Macaca."

There's a monkey perched like a boulder on the top of the wall, watching us. He's stockier than I expect, with a shaggy carpet of drab fur that makes his sunburned face all the more riveting. I think back to the Hanuman figure with its human and animal features not so much merged as mashed together—it's actually a pretty accurate depiction. This guy's face looks as if someone scooped away the nose we would expect on a human face and fastened an imposing animal's snout to the jaw. His pale topaz eyes follow us intently. I have no idea what he's thinking. Macaques have a repertoire of expressions they use with each other, including baring their teeth in a kind of thin-lipped smile of appeasement and staring intently with an open mouth to express violent rage. I'd characterize this fellow's expression as a disdainful scowl.[8]

"We pretend we don't care about him. You can see him?"

The subterfuge works briefly, but then the monkey decides he's had enough of my eager mug peering over Surya's shoulder. He pads hand over hand along the wall to the break. Not running away, just making it clear that he doesn't enjoy our company before he scrambles down the edge and heads into the trees.

The rest of the troop is inside the wall on the ground, where mounds of fresh trash have been dumped. It smells like sour milk and rotting fruit and rancid grease, and it takes me back briefly to the bins in my own back-yard, full of white bags ready to be taken to the curb and carted away. We have a composter for all the tea bags and apple peels we produce, but the majority of the stuff we throw away is similar to the wrappers and aluminum platters and greasy paperboard strewn all over here, packaging with residues of cooked food, globs of stuff that we kept in the fridge too long. The detritus is so fluffy and thick the shrubs seem to be growing out of trash in-stead of soil. The air is humming with flies.

"You see?" Surya says. "Garbage."

As soon as the troop sees us, the trash pit erupts in squealing and screeching and screaming as the older and wiser heads retreat slowly into the canopy. We see females with long-suffering faces carting infants around on their chests and frisky juveniles scampering after each other along the tree limbs. They aren't exactly afraid of us, but they're wary. Some of the troop, not the big male but his subordinates, seem to have taken up position on the chain-link fence above and below us, scouting our movements. When Surya raises his arm, they scatter.

"Maybe the catchers have been here," Surya says.

The catchers are city employees whose job is to lure monkeys into banana-baited traps and then cart them out of the city to a sanctuary. They get paid 450 rupees, or about ten dollars, per monkey, which is a fairly hefty sum in a country where a quarter of the population lives on less than 12 rupees a day. The city is so large that the catchers are spread thin, rarely visiting most places more than once a year. But monkeys have long memories, and they remain wary long after the catchers have left.[9]

The human population has a long memory, too, which may be why monkey catchers aren't more numerous. Even after polio vaccine production no longer needed monkeys, demand for macaques as research subjects continued unabated until 1978, when the Indian government responded to public outcry by banning their export. By then, more than a million macaques had left the country for research labs, reducing the wild population by 90 percent and leaving behind a legacy of mistrust for foreign scientists and the lingering suspicion that trapped monkeys still wind up as research subjects.

Once exports were banned, however, the wild rhesus population rebounded. They have now doubled in number, which may have as much to do with Delhi's monkey conflicts as the abundance of garbage.[10]

Nearly 90 percent of all rhesus monkeys in northern India now live in proximity to humans and depend either directly or indirectly on humans for food. They raid crops, they scavenge in garbage, they eat what the devotees of Hanuman offer them. Only 14 percent live without any form of human contact in the forested foothills of the Himalayas, feeding on shoots and leaves and berries with the occasional bird egg thrown in for protein. That's a complete reversal of the macaque way of life in the 1980s, when research indicated that only 15 percent lived among people.[11] Part of the blame for this shift in lifestyle can be laid once again to trapping. A study by Iqbal Malik, a leading authority on urban macaques, indicated that trapping actually caused forest monkey troops to break apart, because the trappers disrupted the social balance of the troop. Members of the fractured troop wound up migrating to cities, where ironically they have prospered.[12] Today, macaques in northern India are, by and large, city dwellers. For better and for worse.

We drive back down into the crush of humanity, the smells wafting through the windows along with a growing collection of flies. It's slow going in the old city, and I pass the time by counting the saplings that have been dug into patches of dirt along the sidewalk, each one protected from trampling crowds and browsing cattle by a green cage. Each cage bears a slogan in English: "Green Delhi, Clean Delhi." The baby trees have been planted all over the city, it seems, and I've seen versions of the green city slogan everywhere, too. Maybe it's all for show, just another bit of sprucing up for the Commonwealth Games, but it nevertheless makes me think about how little we spend back home on "greening" the city. This city has done far, far more than we have to create an urban forest and clean the air, and they've done so with millions of people living in conditions we would consider squalid.

But I'm not convinced about the clean part. Green Delhi, yes. But Clean Delhi? What does that mean? It means that all the auto rickshaws have a "CNG" painted in yellow on their green backsides, so that we can sit at a stoplight without being pickled in the fumes of innumerable two-stroke engines, for one thing. But when I think clean, I think of the yards in my neighborhood, with every fallen leaf and needle blown into a pile on the curb and hauled away in trucks, the tidy grass where herbicides keep the weeds from sprouting and insecticides keep the ants from pushing up mounds. Ours may be a clean landscape, but that tidiness comes at the expense of habitat.

On Delhi's streets, the first thing that comes to mind is garbage. For someone like me, the stuff that accrues every day and lingers in every corner is a shocking sight. Garbage strewn across the lawn in my neighborhood? Unthinkable. The animal responsible would be shot, poisoned, or trapped. Our neighborhood ritual is not feeding the animals, it's rolling the big green bins to the curb for their Monday morning pickup. That's where visual and olfactory contact with our rotting refuse ends. I doubt any of us have visited the landfill where our waste piles up.

I've already begun to realize that, as Surya says, it's garbage that feeds the animals in the city. There are no pastures for sacred cows to graze here—they eat what people feed them, along with whatever they can scavenge. The food that humans won't eat doesn't go to waste— the cows and the dogs and the monkeys and the pigs and the black kites and the house crows and the rats and the cats all see to it that nothing is wasted. One study found that langurs living in the city of Jodhpur survived a drought in stable numbers, while half their counterparts in a nearby nature park starved.[13] If you clean up the streets, pick up the garbage, and haul it away before the animals can tear into it and make an unsightly mess all over the ground, then you leave nothing for these animals to eat. You will have fewer animals living in the streets, fewer encounters between humans and monkeys, cars and cows. Maybe that's a good thing. Or maybe you don't want to make the city so clean that other species can't live there.

We pull up in front of my hotel as the sun is setting over the rooftops. It's been a long day, and we haven't managed to find many monkeys, which has Surya rubbing the back of his neck, his guidely pride piqued. Where are they all? Usually there are monkeys everywhere, he says. We see them all the time. He's tried the Red Fort, where we found flocks of pigeons across the street from the bird hospital run by the Jain Temple, but no monkeys. He's tried Connaught Place, where we spotted a trio of monkeys way up on the roof of the Parliament, peering down at the gun-toting soldiers on the lawn. He's even tried a sure bet, taking me on a bicycle rickshaw through the passageways of the old market, but even there we saw only one monkey perched on a tangle of power lines, nibbling something out of its palm.

In truth, there have been conflicting reports about the population of monkeys in the city, and conducting an accurate census of these mobile creatures in a sprawling megalopolis has been virtually impossible. The city estimated there were five thousand monkeys when trapping began; other authorities put the number as high as seventy thousand. In 2008, the city declared they had caught all the monkeys and shipped them out to the sanctuary. No more monkey menace. The city's residents, however, begged to differ. They continued to complain that there were monkeys everywhere.

"Maybe they have caught them all for the games," Surya muses. "We just see the leftovers."

My foot is throbbing, and the jet lag is making everything feel like a sleep-deprivation experiment, the kind that ends with the subject hallucinating and babbling incoherently. I'm ready to crawl into bed and squeeze a pillow over my head so that I can't hear or see anything else for a while.

Suddenly Surya's face lights up.

"Jim, they are here," he says, pointing toward the roof directly opposite my hotel. There, silhouetted by the fading light, is a male macaque perched on the rail, and beyond him there are youngsters scampering after each other, females looking after infants, juveniles lounging around, grooming one another.

It's feels like magic, like a physical manifestation of the spirit world. It sounds a bit far-fetched and irrational, but at that moment I feel as if Hanuman himself has decided to send some of his minions to bless me with a visit.

"They have found you," Surya says, shaking his head as if he, too, is aware that some inexplicable cosmic irony is at work here. There hasn't been a monkey sighting in this neighborhood for eight months, I find out later.

I limp upstairs to the balcony. The monkeys are just across the street, which means they are about twenty feet away, too far for them to jump but close enough for me. One group of subadults has discovered someone's balcony, and several of them take turns leaping onto a screen door and trying to pry it open. A juvenile snatches a pair of yellow underwear that was drying on a rack and scampers off with it. Down goes the rack, followed by the hollow pop of a flowerpot hitting the ground. Meanwhile, the dog inside the apartment is going berserk, and his barking puts the entire street on alert. Suddenly, all the complacent street dogs are yammering and lunging toward the rooftops, and all the servants on my side of the street are standing outside, too, pointing and laughing nervously.

The monkeys pay them no heed. The big male sits on his perch, examining his fingernails as a giant jumbo jet rumbles in for a landing overhead. The people whose balcony has been under assault release their husky yellow lab, and he hurls himself at the monkeys, who scatter clothes as they scramble up the gutters to safety. A woman comes out the door behind the dog, brandishing a broom and smiling nervously. She picks up the laundry. Then her adolescent son emerges and takes the broom. He's smiling nervously, too. He can't see the juvenile monkeys sitting on the roof right above his head, but he can sense from the dog that they're there. He tosses what looks like a chunk of Styrofoam insulation up there. The monkeys hurl the chunk back down at him. They seem almost eager for a reply, as if this is a game they're enjoying. The dog barks furiously.

So far everything has been playful. A little light marauding, a little disturbing the peace, no big deal. Then the atmosphere changes. A bloodcurdling scream, followed by the kind of snarling and spitting that erupts when two animals are locked in mortal combat. It's as if an electric current runs through the members of the troop. The big male launches from his perch, twenty feet straight down from the railing, and lands with a tremendous thud on the roof of someone's car. He lets the sound reverberate like a bomb going off, his mouth open wide in a silent howl of fury. Then he scales the wall in a few quick leaps and flings himself onto a flagpole, which he wrenches back and forth in a frenzied display of violence. Whether a rival gang has decided to make a move or somebody in the troop has crossed a line, I'll never know.

I feel blessed he's not on my side of the street.

So that's the monkey menace. Roving bands of thugs, basically, invading your neighborhood and trying to break into your house, biting if you dare to confront them. The city really started going after the macaques in earnest after a senior minister fell to his death while trying to swat them off his balcony with a rolled-up newspaper.[14]

And I thought I had it bad with squirrels.

What I'm still struggling to understand is how people not only tolerate animals like this in their midst but actually feed them, encouraging them to stick around. Letting an animal camp out under the porch I can almost understand: it's not hurting anybody. But these guys?

"This is their place," the proprietress of the hotel says firmly the next morning, after I explain the subject matter of my book. "The monkeys were here first. This is their home."

We're sitting in the lounge, just inside the balcony where I observed the monkey menace. The glass doors are open, and the cool morning air is sifting through the screen door along with the sounds of awakening street life. She's saying that people in the villages live with animals that are dangerous. They know the tiger is going to come and eat one person every year, and they just accept it. That's the way it is.

As she's talking, the male macaque suddenly appears. He's not across the street now. He's on our balcony, strutting hand over hand along the black iron railing, four feet away. A burly fellow, his shoulders packed with muscle. Not someone I'd want to tangle with.

The proprietress leaps from the couch to the screen door.

"I'll just make sure this is locked," she says with a nervous laugh, pressing the top and bottom bolts firmly.

When Surya arrives, I tell him I've seen the menace firsthand. What I'd like to observe is people actually getting along with monkeys, if that's possible. Maybe we can find a place where people feed them, even though it's not Tuesday, the day reserved for Hanuman worship, when temples all around the city turn into all-you-can-eat buffets for macaques.

The street is still waking up, the sidewalk food stalls crowded with people hunched against the cold while they wait for breakfast. We have a new driver. Javinder is a young guy who seems more gung ho about chasing monkeys, although his enthusiasm also seems to express itself in a tendency to floor it when he spots a length of open road, so we hit eighty for a hundred yards and then jolt to a stop behind a truck, whereupon he yawns and scratches the gold chains around his neck before pounding on the horn. Surya sits in front, navigating by a Google map I printed out before I left the States. He doesn't flinch. I sit in back, trying to keep my bad foot up and my chai down.

Feeding monkeys is kind of a gray area as far as the city is concerned. It's an officially discouraged but widely practiced form of worship. If you're seeking good luck, you make an offering to Hanuman by giving one of his holy incarnations some food. It's making a sacrament of an impulse I know from my own monkey-feeding experience in Dania—this deep desire to participate in some kind of gift exchange, to share a meal, break bread together.

Just about any wildlife biologist will say that you shouldn't feed wildlife. If you habituate an animal to handouts, you'll wind up having problems with that animal and its offspring, too. In the back of my mind I can hear Ralph Taylor, a Massachusetts biologist who manages urban bears. "Wild birds don't need to be fed!" he once admonished me. "Why entrain them to your yard for your benefit?" A fed bear is a dead bear, as they say in Yellowstone.

We track down a Jain temple in the Sanjay Van forest, near the wholesale flower market where each tin-roofed stall seems to specialize in a different color: hot pink, orange, white, yellow, ready to be strung into garlands the devout wear to the temple. Yesterday's blooms have been dumped in a pile at the entrance, and nearly all the urban animals seem to be rummaging around in the paisley swirls of refuse, bony cows with long bean-pod ears and moist black eyes, grunting black hogs, pensive dogs, and hopping house crows. All except monkeys. They've already had their fill of the fruit and bread left on a stone platform near the temple. Later, when I mention this feeding station to Iqbal Malik, she says that the platform is a remnant of a previous attempt to deal with the monkeys by feeding them on the city's perimeter and hoping they'd stay there.

The Sanjay Van is the largest remaining chunk of Central Ridge habitat, and like most of the nature parks, it's deserted. A guard from one of the park's ancient Muslim tombs escorts us through the woods, pausing at one point where a dirt track from Mehrauli village is blocked with a mound of dirt. The forest edge here is so carpeted in plastic trash that it looks as if translucent fungus has erupted under the slender trees. I can tell by the way the guard is pantomiming with his hands that something illicit gets dumped here.

"Jim," Surya translates, "he says this is where the monkey catchers come to release their monkeys. They don't want to drive all the way to the sanctuary, so they come here and open up the cage." He chuckles sardonically. "Then the monkeys go right back into the city so they can catch them again."

Javinder is late picking us up on the Gurgaon Road, which is basically a freeway to the suburbs jammed with sixty-mile-per-hour traffic that we have to cross on foot. This is the first time I've seen Surya actually run—anything less and we would be crushed. First we run to one side and wait—no driver. We call his cell. Go to the other side. We scurry back to the other side. No, the other side now—he's turning around. He'll pull off on the other side. It would be comical if it weren't so dangerous.

But Javinder redeems himself: he knows where they feed monkeys all day long. It's right on a bustling street, not far from the expansive ruins of Tughlaquabad, another abandoned former capital in a city with seven of them. We pull over by a cart loaded with bananas, whose owner, a stocky, cheerful man with a silver beard and a long scarf flung over his shoulder, has been coming here daily for fifteen years. He sells a thousand bananas a day, although he's a little cagey about the price—there's one price for me, after all, and another price for your everyday Hanuman devotee. On Tuesdays he sells almost twice as many. Twice a year the catchers come, but they don't seem to make a dent in the population. He's never seen a langur here.

The sidewalk behind him is strewn with banana peels and what on closer inspection appears to be monkey manure. There are monkeys on the sidewalk too. Not many, just some females loafing on the warm concrete, watching their youngsters play. Surya buys some bananas and hands them to each of us, including Javinder, who's decided to get involved. We approach a female who's squatting on her haunches in front of a half-eaten banana. She pointedly ignores us, scratching her backside while a nervous juvenile comes to crouch next to her tail.

Surya motions for me to hang back—she doesn't seem menacing, but you never know, especially with her offspring around. He and Javinder dangle bananas by their knees and make soft *tsst tsst* noises to get her attention. Not interested. Surya peels the banana. Nope. I rejoin them and proffer a banana of my own—no way. Up and down the sidewalk, pedestrians are steering a course between relaxing monkeys and empty peels and poo, all evidence that the morning feed is over.

According to Iqbal Malik, Tughlaquabad was at one time the only place in the city where you could find monkeys and people genuinely coexisting without conflict, because the ruins were covered in the kind of forest that provided adequate food and shelter. The ruins were one of her primary research sites, and she published numerous articles on the habits of these urban macaques.[15] But the archaeological value of the place eventually trumped its value as urban monkey habitat. Renovations stripped away the tree cover to reveal the remnants of life from over a thousand years ago, as well as atmospheric views that stretch across windswept hills to the skyline in the distance. The monkeys have decamped from this treeless landscape—those who once lived among the ruins now live in the woods where the banana seller plies his trade.

Surya and I duck under a chain-link fence, stepping through the trash and trying to avoid the spots where people have relieved themselves along the narrow path through the undergrowth. Eventually, we emerge into the dense shade beneath a stand of tall, skinny trees. Kids are playing cricket in a dusty clearing, but the sandy wash beneath the trees belongs to the monkeys. At least a hundred are all around us, in the lower branches of the trees, grooming each other on the ground, chasing one another in play. Adults stroll past, close enough that I could reach out with a foot and touch them. They aren't approaching us so much as refusing to deviate from their intended path. In here, they seem to be saying, humans don't matter. We may be curious about them, but they're not curious about us. They have their own society, all kinds of clan rituals and responsibilities and expectations, and none of it includes us.

Being in the midst of rhesus society gives you a taste, a small taste, of what it might be like to be a monkey in a human world. On the other side of that fence the human menace bustles past. Urban monkeys are surrounded by people who are wrapped up in the business of being human, although it has to be said that at least some of us stop to toss a banana or two. Come into the shade where a hundred monkeys sit, however, and you find yourself amid a community that doesn't involve you any more than driving to work or going out on a date involves macaques.

And what is it like to be in the midst of rhesus society? Frightening. One minute everybody is grooming each other, and then suddenly, bloodcurdling screams are erupting on all sides of us. We've come in the middle of the breeding season, and the males are particularly on edge, hyperalert to any rivals trying to mess with the chain of command. Adults come racing past us, some huffing and looking murderous, others fleeing in terror. Surya reaches down and picks up a thick branch. "They respect the stick," he says knowingly, as if he's dealt with macaques this way on the farm. "They see the stick, they stay away." We laugh nervously. One of the big males has caught up with an interloper and appears to be punishing him, although it's hard to tell who's winning in that ball of fury rolling in the sand.

Back on the other side of the fence, we leave the stick next to the sidewalk, surrounded by empty banana peels.

One way to deal with the monkey menace, it would seem, is to make sure that the monkeys are well fed. Full monkeys appear to have no interest in people. That's the premise of the monkey sanctuary located on the southern fringe of the city. It makes intuitive sense, which is why I've seen versions of it proposed elsewhere. Give a territorial species everything it needs, and it's likely to stay put instead of roaming around and getting into trouble.

Funded by the Ministry of Environment and Forests since 2007, the monkey sanctuary has been controversial from the start. It sits inside a six-thousand-acre wildlife preserve that was once a quarry providing stone for Delhi's expansions. When the quarry closed, the people stayed. They have stayed in their village despite being notified that the land around them has been declared a wildlife sanctuary. They have stayed despite court judgments declaring their continued residence illegal. And they have stayed despite the arrival of thousands of urban macaques on their doorstep.

I've already been warned that we won't be able to get inside the gates. Iqbal Malik has never been allowed inside. I spoke with a photographer who took some riveting images of the monkey catchers at work, Dmitri Alexander.[16] He said he tried to get permission from the authorities to visit the place, but after a couple weeks of paper-shuffling inertia, permission was denied. I've appealed to Sonya Ghosh, the animal welfare activist who fought for the establishment of the sanctuary and is part of the board that oversees its operation, hoping she might accompany us on a tour of the site. But she is in the former hill station of Shimla, protesting a decision by the government to deal with that city's monkey problems by killing some of them off.[17]

Getting to the monkey sanctuary isn't easy. The place is deliberately off the map, and we wind up spending an hour exploring the heights of the Southern Ridge without finding anyone who's even heard of the place. Eventually, we wind our way through villages crowded with people eating and cooking and standing in line to get their faces shaved on the sidewalk, past mango orchards and walled compounds that Surya calls "swami estates," and at last we arrive at a rutted dirt track that rattles through acacia thorn scrub into the Asola Wildlife Refuge. Two species of acacia are native to the region, but seventy more species have been imported to "improve" places like this, where other trees tend to shrivel up and die. It all looks skeletal and stunted, the leaves of the acacias limp and pale as old dollar bills, the understory bone dry and brown. And this is December; there's another six months of searing heat and little rain to go before the monsoons start again. It's hard to imagine monkeys calling this kind of place home—not if they have another option.

It's no place for your standard taxi, either. Javinder is muttering under his breath by the time we reach the cinder-block shacks of Bhatti Mines village, steering between craters and wincing when we bottom out. An open sewer runs right along the road, a pale, milky trickle clotted with trash and dark mud. People are everywhere, walking, playing in the street, stepping around the stagnant puddles. We pass women in traditional dress getting water from a black plastic spigot poking up from the ground. We pass a small, dusty square with a dozen men squatting on their haunches, playing cards while they wait for trucks to show up looking for labor.

"These are the lowest class of people you can expect to find in India," Surya says.

They are primarily Ods, a formerly nomadic tribe known for their facility with earthworks. Historically, these people roamed the country, setting up camp while they were busy digging ditches and building dams. But in 1975, when the Delhi government took over the quarries, the Ods settled here to work in them. They've been here ever since, refusing to resume their nomadic life after the quarries closed or take the government's offer of land elsewhere.[18]

"How can you have a village in the middle of a forest area?" Sonya Ghosh wrote in an email. She was still recovering from a fever she'd contracted while protesting the monkey cull in Shimla. "If I park myself in the Gir forest, can I complain when the lions come to check me out?" The Supreme Court, she wrote, has decreed that these people have to go, and alternative accommodation has been provided for them. The villagers have the support of local politicians. Ghosh has the writ of the court. The result is a stalemate, with people living right at the gates of the monkey sanctuary.

Not surprisingly, there's been trouble. Take monkeys accustomed to foraging in cities, separate them from their troop and their territory, and set them loose in a range of barren, scrubby hills. Where do a good portion of them wind up? The village next door, of course. And now they associate people with the trauma of being trapped in a cage, so they aren't feeling all that polite when they come to town looking for food.

Monkey bites happen almost every day in this village, frequently enough that the government has set up a clinic to cleanse wounds and give shots for rabies, although they do not offer the victims financial compensation. Many of the villagers have armed themselves with slingshots to keep the monkeys at bay, and a langur has been hired to patrol the local schoolyard. But the monkeys keep coming.[19]

We see them taking in the sun on the top of what was supposed to contain them, a twenty-foot-high wall added in 2007. It's made out of sheets of translucent green fiberglass bolted to a wooden frame, and it looks a bit like the "Green Monster" at Fenway Park. The poorest of the villagers have built their dwellings right up against the stone foundation beneath the green monster, scavenging rocks and bricks for their own walls. They cook and hang clothes in the shadow of the green panels, and they dry cow dung for fuel on the stonewall itself. The monkeys peer down from above, watching.

An imposing metal gate blocks the entrance to the sanctuary, but the keyhole door inside it is wide open. Surya and I step through. Some teenage boys are playing cricket in the dusty parking lot, around what looks like a pen. Inside the cage, we see what Surya identifies as a nilgai, a stocky antelope with stubby horns and a thick neck, munching stalks of sugarcane.

"Jim," Surya says. "You see how he looks like a cow? He is called a blue bull, because he turns blue all over in the fall. Over time, the people have come to associate him with the cow, and for this reason he is not hunted. It is the same with langurs and macacas."

We watch as a cricket player stoops, scoops up a handful of dust, and flings it in the antelope's face. Surya raises his eyebrows, then shrugs. This is how they treat a sacred "cow"? The nilgai appears unfazed.

We walk down the dirt road toward a small concrete building. Dozens of monkeys sit on the ground at the edge of the road, eyeing us like vaguely hostile prisoners.

Two men are waiting for us on the porch, dressed in the knee-length white tunic and baggy pants known as a *shalwar kameez*. The porch is screened in chain-link fencing to keep the monkeys out, and although the doors are sitting open at the top of the steps, it feels as if we're entering a cage.

I listen and nod while Surya addresses himself to the man with the flowing white hair and thick, white moustache. He and the other man are caretakers who also work in the office—the rangers are away because it's a holiday. From what I can catch the conversation seems to center mostly on my camera. Do I have a camera? Yes. I pat my pocket. "Research," Surya keeps emphasizing. "Not pictures."

Once again, he seems to have a knack for placating the suspicions of people we've never met. I have the feeling that a lot is going on here, complexities of caste and social order I can sense but don't understand. We offer the man money, but he declines strenuously.

"The credit goes to Hanuman," Surya says evasively, when I ask him how he does it.

The old man picks up a stout length of peeled wood and walks us back to the car to ensure that we do indeed leave the camera. As we approach the pen, he suddenly begins bellowing at the top of his lungs and shaking the staff over his head. It's not the monkeys—they've already seen the stick and melted away into the scrub. Is it the cricket players? They're laughing. He slams the stick against the trunk of a tree like he's coming to kick some serious ass, a display of aggression that is not all that different from the macaque I saw shaking the flagpole back and forth like a maniac. As soon as you start to focus on monkey behavior, you start seeing people acting like monkeys everywhere you look. We're all primates.

I'M GONNA SMASH YER SKULL TO SMITHEREENS!!! RAAAAAGGHH!!!

With a single bound, the nilgai leaps the fence and trots off down a trail, leaving behind what is in fact not a cage but a monkey feeding station.

I know how the old guy feels. Watching him is like watching myself rampage out the door after that squirrel in the nectarine tree. Been there, done that.

Surya asks to borrow the old man's stick, and the man readily agrees. We set off in the company of two eagerly smiling cricket players, Sunil and Ajay, who agree to be our "local guides." They are both about seventeen, with untucked collared dress shirts and flip-flops on their dusty feet. They speak no English. Surya asks them about themselves as we duck under the thorny acacia branches on a shortcut to the feeding platforms. They tell him they normally work as drivers in the city; they've come home because of the holiday. In this village, Surya says, young people don't have many opportunities. They don't study for very long because they have to earn money for their family.

There's a surprising amount of activity in the thorn scrub. We come upon women from the village, balancing giant bird nests of firewood on their heads. Cows amble past, the bells sending a hollow, soothing clatter into the wind. Surya immediately spots a mongoose darting into a pile of rocks, and the boys pluck a porcupine quill from the sand.

Holding it up, they snigger in the way teenagers do. Surya's translates: There is a saying that if you dig this quill under somebody's house, the family will fight their whole life. I suspect he's giving me the G-rated version.

We emerge on a dirt road that runs straight along the edge of a high plateau before curving down into a narrow, boulder-strewn ravine. We've come maybe half a mile from the office. This is the route the food truck takes each day, arriving with a load of produce to stock the feeding platforms. The mix of worn boulders and scrubby trees makes it seem like the set for an old Western. Our local guides set a brisk pace in their flip-flops, and Surya is more than capable of keeping up. I bring up the rear, my ankle throbbing.

When the first feeding platform is in sight, Surya calls for a halt. He hands me the old man's staff. I'm clearly the weakest and most vulnerable member of this expedition—if the monkeys are going to go for anybody, it'll be me.

The platform looks like something the National Park Service would construct to blend into the landscape, an artful column of stone. A cluster of monkeys is sitting on top, munching cucumbers. When they see us, they retreat to the boulders. The warm smell of fermenting bananas wafts toward us as we watch a monkey farther down the ravine begin shaking a small tree as a warning that we are coming. In response, the troop emerges from the shade to perch on the rocks and observe us. It's a far cry from the scene outside my hotel. If these monkeys were once savvy city-dwellers, there's no recognizable sign of that high-strung indifference here. There's no balcony to climb on, no kitchen to raid, no one nearby. And there's plenty of food, at least when the nilgai don't get it.

Around the bend, there's construction going on. Two women are lugging bricks on top of their heads while the menfolk attend to the finer points of laying the foundation. It looks like they're building a house, but the foreman says they're making new platforms. The old ones, at six feet, are too low. The nilgai can jump right up on top, and the cows can crane their necks and tongue a few morsels down. The new platforms will be ten feet high, with a roof, so that only the monkeys can jump up.

Soon enough, we encounter other uninvited guests at the monkey buffet—camels. A groaning and grumbling trio of them plods right past us on the road, brass bells jangling on their frayed halters. We watch as they nudge aside some cows and begin to chow down on what's left atop a feeding platform. Even ten feet may not be enough.

As we walk, Surya gives me the history of land tenure in the region. It's hard for me to imagine how a place like this could have escaped development. How is it that such a great expanse of land is uninhabited, so close to a city where every inch of concrete seems to be occupied?

Surya attributes this de facto greenbelt to the legacy of the British rule. When the British mapped out the country, he says, they set up two kinds of land designations, revenue land and forest land. The former was cultivated land, usually owned by a local ruler who paid taxes to the Crown. Forest land was reserved, at least in theory, for timber and other sylvan pursuits. By law, it could not be converted into revenue land, meaning it couldn't be developed even as the city swallowed up villages nearby.

It's not clear to me what it is about this place that has inspired such secrecy. What is it that the government doesn't want the outside world to see? Is it the treatment of the monkeys? They seem to have it pretty good. Or is it the treatment of the villagers?

This sanctuary is a big step up from the city's prior attempts to deal with monkeys. After trapping for export was banned and the population began to rebound, the monkeys had to go somewhere. For years, many were transferred to areas surrounding Delhi, including Vrindavan, a small city where Hindu pilgrims come to worship at the many temples devoted to Lord Krishna, who according to legend was born nearby. Iqbal Malik helped with some of the initial translocations of several hundred urban macaques to this area and pioneered many of the strategies for rehabilitating urban primates to the forest. But eventually, she said, "so many monkeys were being born due to their very high productivity rate that it had become a situation where the humans were in cages and the monkeys were free."[20]

By the early 1990s, Delhi was forced to stop exporting its problem primates, and the city wound up holding them in a concrete-floored cage, hidden away on the edge of the Sanjay Van forest. The discovery of this pen in 2002, stuffed with hundreds of monkeys that had been thrown together from various troops, caused a furor among the faithful and prompted the notoriously bureaucratic government machinery to move on a sanctuary with uncharacteristic speed.[21]

It's still early days here, and as the redo of the platforms suggests, the place is still learning what works. Malik had originally proposed a much different version of the sanctuary, with fewer acres and more local people involved in the care. She envisioned the kind of place that tourists might visit and had recommended a list of forty trees species that would provide better forage. Malik had also suggested neutering monkeys in the city as a way to control their population growth there.[22] None of these proposals have been taken up so far, and she no longer consults on the management of the sanctuary.

I asked Ghosh what they planned to do about limiting the growth of the monkey's population. It seemed to me that the monkeys might have it a little too good. After all, if you keep bringing monkeys to a place with few predators and plenty of food, the population is almost certain to grow. Malik's research on the Tughlaquabad monkeys showed that the urban rhesus population is capable of doubling every four years. When the main group gets too large, small groups of females splinter off to colonize fresh territory and create new groups of their own.[23] Eventually, you have to wonder how many monkeys the sanctuary could contain before such splinter groups began colonizing their way back to Delhi.

Ghosh said they could deal with population growth by creating more sanctuaries in reserved forest areas. But where? Even if this sanctuary proves to be a model, isn't the conflict with the villagers here likely to be repeated elsewhere around the perimeter of this booming city? How much are you willing to invest in the care and provisioning of monkeys in a place where people live with so little? I think of the starlings we kill by the millions, the brimming host of nuisance animals shot and trapped and poisoned because they get in the way. How much would I be willing to sacrifice to let these creatures live?

One solution might be sterilizing monkeys, which is already being tried in Shimla.[24] However, as might be expected in a country that exported so many rhesus monkeys for medical research, the idea of technicians chasing monkeys around with scalpels has met with plenty of skepticism. Ghosh, for example, said she didn't think there were enough monkeys in Delhi to warrant sterilization. "The monkey population is not so high in Delhi," she wrote. "In Shimla they sterilize monkeys because the population runs into lakhs [hundreds of thousands] and there have been cases of unprovoked monkey bites." She also suggested that sterilizing monkeys makes them vicious and prone to attack for no reason.

The real problem here doesn't seem to be indifference to the plight of animals so much as caring too much, the volatile mix of religion, animal rights, and science creating rifts between those who want to help. It isn't just monkeys. The director of an animal shelter in the city, described what would happen when the shelter tried to help cows that had been hit by cars. The ambulance would be met by "this fanatic religious lobby" who refused to allow the shelter staff to administer painkillers to the wounded animal. When the staff tried to euthanize a cow whose back was broken, they were beaten up. The shelter doesn't respond to calls about cows any more. Instead, she said, the sacred animals are taken into custody by priests and left to die on the banks of the sacred Yamuna River or dragged to the grounds of a temple and given water from the river to drink but nothing for the pain.

At the same time, animal welfare has support in powerful places because of the sacred stature of the animals, their central role in the ethos and imagination of the culture. You wouldn't have funding for a monkey sanctuary without keen awareness of their spiritual significance to people who vote.

I can see why someone with reverence for the natural world might say, Look, let nature take its course here. It's not our place to intervene. Leave the cow by the sacred river. But then, this is the city, and this is an animal suffering in our midst. To empathize with the plight of an animal, to do something about it, is to go against the natural course of things.

So be it, I find myself thinking. It's in our nature to do something about suffering.

By the time we reach the quarry pit, more teenage boys have joined us, and they've taken to ribbing each other and passing around some kind of lemony condiment that comes in a blue tinsel sachet. We've seen hundreds of monkeys crowding the platforms, stuffing guavas into their cheeks and gnawing on reddish stalks of sugarcane, snorting challenges at each other. They haven't approached us. I haven't needed the stick. I wonder, though, about Malik's vision of this place as an ecotourism spot. Could you harness the human desire to feed monkeys to feed the villagers, too? Could Ajay and Sunil become guides instead of drivers, showing people like me around? Or is it best to keep people away from these creatures, resign ourselves to the fact that people will be people, macaques will be macaques, and inevitably someone will get hurt in the encounter between the two?

There are plenty of nearby venues where you can see local people serving as guides for the wildlife riches at their doorstep. Keoladeo, a watery mix of river and swamp a bit further south, has plenty of guides ready to help you find and identify hundreds of bird species. In

Ranthambore, guides stand ready to do the same with tigers. Both of these involve just looking at the wildlife, however, preferably through binoculars. With monkeys, the appeal lies not just in observing but in feeding. That's the sacred practice, and it involves getting up close and personal with the animal, extending a hand in friendship or devotion, taking the risk of a bite in exchange for a blessing.

The last platform is perched on the edge of a sheer sandstone cliff, with water glittering hundreds of feet below in the old quarry pit. The cows have managed to pull most of the food down and are munching on the sugarcane, while a handful of monkeys squat on top of the platform, gnoshing guavas. This is the end of the road for urban monkeys. When you think about all the other places they could wind up, it's not so bad. In every direction, desolate rocky hills and thorn scrub are lit by the pale winter sun. It seems to go on and on, as if the chaotic hive of humanity we left behind is not ten miles away but ten thousand.

"You made me see this," Surya says, shaking his head in bemused appreciation at the monkeys and the cows and the vertiginous view. We joke about how far off the beaten track we are—the name of the company he works for is Wild Frontiers, and we have definitely lived up to the name. I don't think either of us could have imagined we'd wind up here.

We take turns with my binoculars, watching coots and

some white-breasted ducks stir the shimmering surface way down below.

"Say *binoculars*," Surya says, before he will hand them over to the boys.

He's joking, but he's serious, too. He's trying to show them something, and it has more to do with the possibilities for a life outside the village than with a look through the American's glasses.

Ajay, who goes first, doesn't know how to hold them to his face. Surya shows him how to widen the spread between the lenses and adjust the focus, but only after Ajay mouths a soft and slightly embarrassed *Binoculars*. Behind us we can hear the monkeys, the quick patter of their footfalls as they cross open ground.

Ajay hands the binoculars back. Surya offers them to the others, but they are too embarrassed to say the word.

Surya is not a nature guide. He's a registered guide in historical subjects, having passed the exams to certify his expertise in those areas. But he knows a thing or two about the natural world, and gradually he's adjusted his observations to fit the work at hand. Back in the city, he'd already taken to identifying the trees we encountered. This one is *peepal*, he'd say. This is *peelu*, and this is *ashok*. That one we use for antiseptic. This one for toothbrushes.

On the way back, he points out a male peacock hopping silently across a boulder field. The thorny knee-high scrub we walk through is a kind of "plum," he says, pointing out a small, translucent yellow fruit tucked under the leathery leaves. The monkeys could eat these. Not far from the smoke and noise of the village, a bird bursts from the ground cover and zooms into the evening sky before I can raise my binos.

"Lapwing," Surya says.

Not bad for someone who professes no knowledge of nature.

The boys lead us along the wet, milky path of an open sewer to where the green fence looms. The sewage runs into the park from beneath it, near a gap in the fence where the green panel is missing.

The monkeys see us coming. They start shaking the green panels in warning, announcing our arrival with a thumping drum roll. We duck under the wooden framing and find ourselves in the middle of a tent camp, the huts made of mud bricks covered in a jigsaw of tarps and corrugated tin sheets. This is where the boys live.

Ajay invites us in for chai. His mother is bent over a fire pit on the ground, smoke rising from the circle of stones around a blackened pot. The sun is setting, and Surya knows I can't drink this water without consequences. He declines for us. Still, I imagine what it would be like to share a meal with Ajay and his family, to gather on the stones and eat our food while the monkeys watched us from the wall. I think of my own backyard, the permeability of my own walls. What we live with, and live without.

Surya instructs me to give Ajay a hundred rupees for his services, which is about a week's salary for most people here. He says something to him, something about the possibility of being a guide, perhaps. Then he tosses the stick on the ground and commands him in an abruptly authoritarian voice to take it back to the old man. We head back to the car, where Javinder is still stretched out in the reclined seat, deep in a nap.

When neither the guide nor the driver knows where you're going, that can either be great—you're way off the beaten track—or a recipe for disaster. The place we're looking for has recently become something of an urban myth, sometimes called the Madari Village but more often referred to as the Kaputhli slum. You won't find it on a Google map, apparently, but this is where the city's array of circus acts, the drummers, dancers, magicians, and musicians known as *madaris,* live.

The people we're hoping to find are a distinct subculture: the Kalandars, a nomadic Muslim caste who for generations have made their living performing with trained wild animals. They often work with other street performers and are traditionally associated with trained bears. Not long ago, shaggy black bears shuffled backward through the lanes of oncoming city traffic, forcing the cars to slow down. The only way to get an animal out of the way was to hand some coins to the owner.[25]

Their livelihood is fast disappearing in this modernizing city. Bear shows were the first to go: those have been outlawed, and animal welfare groups have confiscated many ursine performers and taken them to sanctuaries. Forbidden bears, the Kalandars turned to monkeys, and even today rest stops and tollbooths outside the city are thronged with trained macaques performing tricks and leaping onto tour bus windows to demand *baksheesh*. In the city, however, monkey performances have been banned, and the once-common sight of a dancing monkey has gone underground.[26]

Why talk to these people? This is another story of life with monkeys, a story that lies at the uncomfortable edge of coexistence. In this city there are the people who feed the monkeys and consider them sacred. There are people who take the "modern" view that they have no spiritual significance at all—they're just pests. And then there are the Kalandars, who make their living from domesticating wild primates and in doing so present another challenge to the notion that there's a hard-and-fast boundary between the wild and the tame, rather than a spectrum of possibilities. This is a part of the world where elephants do physical labor and falcons perch on the wrists of hunters. There's a trajectory here, from circus to zoo to captive-breeding program, in which the goals and methods change but the fundamental circumstances do not: each situation involves an intermingling of the lives of people and wild animals. I haven't given up hope that the *zoopolis* I envisioned at the start might lie further down this same path, an evolution of the way we live with other species.

That's not to say that every relationship between humans and other species is benign. Domestication is a process that typically involves great cruelty. Bears usually have their nose perforated so they can be led around with a metal ring. Often their canines are yanked out. Monkeys endure beatings when they don't get their routines right. And yet, the Kalandars are people who know the ways and habits of monkeys intimately, who have accumulated centuries of knowledge of what it takes to live with them. In some ways, they are the people who appreciate them most.

Start asking around for the guys who keep trained monkeys illegally, and you're likely to wind up going around in circles. Has the slum actually been torn down to make way for the Commonwealth Games? Maybe. Where was it in the first place? Nobody knows. Even Surya gets the runaround. We find the place where we think it is—behind a temple devoted to "five-faced Hanuman," a multispecies representation of the demigod that includes a lion, boar, and bull in addition to man and monkey. There's a male monkey on a leash in the stall beneath the temple, clutching a banana and watching the street traffic impassively. But the people here tell us the madaris we're looking for have been moved across town.

We delve into the ancient villages that have been subsumed into the metropolis without gaining any of the amenities of urban life, like paved roads or underground sewage disposal. The streets are narrow, clogged with auto rickshaws and pedestrians and donkey carts and cows, and look as though they have been scooped into potholes for a motorcross event. Javinder winces as we bottom out the taxi.

Because he's from this part of town, he gets out with us at a rickshaw repair center, and the three of us cross a road near an enormous fruit market and head toward a broad open sewer with high concrete walls to keep the monsoon floods inside. Pigs are rummaging in the soggy mounds of trash between the walls. The air is putrid; it smells of rancid milk and rotting waste, a collection of odors far sharper than anything you might detect down-wind from a sewage treatment plant. A row of shanties has been built on the packed dirt next to the wall of the sewer. This is the kind of place where the risk of zoonotic disease, the risk of microbes making the leap from animal hosts to human hosts, seems frighteningly real.

We duck down beneath the ropes holding up the tarps into a path where all the tents open up onto cooking fires. It feels as if we have entered the private space of a dwelling, although we are outdoors. In the first tent, a man is watching a game show on a television that is somehow attached to the grid. Kids are squatting and playing with marbles in the path, snot oozing from their noses. Flies are everywhere, and the kids reflexively flick them away. They land on us also, persistent, too numerous to keep away.

The report of our arrival precedes us. An American? With a government-certified Rajput guide and a local driver? Here? A commotion arises from the end of the path, and a dark-skinned man with an eager face comes down the path buttoning up his shirt. He talks loudly and excitedly, ordering one of the kids away to fetch something, then showing me a trick with his eyeballs— *Look! Look!* he says in English, as his eyes appear to vibrate in their sockets. *See! See!* The crowd yanks a jute rope cot out from a tent for me. *Sit! Sit!* I sit. Everyone else stands around me. I try not to wave at the flies.

The boy returns with grubby, zipped-up, vinyl document bags, which are full of scrapbooks. The man with the quivering eye trick leafs through, showing me the airline tickets and photos and pamphlets he's preserved. He's a traditional monkey dancer by trade, dressing up in a fur costume and a grease-painted face to look like a langur: there he is at the 2002 Smithsonian Silk Road Festival in Washington, cavorting with his long tail on a big stage with a multitude of other performers. On the next page there's a VIP ticket to an international festival in Brussels. His passport has expired, but it's filled with stamps to places all over the globe. He pulls out a small drum with a string attached—a tambura—and begins plucking a thin, wavering tune from it.

None of us can stop him—he's going fast, aware perhaps that he has our attention only briefly. None of us have the heart to say, *Sorry, this is a mistake, We want the people who work with monkeys, not the people who dress up as monkeys.* Instead, I listen, trying to make sense of the strange juxtaposition of these artifacts from where I'm from and where we are, beside this open sewer. He's apparently made many trips between these worlds. I can't understand why he would ever come back to live like this, and it seems rude to ask a question like that.

It falls to Surya to interrupt. We must go. The man refuses all offers of money, and we duck back through the camp to the street. Glancing back at the tarps by the sewer one more time, I think again of how we define life in the city. I have imagined trying to live with other species, but I have never imagined any place like this.

Back in the car, Surya and Javinder are laughing at me.

"If we just got you off the plane and took you here and said this is Delhi, you would be . . . ." Surya puts his fingers to his temple and makes a mind-blowing flick.

"You wouldn't believe."

Javinder says something in his broken English, something to the effect that things are about to get more world-shaking. He pulls up near the five-faced Hanuman, and it seems obvious now that we were in the right place after all. Bands of small boys are strolling along the alley with big, booming drums strapped to their chests, pounding out beats under the tutelage of several men.

Many people seem to be coughing. It's not just the acrid smoke from the morning fires—there's fresh phlegm in the street in addition to the usual food waste and excrement.

Somehow, Surya quickly enlists the services of a slender young guy with soft, slightly protruding eyes—a fellow Rajput, cellphone pressed to his ear, who leads us through alleys so narrow we almost shimmy through.

He seats us on milk crates next to a chai stall to wait for someone named Mahesh. An old woman sits cross-legged under a tarp ladling the milky tea through a strainer into small glasses. Three guys sit down next to us with their chai. They are magicians, Surya says. We are in the right place.

Twenty minutes pass. Many cellphone calls are made. Then Mahesh arrives. We talk a bit about his travels—he's a puppeteer, and he shows me a picture on his phone of the oversized figures they maneuver with sticks. His next gig is Amsterdam, in the New Year.

More calls, and then a small, fearful man with pock-marked cheeks arrives. A Kalandar. He looks both shy and terrified that he's going to be arrested or persecuted. He can barely bring himself to sit. More calls are made. The small man keeps shaking his head, and Mahesh keeps cajoling him. They are not filmmakers, he tells him. No cameras. Surya sits impassively.

"Come," Mahesh finally says, and we set off down the street. It occurs to me that this is how journalists get kidnapped. Do I have any idea what has been said in all these phone calls? Do I have any idea where I'm going?

We turn into an alley that follows another concrete-walled sewer, stepping over toddlers playing with plastic toys and skirting women tending charcoal pits. The alley gets narrower, and we dodge stacks of dirty breakfast dishes left outside doorways and squeeze shoulder-to-shoulder past people heading the other way.

A heavyset man is waiting for us in a small courtyard draped with laundry lines. He stubs out his cigarette. Here is a monkey: a female with a chain around her neck, crouching inside a wooden crate and gnawing agitatedly on a sugarcane stick. When a kid gets too close she lunges at him, exposing her flanks, where the fur has been worn away. She looks miserable and disturbed and likely to bite.

This isn't what they want to show me. After a minute or two, the show is ready. We turn the corner—a crowd of men and boys has gathered behind me now—and find another small, sad-eyed man crouched in a doorway. He's dressed in traditional garb, which Surya identifies as the *lungi* and *kurta,* undyed cloth draped around the legs beneath a long tunic, topped with a small, round cap. The man has two leashed monkeys with him, a stocky male and a juvenile female. Compared to the monkeys I've been seeing around town, this pair has the sleek and glossy look of well-groomed pets. Their faces in particular are noticeably pale and smooth compared to the scabbed and blistered complexions of the city monkeys I've seen. It makes me wonder if they spend much time outside. I recall the monkeys in the sanctuary, their contact with people reduced to a minimum. Are there options in between?

I'm ushered to the front. The monkeys are nervous. They cling to each other, trying to squeeze out of sight behind the man's flowing sleeve. Their eyes flicker over me, then move around the crowd. From inside his kurta the man produces a card, which Mahesh hands to me. It's the business card of a government official. The man performed with his monkeys at a birthday party for this guy, Mahesh explains, a couple of weeks ago. Nowadays, birthday parties are his main source of income.

The man has a small drum and a smooth stick about as long as his arm. He taps the stick and begins to chant in a low, sing-song voice. When his voice rises, the male monkey readies himself. The man raises the stick and the monkey does a somersault. A ripple of delight flows through the crowd. He does another. And another, springing effortlessly in place. Meanwhile, the juvenile female has discovered a glittery candy wrapper on the ground and is shuffling it toward her mouth. The man plucks it away, still chanting.

After the somersaults, it's the female's turn. The man begins tapping the drum as he sings. He tugs the leash, and the female begins shuffling in a semicircle on her hind legs. The male does the same. Every so often, the man tugs the female back on her leash, eliciting a chuckle from the crowd.

"That's the wife," Surya explains. "That is her husband. She is trying to stray, but he always gets her back again."

After two more dances, Mahesh escorts us back to the chai stall, where we see the kids pounding their snare drums. This is the future for Kalandars, he tells us. Learning to perform with something that isn't wild or alive.

I find myself wondering about that future. Isn't this what always happens in the move to a modern economy—working animals become superfluous, along with the skills and knowledge needed to live with them? Maybe there is a way to keep people involved in the lives of wild animals, to draw on the accumulated expertise of the Kalandars and the proximity of the Ods to devise an enduring engagement between the species. I've been lucky—I found a guide who happens to know more about the natural world than he normally gets paid to know. We've gone places and seen things I wouldn't trade for a glimpse of a tiger from the back of a jeep.

I think of all the "local guides" we've had along the way, and it strikes me that there are plenty of people who would be a natural fit for this kind of work. I'd like to have guides like Surya—resourceful, imperturbable, knowledgeable—who also know their way around the wildlife of the city. I'd like to have guides whose work helps us figure out how to coexist with other species, who can tell overwhelmed outsiders like me all about the connection between the spiritual history and the natural history of the place.

That's the kind of development I'd like to see.

Heading back to the airport, it feels strange to see the same sights and realize how acclimated I've become to the ferocious onslaught of stimuli. The horns, the reckless pedestrians, our seizure-like progress—none of it hits me like it did before. I hardly notice the smoke hanging over everything.

When we were walking back to the green wall in the monkey sanctuary and following a cloudy stream of sewage through the woods, it occurred to me that what I wanted to create in my backyard might not be possible, that I might be wishing for a reconciliation between forces that ultimately cannot be merged. Diversity doesn't come from balance, I thought. It comes from chaos.

I want harmony and diversity in my backyard, but that's not how the natural world works. There's nothing orderly here. That's why the streets are full of life. I think of the carpenter bees in the eaves, the squirrel in the fruit tree. I want to create a sanctuary for wildlife. But I'm not sure how much chaos I can embrace.

5

The Night Visitor

FACT: Based on estimates of one rat per person, approximately 250 million rats inhabit urban and suburban areas in the United States. An estimated 1 billion more inhabit poultry farms, causing $19 billion in feed losses per year.

—————————

It begins at 4 a.m. I'm drawn to consciousness by a rattling, scraping, thunking sound in the bathroom. It sounds almost like someone has shut themselves in there and can't figure out how to get the doorknob to turn, which sometimes happens when you have two kids under the age of five. But not at 4 a.m. I tune my parental antennae to the sounds of breathing across the hall—two regular sets of rises and falls, a soft snuffle. All is well there. But someone, or something, is stuck in the bathroom.

This has the feeling of a nightmare about it.

I creak across the floor and tap the door aside with my foot—it's already partly open. The nightlight is casting a soft, warm glow on things, the toilet, the towels, the tub. I don't see anything I don't expect to see. I'm in the middle of emptying my bladder—I figure I might as well make the trip worthwhile—when I hear it again. Right there. Right there in the bathtub about a foot from my heels. Something quite sizable, and by that I mean I can hear the sound of its hair brushing against the wall of the tub and the clack of its scrabbling claws.

I should say at the outset that I am reasonably genial character by day. But at night I'm closer to instinct, especially as a parent of two young children. When they wake me up at 4 a.m., I restrain myself. But anything else—sleep is precious. I can't be held responsible. Which is why I first take a startled leap forward, splashing my hand with the contents of my bladder, and then I lurch around with an incoherent roar and rip aside the shower curtain, ready to pulverize the intruder.

The tub is empty.

The children sleep soundly on. But not my spouse, Nicola, who pads into the bathroom and confronts me with a heavy-lidded glare. She likes her sleep, too.

"What are you doing?" she hisses.

The visitor begins again, freezing us. He's not in the tub. He's under the tub, rattling the PVC pipes like a pair of bamboo wind chimes. Our eyes meet, registering the fact that he's real and he's big. No mouse. No palmetto bug. I receive tacit permission to disturb the peace.

After I've filled the house with the conga beat of my

fist against the side of the tub, I pull back. My pain threshold is much higher when I'm still half asleep, but still, the meat of my hand feels tenderized. We exchange another look: *He's gone? Scuttled away? We can go back to bed?*

He answers immediately, clawing his defiance into the pipes. I wonder if he can peer out the overflow drain and see us—a pair of half-dressed homeowners staring dumbly at a blank sheet of porcelain. I don't know if I'd be stricken with fear either.

"What is it?" Nicola says.

"I don't know," I say. Could it be that the tub is acting like an amplifier, that really it's just a tiny mouse? I offer a range of other possibilities—a squirrel? We've got lots of those running around. A possum? Raccoon? Cat? Rabbit? I leave unsaid the one possibility I know we both dread. Rat. Plump, beady-eyed, and cunning. With that tail—it's the half-naked tail that gets me.

I can't do anything more. Our visitor keeps up the racket, frantic intervals followed by an almost calculated pause. I can see dawn glowing through the slats in the blinds. Soon the kids will be up and we'll be pulling off pajamas and pouring milk into cereal in a deeper than usual stupor. Not for the last time, I want to kill whatever is under there.

Most houses I've inhabited have included a basement. These were not always pleasant places to visit—I recall showing my mom a slug I found by the washing machine one time that looked a bit like a mottled brown pickle and left a broad swath of slime in her quivering palm. But in the South, where we live now, the crawlspace is the norm. And although neither venue is particularly salubrious, at least in the former you can wander around upright, maybe even set up a Ping-Pong table. In the crawlspace, however, as the name implies, recreation is the furthest thing from your mind. You are sliding on your stomach through the dirt, burrowing into the entrails of your domicile, hoping you don't come face to face with Shelob's cousin. Nobody ever called a crawlspace "garden level."

This is where I'm bound. A small square of painted plywood along the side of the house marks the gap in the brickwork that serves as the entry to this underworld. It's surprisingly small. Homeowners were apparently smaller in the 1940s, when the house was built. A lot smaller. When we bought the place, I watched the home inspector wriggle through the opening and worm his way around under the floor joists and ventilation tubes with a flashlight. When he came back, he had to twist himself sideways to get his shoulders out. He looked like he was being born.

I'll say it again: this has the feeling of a nightmare about it.

I delay as long as possible, even though the visitor comes back every night at the same dark hour and steals my slumber. I do research. I find examples of squirrels nesting under tubs. I find examples of various creatures taking up residence under porches. They all bite and stink and carry disease while occupying the interstitial space of someone's home. Not the kind of thing you want to confront unarmed and lying prone on your stomach.

I ask around the neighborhood, too. I tell people I haven't actually seen the intruder, just heard it at night. Their answer: *Sounds like you got rats in the walls.* The phrase recurs regularly enough that it feels like part of the vernacular, a local version of *I smell a rat!* or *I don't give a rat's ass!* Rats in the walls, I'm guessing, are about as common as crawlspaces around here, and I have a feeling the two are connected.

Telling people about the visitor, I feel a twinge of shame. It's as if one of my kids has been sent home from school with head lice: no matter how many times the people who know better say that lice prefer clean hair, having lice invokes a deep-down embarrassment that has to do with cleanliness. Having rats in the walls comes across as a similar expression of poor household hygiene. *We're clean enough,* I feel like reassuring the neighbors. *I mean, the kids do paste the floor around their dining chairs with applesauce and ground-up cheese puffs, but we clean it up! I swear! We're not rat people!*

As it turns out, with the exception of those who live in isolation near the polar ice, we're all rat people. Our history of commingling, of sharing cuisines and taboos, crops and tools, is also the history of our fellow travelers, unwelcome as they may be. Think of all the names we've given them: wharf rat, sewer rat, roof rat, ship rat, Hanover rat, Alexandrine rat, Norway rat, drain rat, stack rat, and, most indicatively, house rat.[1] When humans first learned to sow and harvest grain in the ancient fields of Mesopotamia, rats were there to reap the harvest, too. When we learned to sail the seas, so did rats. One species learned to sail with the Polynesians; black rats and brown rats voyaged with European explorers. Wherever we went, the rodents went with us, disembarking at every port, writing chapter after chapter of shared history, sketching a shadow map of our own geography. There are rat colonies on tiny atolls in the South Pacific. There are rats on the ships breaking ice near the Arctic Circle.[2] To put it another way, wherever we call home, the rat calls home. Wherever we belong, the rat belongs.

The irony here is a bit too penetrating for my taste. Here I am with piles of material about invasion biology stacked up around the comfy chairs in the living room, all in preparation for writing a book about how learning to coexist with other species can make us feel more at home in the world, and suddenly there's an invasive species not on my doorstep but actually inside my comfort zone, invading my personal habitat.

Maybe because it's so close to home, at first I don't make the connection between what I'm reading about and what's going on in my life. Somehow the rat feels different from the brown tree snakes and woolly adelgids, kudzu vines and zebra mussels in my books; it feels like a homegrown scourge. Only later, when I'm lying awake in the wee hours listening to the visitor paw around in the plumbing, does it dawn on me that deep denial must be at work here, that we don't ask certain questions about ourselves. To call the rat an invasive species, to call attention to its origins, is to call attention to our own origins in other places. To say it belongs in one place and not another is to raise that question about ourselves. It's easier to think that rats have always been everywhere, a universal bane of our existence.[3]

I used the word *interstitial* earlier, *the interstitial space of someone's home.* The wall of the house is the divide between nature and culture made tangible. Outside they live. Inside we live. Their home. Our home. But the rat *in the wall?* Suddenly we discover there's a standard three-inch space between the bricks on the outside and the plaster on the inside, literally interstitial. "The outside wants to come in," Joyce Carol Oates has argued, "and only the self's thin membrane prevents it."[4] The home is an extension of the self. It's more than a roof over our heads—it's the exterior we show the world and the decorated interior that helps define who we are. The walls are another layer in the self's protective membrane, but as it turns out they are hollow, and apparently inhabitable.

The rat has not come in, yet, but it's not outside, either. And I don't spend all that long thinking of ways to accommodate it. This isn't the Karni Mata Temple in Rajasthan, where having a rat run over your feet is supposed to bring good luck and sharing a bowl of milk with some of the twenty thousand temple rodents is considered a great blessing indeed. Generally speaking, harmony is not our interspecies history—we've been killing each other for millennia. The list of diseases a rat can carry is long and nasty. It begins with the Black Death, of course, but there are also unsavory microbes and parasites lurking in the rat's droppings, and their mouths are brimming with infectious agents, too.[5] To keep from playing host, people have deployed ferrets and terriers, cats and mongooses, set traps and spread poisons, "rat-proofed" with wire mesh and even dropped little sachets of crystallized bobcat urine into the walls.[6]

The space between the walls is contestable space, not quite outside, not quite inside, a frontier zone. On one side of the plaster the diurnal creatures go about their business. And on the other side, the night crew awaits, listening for that moment when the last groan of a faucet subsides and it's just the ambient noise of the appliances running through their cycles in the dark.

Their turn to start making noise.

Chopping a wiener into rat-sized bites feels a bit strange—I'm making a plate of canapés for an uninvited guest as a prelude to snapping his neck. I feel as if I should disinfect everything, as if the rodent's half-inch incisors have been nibbling at my fingertips.

My adversary is invisible, which doesn't help. I certainly don't want to see the thing inside, but I'm a visual creature dealing with something that doesn't care much about visual cues, something that can call the suffocating dark of a three-inch crevice home. I'm less than delighted to learn that there are two species in these parts, each with its own habits. The humongous brown kind, *Rattus norwegicus,* likes to tunnel in the dirt. It particularly likes crawlspaces, where it can poke around in the twilight and build its own catacombs, a subterranean extension of your house. The black kind, *Rattus rattus,* is slightly more effete, with a lengthy tail it uses for balance as it scrambles along the wires that lead to your attic. Both are exponential breeders: brown rats can produce five litters per year, with a gestation period of twenty-one days. Each litter can number in the double digits, with the offspring reaching breeding age in five weeks.[7]

Which one am I dealing with? Supposedly, you can distinguish the two by the way they eat an orange, one species hollowing out the flesh and leaving the peel almost intact, the other pulling a smash-and-grab on the fruit. I don't have this kind of evidence, but I do find signs of occupancy in the attic. And in the crawlspace, right by the door. Droppings. Smaller than coffee beans, about the size of a clove. Too big for a mouse, too small for a raccoon. But not for a squirrel, maybe. I'm still reluctant to give up the notion that this is another kind of rodent, one with a bushy tail and a less scurrilous reputation.

I spread out a sheet of plastic and get as far as having my entire torso under the house (I'm in the crypt with only my shins poking out) when I lose my nerve. There are no bugs or cobwebs—there's nothing under there in the beam of my light. That's what makes it feel so creepy. I can see shards of brick, a length of black television cable, and fallen tufts of pink insulation, but mostly it's a lunar landscape, layers of sand and dust doused with termiticide. Not a place where the living belong.

Rats are supposedly wary by nature, and any change in their environment is supposed to disturb them (except pounding on the tub, apparently). This is why, if you're trying to trap or poison them, you're advised to give them a few free meals first, so that they learn to trust their executioner.[8] With this principle in mind, I decide on a two-pronged approach: attraction and aversion, carrot and stick. I buy a pair of wooden rattraps, each as long as a shoebox. And I juice up the headlamp I use for cycling to work at night. I'll tempt them with their favorite foods—the agricultural extension office advises hotdogs and peanut butter over cheese—while blasting the crawlspace with a one-watt dose of flashing, phosphorescent LED light.

As dusk falls, I shut the door on a plate of hotdog bites

lit up by the flashing of a bike headlamp. It pulses through the ventilation slats in the brick, haloing our shrubbery in what looks disconcertingly like a police bust in action. I can see the neighbors walking their dogs, wondering what the hell I'm doing. I wave good-naturedly.

Don't worry! Just rats in the walls!

The lethal traps don't work out so well. First of all, you're dealing with something that probably hasn't changed much in a hundred years, which means no bells and whistles like safety latches. You bend the metal bar back, tamping down the spring, and try to keep it back with a metal wand that catches under the little metal plate where you put the food. The trick is to get the wand to catch under the food, but not so securely that a wary, snuffling nose won't trigger a snap. The slightest tremble should set it off. You might think you've done all this before with a mousetrap, but it's not the same when the trap is the size of a shoebox. The first time I lift my fingers from the wire it's like a landmine detonating. The wooden base back flips into the air about an inch from my nose, just missing my petrified fingers. It's so loud that for half an hour afterward, I can barely hear in my right ear. It occurs to me then that any trap meant to snap a rat's neck stands an equally good chance of snapping a finger bone like a twig. I take the old-timey traps back.

There are other, more modern options. Glue traps are shallow black trays full of what looks like glistening rubber cement, laced with an anesthetic that keeps the victim from struggling too much. These work with cruel efficiency—my parents have told me of the red squirrels, chipmunks, and even flying squirrels they've trapped this way in their rural home in Massachusetts, how you come home in the evening and find a rodent glued like a statue in an expression of torturous immobility.

Each has its disadvantages. Let's say I actually succeed in conning the rodent into a "live trap," a plastic box shaped like a coffin, what am I going to do with it? Let it go down the street near a neighbor I don't like? Drive it to a park and let it scurry away? Suffocate it somehow? An electrocution trap could work, but something tells me I shouldn't be messing around with high voltage. And glue—well, I do want to kill them, but not with extreme prejudice. At least, not yet.

I settle on a lethal trap that looks like the head of a mamba, ominously black, with rows of jagged teeth that open wide when you step on a lever at the back. The rat is supposed to stick its head between the jaws of the snake for a taste of peanut butter, which seems a bit of a stretch, but at least I won't risk chopping off a digit. My neighbor happens by when I'm outside testing the things, prodding the plate with sticks until the jaws clamp down. He observes for a moment, then makes my skin crawl by suggesting I tie the traps to something outside. *You don't want them dragging it way back in there,* he says, and something about the way he cocks an eyebrow suggests that he knows from experience.

The real solution is to reconfigure the creature's map, to find the place it's getting in and seal it off.[9] The vents in the eaves are open, and there's evidence, once I get up there, of a variety of species using them as a place to loaf and have a snack. A bird of some kind has built half a nest inside one eave. Something else has nibbled the seeds out of a pinecone. I staple line after line of squirrel-proof screening across the slats. I hire someone to climb up on the roof and seal off the top of a hidden coal chimney with sheet metal.

Neither of these fixes works. The rats have a clandestine vision of my home, apparently, their network of passageways invisible to the human eye. Or perhaps their map is more complex than my own, a city's worth of on-ramps and exits, cul-de-sacs and thoroughfares that the next generation can follow from the line of bushes at the property line to the cable wire to the eaves, behind and underneath and overhead. How long has this shadow city existed? The house was built in 1940. I have spread my superficial map over the intricacies of the rodent's world.

To reconfigure things, I'm going to have to start taking a rat's-eye view of my home. But how far am I willing to go in this direction? This varmint already has me on my abdomen in the dirt, squeezing into spaces that are too tight for comfort. It already has me parsing its scat, trying to decode its particulars, and I'm no scatologist. I don't want to be a scatologist—my kids are potty-trained, thank God, and that's a realm whose mysteries I have no further wish to plumb. It seems as if everything our society goes to great lengths to disguise the rat is going to lay bare for me. I find this invasion of my consciousness even harder to bear.

I could just throw down poison, but that's another kind of nightmare waiting to happen. When I was a ten-year-old living in a tiny house in rural Massachusetts, we had a visitor. The house was situated at the edge of a sawmill, surrounded at the back by piles of offcut lumber that looked like shreds of hard cheese, scaly and round on one side, smooth-tapered on the other. It was a great place to find snakes—I recall finding a green snake, a ring-necked snake, a red-bellied snake, a wood snake, and a garter snake all on the same afternoon, simply by lifting up planks. It was great habitat for lots of creatures, actually, including the things that left mold-frosted tunnels through the duff beneath the boards. Voles, sure. And something else. Something that decided it preferred indoor amenities to life under lumber. We'd hear it at night, knocking things around on the counters like someone groping for a light switch in the dark. In the morning we'd find the garbage pail sitting in the middle of the room, at the end of a trail of whatever we'd thrown away the day before.

The next thing I recall is the smell. The smell of carrion has been described as cloying and sweet, and I suppose it is those things. In fact, it's all that and more. It's a lesson in the figurative limits of the senses—most smells can be described in terms of something else, such as, that wine smells like a mix of chocolate and cherries and freshly tarred road. But if you've ever passed something dead on the side of the road, you know that death is a primary color in the olfactory spectrum. It doesn't smell like other things. Death smells like death, and I daresay we are genetically programmed to keep that smell out of our homes by whatever means necessary.

A dead rat doesn't become instantly pungent. It ripens over several days, which means that at the beginning it's almost like a shallow mood, a whim, a passing thought. You catch a whiff and then it's gone. It's only after a few days that you can begin to pinpoint the smell.

It was a week between the evening my dad put down the little tray of poisoned granules and the discovery of the body. Rat poisons contain anticoagulants, the same kind of thing that cardio patients take to avoid the clotting that can lead to strokes. Supposedly, the poison makes the rodents desperately thirsty. The rodents are supposed to evacuate the house in search of a drink before they keel over, leaving the home rodent-free and the homeowner free from the burden of a poisoned corpse.

That's the theory, anyway. We found ours stretched out under the chair by the woodstove, the spot I liked to occupy with a good fantasy novel before bedtime. My first impression of the visitor as my dad pinched him by the tail and held him over a plastic bag for inspection: big.

Bigger than several generations of mice all piled together in a mound. A brown rat, stiffened into a menacing torpedo of decay.

On the first night after I set the snakehead traps, one of them goes off. It's 4 a.m., as usual, and the trap resonates like a gunshot even though it's under the floor. Instantly, I'm wide awake and bolt upright in bed, listening for the sounds of success and wondering what I'm going to do about it. There's no further sound. I've got two hours to kill before daylight, and I lie there imagining this creature writhing in its death throes under the thin membrane of the floorboards. When I drift off, I see rats squeezing up through the heating ducts and swarming over my bed, eager for vengeance.

The morning sun warms my back as I pry open the door to the underworld. I have to duck down farther and lean face first into the hole, where something scaly and hairy and disease-ridden could be waiting, something I've inflated to the size of a parade float.

I track my headlamp beam over the barren ground and come to the traps. Cool, musty air wafts through the white filter of my dust mask.

Nothing. No stiffened tail. No pale splayed feet. No chunky brown corpse. No oily black corpse. Just a few stray wiener chunks to linger in my imagination.

We never hear from the night visitor again, although

it's not as if he disappears without a trace. Later that morning, two zebra-striped trucks pull up in front of the house a couple doors down: professional wildlife removers, people who know their way around a snap trap.

Squirrels in the attic, my neighbor says.

6

Backyard Bruins

FACT: Approximately three thousand black bears inhabited Massachusetts before European colonization. By 1900, that number had been reduced to fewer than one hundred. Today, the bear population has reached three thousand again and is increasing by 8–10 percent each year.

Thanks to my hours on the couch with the kids, I have a picture of ursine family life that looks like a woodsy version of our own. Sure, they live in a hollowed-out tree, but it's in a nice neighborhood, and they have curtains and comfy chairs and baseball gloves. If you're a parent, you undoubtedly know the cartoon I'm talking about, and I apologize if I've brought back a tune from *The Berenstain Bears* you couldn't shake for years. If you're anything like me, you'll be standing in a supermarket line and suddenly you'll find yourself humming along to Lee Ann Womack again.

What is it about these creatures? Why is my son's bed

piled high with stuffed bruins? What made people come to the conclusion that a wild animal often weighing more than the average human adult was actually a cuddle-worthy friend? Where are the teeth on those teddy bears?

In Northampton, Massachusetts, the cartoon character has come to life. Here, when the kids get on the school bus, the bears come out. Out from under the decks and porches and into the backyards where the bird feeders hang. They get up on their hind legs. They perch on privacy fences; they hang from branches and tug the feeder sideways, then scoop up the spillage from the ground.

The human occupants get home from work and the feeder's empty.

Again! Damn squirrels!

They fill it with nutritious, oil-rich sunflower and black thistle seed, maybe some corn nuggets, or even the birdseed that's dipped in beef tallow for an extra energy boost. Americans spend $2.7 billion on birdseed every year, making sure our feathered friends get enough to eat.[1]

Bears love that.

As Ralph Taylor, the district manager for the Massachusetts Division of Wildlife put it, "When people go to work these guys turn into Yogi Bear. Then at two o'clock when the school bus pulls up, they go back to being normal bears again."

The lives of these animals, it seems to me, must hold clues to the qualities that allow some animals to thrive in the urban environment even as others are doomed to persecution and failure. Their circumstances suggest something about tolerance, about the limits of what humans and bears can live with and the degree of risk both species are willing to endure. And with the animals coming home to roost in my backyard, I've got a personal stake in all of this.

I wonder what it would be like, watching *Berenstain Bears* or *Little Bear* or even *Yogi Bear* on the couch, knowing all the while that underneath the floorboards a sow and her yearling cubs were hunkered down, waiting for you to refill the bird feeder.

It's a gray and diaphanous morning in western Massachusetts. Daffodils are poking up from the bare soil, but the canopy is still a watercolor wash of buds breaking into deep velvety maroon. Two days ago, an inch of snow dusted the ground here. It's creating a bit of weather-related whiplash for me—weather like this is a distant memory in Columbia, where the routine of afternoon thunderstorms ballooning over sun-parched lawns has already begun.

Dave Fuller, a state wildlife biologist who specializes in bear management, has agreed to let me join him as he checks in on Northampton's bear population. Every year in late winter, biologists climb into den sites where females have given birth to measure and weigh the cubs. Then, after the adults have emerged in the spring, the biologists set traps for them made from two steel barrels welded together. They gather data on these adults, sometimes swapping out the batteries on a previously collared bear, sometimes attaching radio collars to new bears so that they can track them through the city. There are currently six radio-collared bears in Northampton, providing a wealth of data about their habits. Signals have come from the outskirts of the city, but they've also come from Main Street, right in the center, with its trendy restaurants and buskers and college students. Bears have been spotted in neighborhood parks and on the Smith College campus. And they've shown up frequently in various backyards.

Fuller is waiting for me in a green state pickup at a gas station, just off Interstate 91 in Deerfield. He has sharp features and watchful eyes, and although he's been out in the field quite a bit recently, his skin is still winter pale. He's dressed for a day hike, a green canvas shirt tucked into jeans and low-cut hiking shoes. This is the urban wild, after all, not some remote corner of the Alaskan bush.

We head up into hills above an old dairy farm and apple orchard, onto a winding dirt road that climbs into hemlock forest. It's the patchwork geography of western Massachusetts: old factory towns built where the rivers narrowed, hazy expanses of corn and tobacco where the river spread wide its rich alluvial soil, and then the dense, brooding hills above the valleys, the hill towns cloaked in second-growth forest.

The landscape is a study in the ironies brought about by the passage of time: when these dirt thoroughfares were actually in use more than a century ago, farmers clopped around on horse-drawn carts and bears were scarce. Now there's a freeway funneling traffic away from the old roads, hardwoods are maturing on what would have been pasture, and bears are common. The interstate pulses down below, the whole urban corridor of the East Coast stretched out to the south of us while to the north lie the bucolic hills of Vermont.

Fuller pulls over where the road becomes a gravel wash between the trees, almost but not quite four-wheel-drive territory. The road has leveled out—we've reached the top of a narrow ridge. There's nothing here that screams *Bears!* to me, but Fuller has chosen this site carefully. He tells me they set traps on the top of ridgelines like these so that the scent of the bait will waft down, enticing bruins from all directions. Bears like to travel along ridges that rise above swamps, and they also like stands of conifers, which keep them cool. Everything they like, in other words, including jelly donuts, is right here in this patch of woods. What's disconcerting to me is that the places bears apparently like are the very places I used to frequent as a young angler—streams flowing through skunk cabbage swamps and beaver-dammed thickets, the ridgelines above draped in solemn hemlock. I spent quite a bit of time trudging through places like these and never saw a bear. I wonder if they saw me.

I wonder, too, how a bear in a trap is going to behave. Will it snarl a warning, poke its hefty claws through the vents? Will we smell it before we get close? I find myself rummaging through various smells I connect with animals, wet dogs, zoo exhibits, barnyards. Nothing quite seems to fit. Fuller pushes his way through the dead hemlock boughs, alert but unconcerned. Before he joined the state's wildlife division, he was a graduate student at the nearby University of Massachusetts in Amherst, studying the population dynamics of bears in the area, which means he's had a lot of face time with the area's ursine residents. For the most part, the bears we're tracking now are the offspring of the female bears he studied twenty years ago.

Things have changed since he was in grad school in the late eighties, however. The population of urban bears has exploded, and the human population has grown, too, pushing out into what were once agricultural fields and uninhabited tracts of forest. A bear population that once lived at the edge of the city is now right in the heart of it, and den sites that were once out in the woods are now in someone's backyard. But urbanization hasn't put a dent in the bear population. In fact, bears have expanded their range even as the suburbs have grown, and they are now moving eastward toward the satellite cities of Boston.[2]

My human sense of smell is hundreds of times less

acute than a bear's, but as we get close to the two traps even I can detect the pungent olfactory beacon of grease and sugar and ripening cheese. The traps, by design, don't look like much. They've been crafted from fifty-five-gallon steel barrels welded lengthwise into a long, narrow tube and then painted a drab shade in keeping with the forest floor. They look like the cardboard tubes left over when you run out of paper towels; I would never crawl inside one myself, and they look too claustrophobic for a stocky bear, too. But Fuller assures me the bears can indeed squeeze all the way to the back, where a trigger plate sits under the mound of pastries. Once their bulk hits the plate, the door slams down behind. They've caught three-hundred-pound males in these traps.

The traps work best when the bears first emerge from their dens and their natural foods are still scarce. I can see why it would work: they must come snuffling through the melting snow and barren undergrowth, finding just a tidbit here and there, and suddenly this tendril of rich and decadent scent fills their nostrils.

When we get close, we can see that the untriggered trap doors are still raised high. No bears. Although they trapped fourteen bears last year, this season they haven't caught a single one. Fuller attributes the lack of success to the wet weather, which has prompted earlier growth of the plants bears like to eat, like skunk cabbage. The damp air doesn't help either; it doesn't broadcast the smell of rancid donuts quite so enticingly.

Something has been stuffing its face here, however. The floor of the tube is glossed with powdered sugar and the innards of cherry jelly donuts and cheese danish, and there's a trail of crumbs leading away from the mouth of the tube.

"Raccoons," Dave grouses as he unlocks the case around a camera that's bolted to a nearby trunk. The camera has a motion detector, and when something ambles toward the traps at night it triggers a ten-second flash of infrared light while the camera shoots multiple frames. Fuller pulls out the memory card and slides it into another camera and thumbs through the frames. Sure enough, there are the black-ringed eyes and inquisitive snout of the bear's fellow omnivore, another creature adept at scratching out a living among us.

One picture book on my son's shelf features a cute young raccoon dealing with his peers at elementary school, but that's it. For some reason, this creature with the shambling gait and dietary habits of a miniature bear hasn't sparked the human imagination in quite the same way. I'm not sure why; it's an appealing animal, no less round and cuddly than your average bruin, as the photos attest. And nobody has ever been devoured by a raccoon, although rabies is a serious concern. Beware the raccoon you see rambling around your yard in broad daylight. Bears, however, almost never get rabies.

There are 450 photos of this raccoon sniffing around the front of the cage but not a single image of a bear.

We're going to have to head down into the warmer and more settled precincts of the city if we want to find one.

I tend to think that an animal has to be small to thrive in the city or live way up high and out of our reach. But the black bear, perhaps even more than the white-tailed deer, is living proof that a large animal can live among us. They may be smaller than grizzlies on average, but that doesn't mean they're small compared to us. An average white-tailed deer weighs about one hundred and fifty pounds, which is sizable enough to total your car but nothing compared to an adult male black bear. While adult females average about 200 pounds, male bears are usually much larger—they often weigh over 300 pounds, and bears in excess of 800 pounds have been confirmed in places as far from each other as North Carolina and Manitoba. According to Fuller, the biggest bear recorded in Massachusetts was a 525-pound "boar" shot by a hunter in the Berkshires, a mountain range west of Northampton, in 1980.

Humans with guns are one of the primary threats to an animal of this size, and the four-wheeled predators we use to get around town are another. Nevertheless, human habitat does have its appealing features. Unlike the grizzly, which evolved to survive in the treeless terrain of prairie and tundra, *Ursus americanus* evolved to depend on trees as a refuge, although these bears still spend most of their time foraging on the ground. An unbroken blanket of old growth doesn't suit them nearly so well as a patchwork of meadows and wetlands and woods where various edibles are coming into season at different times of the year. And that kind of "mixed forest" is exactly what they get in a typical small New England city like Northampton, right down to the fabric of the typical yard with its shade trees and flower beds and lawn.[3]

Black bears are omnivores, but by and large they tend toward the vegetarian side. Although they'll dine on carrion and whatever they can catch, the bulk of their diet typically comes from sprigs and berries and nuts. In the spring, they'll wallow in the swamps that are too wet for anybody to build on, dining on skunk cabbage while spring peepers fill the leafless thickets with urgent noise. During the summer they'll ramble around their territory, plucking blackberries in abandoned fields and gnoshing bugs, waiting for the "hard mast crops" to ripen, the acorns and hickory and beech nuts that are plentiful in the woods as the days grow shorter. When these become scarce, they'll usually find an uprooted tree and slow way down for the winter.

I've sanitized the urban bear's lifestyle a bit here. This is what ursine life would look like in a habitat created by people, but without any people actually living there. In real life, urban bears live around people, and their routine revolves around our schedules and behaviors. Sure bears like skunk cabbage in the spring, but a bird feeder full of sunflower seed also hits the spot. So does a bag of garbage on the curb. In the fall, the cornfields along the Connecticut River are mighty tempting, and bears are known to gluttonize in these fields, gorging themselves until they vomit. When the snow begins to fall, normally it would be time to find a den and hole up in there until spring. But if people are going to put out seed and suet for birds all winter, why hibernate? Many urban bears den only when the weather gets really bad, emerging as soon as there's a thaw for a birdseed snack and then clambering back under the porch of somebody's house.

On our way into town, I mention to Fuller that my knowledge of black bear behavior comes primarily from the book *Bear Attacks,* whose lurid pages I perused while sitting at the backcountry desk in Yellowstone.[4] To get a permit to camp along the trail, hikers would have to stand at my desk and watch a video of the dos and don'ts of bear country. Then I would give them a brief follow-up lecture, which included the usual advice to make lots of noise to avoid surprising a sow and her cubs. If they nevertheless found themselves with an enraged mother bearing down on them, my advice was to try to climb a tree, and if that was not an option, then to lie down and play dead. And *pray,* I often added silently, my head full of bloodthirsty marauders tearing open tents and dragging people off in their sleeping bags like fat, wriggling caterpillars. Of course, I never saw a grizzly that summer, not in the hundreds of miles I logged patrolling the backcountry trails.

As I'm confessing all this, Dave is shaking his head. Most of what I think I know about bears is not altogether wrong, but you have to understand the context of each encounter to know how to behave, and you can't confuse a black bear with a grizzly or a polar bear. Polar bears evolved to hunt and devour meat, and human flesh is on the menu. Grizzlies, with no place to hide on the prairie, evolved to charge first and ask questions later. But black bears, Dave says, are by and large very tolerant of human presence. Surprisingly tolerant. Unlike grizzlies, female black bears in particular rarely exhibit aggressive behavior toward humans, even in the presence of their cubs. Most black bears either know better than to tangle with humans or they're simply indifferent to us.

Which isn't the same as giving us a wide berth, apparently. Dave points out a tree as we cross a bridge. The tree overlooks a bike path that was once a railroad bed. He once tracked a collared bear to a crook in that very tree, where it was napping in the shade with its cub playing among the branches while cyclists and joggers and children in strollers passed beneath, unaware.

Nobody has been ever been eaten, or even bitten, by a bear in Northampton, which makes a lot of sense. Black bears have to tolerate us; it's the fundamental law of urban life, the key to their survival. They can't behave like grizzlies or polar bears—they can't charge everything that crosses their path or stalk us as they would a plump seal. We don't tolerate that behavior. Mountain lions that wander into town get dispatched with a bullet, ASAP. You can't treat us like prey and expect to survive.

Fortunately, black bears don't see us as prey, for the most part. But the fact that they do occasionally cross that line lends substance to our nightmares. There is some research, Fuller says, based on bear behavior in Ontario's Algonquin Provincial Park, to suggest that black bears there have learned to lean more toward the carnivorous side.[5] They bring down adult moose in the park with some frequency, and researchers suspect that this experience with preying on larger animals leads this population to view us as potentially easy pickings. Most black bear attacks happen in rural areas like this, where the bears have had little interaction with humans. The more they get to know us, the more likely they are to look for a handout instead of biting our hand off.

Predatory black bears are almost exclusively adult males who stalk their human quarry as they would any other large prey. The highly unlikely but plausible sight of a large boar following you quietly down the path should set off alarm bells, but make sure you heed the right advice. Don't, under any circumstances, do what I told the Yellowstone campers to do. With grizzlies, you need to worry about getting between a female and her cubs. She's not interested in eating you; she's defending her vulnerable offspring. Playing dead works well in that case—it demonstrates that you're not a threat. When a male black bear approaches, on the other hand, if you play dead you might wind up being dead meat.[6]

It's easy to get worked up about the possibility of a bear attack. We have a library's worth of books that feature friendly cartoon bears, but still, there is this one slim volume of horror stories sitting on the shelf. It's probably been checked out more than it should be; after all, in real life the likelihood of getting hit by a car or savaged by a dog is far, far more likely. According to a study by the Centers for Disease Control, in 2001 there were more than three hundred thousand dog bite cases in the United States that were severe enough to require a visit to the emergency room.[7] Meanwhile, according to Fuller, the last record of a black bear attack in Massachusetts was in the early 1800s.

There's something deeper here, an uneasiness about an animal that doesn't always treat us as we expect to be treated. With something like a great white shark, you know where you stand. It's a meat eater, no questions, no apologies, no ambiguities. Same with a polar bear. But with an omnivore like the black bear, the food chain dynamic between us isn't so clearly defined.

There are people—knowledgeable researchers in fact—who argue that black bears aren't aggressive toward humans at all. They spend their time trailing bears around, often just a few feet away.[8] Then there are people who not only believe bears are harmless but think it's a good idea to feed them. Our first stop is a cul-de-sac where three or four small houses sit beneath a mature canopy of shade trees, their lawns bordered by an unplanted field. Here, the resident of one otherwise innocuous ranch has established a regular bear-feeding station. It's not the only one in town, Fuller says, and the biologists can't do anything about it. Feeding wildlife isn't illegal in Massachusetts, even if that wildlife is quite a bit larger than the average songbird.

We pull up, but we don't get out—although Fuller isn't the type to wear his emotions on his sleeve, I sense that there's not a lot of love lost between wildlife officials and this guy. They've warned him, they've requested that he desist, but they can't stop him, even if it's turning bears into nuisance animals who later get shot. There's no law against killing nuisance bears in your yard either.

Fuller points to a large, leafless tree in the front yard. There's nothing on the ground beneath it now, but this is where the owner typically spreads birdseed for the bears and watches them come in to feed. To get here, however, many of them have to cross the two-lane highway that runs parallel to the freeway, and they may have to cross the freeway, too.

"He's boasted to a research biologist that he's fed over twenty bears over the years," Fuller says. "We try to tell him that it's not good for the bears—last year two bears wound up getting hit by cars just down the road, presumably trying to get here."

He shakes his head, noting the small metal swing set next to the feeding tree.

"For his grandkids," he says, his tone hinting at exasperation.

I figure maybe the swings are there because the guy isn't feeding right now. Maybe he knows the bears won't be around this time of year, or his grandkids won't be coming to visit until the summer. Still, I wouldn't feel comfortable with my own kids *inside* the house if there were bears around, let alone playing under a tree that bears normally associate with food.

It's not hard to imagine an incident happening here. And all it would take would be one. One attack, and suddenly the whole premise of these animals living next to people comes to seem far-fetched and dangerous. A city of bears and people could easily become a city with no bears.

We don't stay long. Instead, we cross the interstate and pull off to the side of the on-ramp. Traffic is roaring below, the concrete of the overpass reverberating with air brake thunder. Growing up on the eastern side of the freeway, I was told there were no bears in our neck of the woods because they couldn't make it across this road without getting hit. That was back in the late 1980s, when the bear population boom was just taking off. Now there are bears knocking over bird feeders on the eastern side of I-91 all the time; my parents have seen them in the yard, and reports of bird-feeder raids ripple across the municipal listserv for their small town every spring.

Fuller points to a mane of junipers cloaking the patch between the freeway and the off-ramp. Bear den. Yes, that's where number 341, a scruffy two-year-old female who weighs about 120 pounds, denned this past winter. The biologists give the radio-collared bears numbers instead of nicknames, so they don't become too attached to them. This bear clearly hadn't read the studies that suggest bears avoid crossing roads with traffic greater than ten thousand vehicles per day and in fact tend to give these kinds of thoroughfares a wide berth.[9] Thirty-five thousand vehicles roar through this stretch on an average day. It's gratingly, grindingly, overbearingly loud here. But it's still habitat.

Number 341 was one of three cubs born to another collared female, one of the constellation of bears known to frequent the yard with the birdseed and the swing set. This past winter would have been 341's first on her own, since sows typically force their offspring to fend for themselves after about a year and a half, usually in late June, when it's time to breed. Newly independent males tend to wander far afield in search of an unoccupied territory—ear-tagged males from Northampton have been shot in the Adirondacks and Vermont. But females tend to stay close to home, rubbing shoulders with their mothers and sisters. In fact, as Fuller describes the family dynamics of the Northampton bears, it soon becomes clear that everybody is related to everybody else through their matrilineal line. The first bear they radio-collared here, on the outskirts of town in the 1980s, is the great-grandmother of all the bears in the city. Because the adult males tend to roam, most of the stories that have accumulated over the years are of female bears and their offspring, the legacy of this one ancestral female.

Number 341 is basically an adolescent, still learning to make her way in an already densely populated ursine world while avoiding the menace of oncoming traffic. It's a precarious transition: her littermate was one of the bears who got hit trying to cross the road to the feed corn.

Less than half a mile away, we pass the place where her mother denned this year, in some cattails by a fertilizer company. Another half a mile, and we pull into a big parking lot edged with nondescript buildings that cater to small businesses. Behind some green dumpsters is a strip of scrubby trees and trampled brush, and beyond that is a chain-link fence trembling with freeway noise. I know this area, although I can't say I ever paid any attention to it. It's across the street from the Subaru dealer, in an industrial pocket that harkens back to the days before Northampton gentrified into a happening cultural scene. I'd be tempted to call it a wasteland, but that's not how wildlife sees places like this. Vacant lots, overpasses, weedy corners pulsing with noise—what I'm coming to see as typical urban wildlife habitat is what I might call the landscape of neglect, an unclaimed and untidy swath of urban decay.

Fuller leads me on a path through last year's nettles and bramble canes, stepping over a pile of leaves someone has blown off the parking spaces. The nearest office building has big windows looking out on this patch of roadside vegetation, and about a month ago the manager looked out one morning and saw a four-year-old bear known as 323 ambling down the path about fifteen feet from the window. I can only imagine how startling the disparity between the world of the office and the wild outside the window must have seemed that morning. Look up from your coffee and glance idly out the window, and what's that on the other side of the glass? A loose . . . Wait! That's no black lab . . . .

We see where she denned. A tree has come down, roots splayed in the air, and under the trunk at the base she had created a dry nest of matted grass. It looks freshly compressed, as if she just got up when she heard us approaching. Beyond the tree, we can see the path she followed to get here, the tawny hummocks and black, shimmering pools of a marsh leading away from the building. At one time, this entire office park was probably a wetland, at least in the spring. Another feature of the landscape of neglect: spongy, squelching swamp gas belching muck. We humans don't like places like this; there are no views, the bugs are thick, and we can't walk the dogs without getting our feet soaked. A trash-lined marsh meandering along the edge of a highway—that's exactly the kind of corridor wild animals use to get around town.

The manager called the cops, who called in the state biologists. When Fuller and his team arrived at the scene, 323 was still here, curled up under the trees. She probably wouldn't have noticed anything amiss when their truck pulled up by the dumpsters—after all, she was accustomed to the sights and sounds of car doors slamming and people trudging across the lot. When biologists approach a bear curled up with cubs in a den, they often use a dart stick, injecting anesthetic through a needle at the end of a probe. But this bear was clearly visible and could easily take off if disturbed, so Fuller took aim with a dart gun. Some darted bears will run, but many simply curl up tighter in their den. Number 323 stayed put.

After the drug took effect, the team loaded her into a cage and drove her to a more remote corner of her home range, where they released her. Since she's a radio-collared bear whose whereabouts are recorded and mapped, the biologists knew that she'd previously spent time in this less developed country. But she's drawn to the birdseed feeding station, too, which means she's almost certain to be back. Translocated bears have been known to travel more than forty miles back to their original home range; even females, who tend to roam less than males, have a well-developed homing instinct.[10]

The typical home range of Northampton's female bears

is just two square miles, far less than the fifty miles it might reach in some regions of the West. The size of this territory is a function of food scarcity, and Northampton's bears don't need to cover a lot of ground to find enough calories.[11] According to calculations Fuller has made, every year the city's homeowners put out twelve tons of birdseed in the two-mile home range of a single female bear.

Number 323 hasn't gotten into trouble again. Not yet. Maybe she's figured out how to walk the line between human habitation and bear habitat this time. For now, maybe she's feasting on skunk cabbage in a swamp where no human cares to tread.

It's early in the season.

We drive through downtown, past the Smith College campus and the high school. On the way, we pass a patch of swamp that bears and the people who track them know well, a two-acre parcel that at times has hosted five radio-collared bears at once. It's nondescript, which is exactly as you'd expect urban bear habitat to be, just a patch of dry bunch grass and leafless brush reflected in pools of snowmelt, surrounded by houses built on higher ground. People must walk right past it all the time. We pass Child's Park, a triangle of greening grass and benches where the previous ursine matriarch used to like to ramble around with her cubs in broad daylight, oblivious to the attentions of human observers.

From there, we wend our way through neighborhoods along the Mill River, passing mills that testify to the time when Northampton was a factory town that happened to have a women's college in it. The river leads us into a large but semiforgotten corner of the city: "Hospital Hill," the grounds of the former state mental hospital, built in the mid-nineteenth century. One hundred and seventy acres between downtown and the freeway, once bustling with hundreds of workers and thousands of patients, then declining for decades with the advent of better treatment options for the mentally ill. By the time the bears were making their way into town in the 1980s, the last patients were leaving the premises and most of the buildings had been abandoned to the elements, ruins from the Victorian Age. The grounds were left alone, too, which was good for bears.

After two decades of little human traffic, however, the state and the city got moving on redevelopment. The buildings were razed; part of the land was turned into the first phase of a housing development. There are plans to transform the pastures and fields that once provided food for the hospital into hundreds of housing lots and an industrial park with spacious parking lots. Good for city tax revenues, but not so good for keeping bears away from people.

We park in a gravel lot at the base of the hill, next to a new dog park and new community garden plots, their compost bins erupting like black mushrooms from the unplanted earth. A few low strands of barbed wire enclose what looks like unmowed cow pasture heading upslope toward the unsettled gray sky, the grass dotted with hawthorn and spindly clumps of multiflora rose. You don't see many places like this in western Massachusetts, where trees need little encouragement to turn fields into forest. It resembles a windswept and dank Yorkshire moor, a fitting setting for the institution it once housed.

Fuller gets out his tracking antenna and starts sweeping the air for a signal. The bear he's seeking is 269, an eleven-year-old female with young cubs who has assumed the mantle of the city's dominant female and who also happens to be 323's mother and 341's grandmother. Fuller hasn't had a chance to check on her this year; he's eager to find out how many cubs she has. Most of us just see individual bears, if we see anything at all. Fuller sees generations, sees the influence of the mother and the grandmother in the behavior of the offspring. It must be hard to know the genealogy of all these bears, to study the fabric of this matrilineal society, and still maintain any kind of objectivity.

Number 269 has achieved some notoriety as a problem bear—there have been reports of her breaking windows at night and raiding breezeways for stored birdseed, and she's reputed to be persistent, coming back even after the cops have shown up to scare her away. Her behavior is not all that different from her predecessor at the top of this urban bear society. The former matriarch was also known for her brazen forays into human habitat, and she could often be found wandering through the city in broad daylight with her yearling cubs trailing behind. She met her end in someone's backyard; the city's police had received reports of a bear acting "somewhat groggy," and fearing she might be suffering from a rare case of rabies, they shot her, even though Massachusetts hasn't had a confirmed case of a rabid bear in recent memory. Fuller suspects she may have finally worn out her welcome; the police get over a thousand calls a year about bears in the backyard, and she was responsible for a good many of them.

Bears communicate their territory primarily by smell; when 269 discovered that the old matriarch was no longer marking the boundary they shared, she took over all the "hot spots" in town. Like the former matriarch, she's teaching problem behavior to her cubs; one of her offspring was killed recently after breaking a kitchen window and going for the fridge. The same bear had broken into the house twice before, and it appeared unfazed by the approach of the authorities who ultimately dispatched it. Right now, her cubs are too young to join her in her foraging expeditions, but in two months they'll be out there in the neighborhoods, learning her foodways. It's not a recipe for long-term survival.

A ping emerges from the static on the truck speakers, getting stronger as Fuller turns the wand toward a dense stand of pines and hemlocks on the ridge above us, then fading as he twists toward the bare slopes beyond. She's somewhere in that direction, probably in those woods. To find her location, we need to triangulate by picking up her signal from the opposite side. Which in this environment, crosshatched with roads, is as easy as getting back in the truck.

On our way around the hospital grounds, we stop in a cluster of townhouses to inspect 269's previous den site. It's just off the freeway, on the edge of a junkyard, in a narrow strip of woodland that was once a railroad right-of-way. We're maybe a mile by freeway from 323's den in the mixed-use office park. The kind of place I've come to expect urban wildlife to use, an eyesore, basically.

Or at least it used to be. We slide down through the leaf litter and climb over a split-rail fence that still has the raw chemical smell of pressure-treated lumber. On the other side is a strip of fresh tar—a brand-new bike path. It may not be the most scenic place to ride, but the trail has turned what was a wildlife corridor into a path for people.

Number 269 apparently learned about this transformation the hard way. Her den site is easy for us to find, a live tree with a hollowed-out base that happens to be only a few feet from the edge of the bike path. When this was a defunct railroad track, it was a probably a good place to hole up with her new litter of cubs. Not anymore. Someone was strolling through here not long ago, enjoying their new access to nature while their dog followed the scent of something wild to the base of the tree. The dog poked its snout into that dark cavern; maybe it barked. Not surprisingly, 269 took offense at this invasion of her privacy and swatted the hound across the face.[12]

This kind of canine confrontation is actually pretty unusual, believe it or not. Plenty of people chain dogs up in their yards, thinking it will keep away bears. But according to Fuller, the dogs and bears usually wind up accommodating one another. In one case, a homeowner, fed up with the old matriarch constantly emptying her bird feeder, decided to dangle the feeder directly over the doghouse inhabited by her German shepherd. What happened next was not the fur-flying brawl one might expect; the dog simply watched as the bear teetered over the privacy fence, scrambled on top of the doghouse, and made short work of the feeder.

In 269's case, scared dog and scared owner retreated; the owner called the cops. Meanwhile, 269 headed for a more secure location: the old hospital grounds. We find her signal from the edge of a field on the other side the woods—she's somewhere in the hospital's sliver of a forest.

When we emerge from the truck at the edge of the woods, Fuller whispers that we shouldn't talk. We're in stalking mode now. We cross the barren slope into the woods, then creep along the edge of a skunk cabbage swamp, ducking under the canes of the multiflora rose. Classic bear habitat: fresh green forbs, then a ridge beyond, with a stand of mature conifers for the cubs to climb if there's trouble. I follow Fuller's lead; he's tiptoeing, his feet making small squelching sounds in the muck. Everything is soggy. I place one foot on a tussock of grass and try to shift my weight off it before it sinks. Fuller sweeps aside a dead branch and holds it for me, carefully, so it doesn't snap. I whisper that the nonnative rose here is pretty bad—the canes droop across the drier islands like barbed tentacles, and we have to try to pluck them out of our shoulders while simultaneously keeping our feet dry and not making a sound.

"Bears love it," Fuller whispers back, keeping his eyes fixed on the wooded slope ahead. "Keep your eyes peeled for what looks like an unnatural black blob."

Right then I see it. It's an unnatural black blob, sitting up on its haunches and staring at us. It has ears and everything.

"Not black enough," Fuller whispers. "But you're right, it does have ears and everything."

Just a rain-slicked stump, half hidden by rose canes. Still, I could swear the thing is watching us, ears swiveled toward us in a state of heightened alertness.

We start climbing the ridge, then Fuller stiffens, suspended in midstep.

"Stay right behind me."

He leans into the trunk of a nearby tree. Beyond us,

there's shaking in the bushes. My heart begins to thump, and I feel a frisson of fear. This may be old hat for the citizenry of Northampton, but I've never been this close to a wild bear. Female with cubs, no gun, no bear spray: this goes against all my Yellowstone training.

Fifty feet from us, I see a black shape scurry across a patch of open ground. It looks like a chunky puppy.

"There's a cub," Fuller whispers, and even though he's been doing this for decades, there's excitement in his voice.

They're playing; another cub is chasing the first one, and when it catches up, they start rolling over and over each other. It's the kind of thing you see on nature shows, but this is unfiltered by the camera. It's happening in real time.

"She's seen us," Fuller says after a few seconds.

How does he know? I can't even see her.

He raises a finger, alerting me to a sound, like a horse clearing its nose, a kind of breathy snort. Deer make a similar sound when they're startled.

"There go the cubs," he observes. We watch one cub scramble halfway up the bare trunk of a tall pine, its claws making small scraping sounds against the bark. It pauses, peering at us over its brown muzzle. A second cub follows.

These cubs would have been born sometime in late winter, so they're probably a couple of months old at this point. They would have been virtually helpless at birth, blind, hairless, weighing about half a pound. But they develop quickly; a bear's milk is twice as rich in calories as human milk, and by the time the cubs are ready to emerge from the den in late spring they're about the size of a small cat.[13] Whether they make it to adulthood depends on a lot of factors, but the most important is the experience of the mother. Young females raising cubs for the first time tend to have little success; they're still learning to fend for themselves, and they haven't built up the fat stores it takes to feed a family.[14]

Cubs are relatively safe in the den with their mother. But once they emerge they're vulnerable to a host of potential threats. Most cub deaths occur in the first three months outside the den. By early summer they've gotten big enough to avoid being eaten and savvy enough to avoid getting run over. In fact, cubs are surprisingly precocious when it comes to making their way in the world. Fuller says he's seen orphaned cubs in the area survive on their own at five months.

These cubs haven't got there yet. Although their mother is still panting her warnings—she sounds like an out-of-shape jogger lumbering up a steep hill—her third cub isn't paying her any heed. It's still rolling around in the brush without a care in the world, probably waiting until she sounds like she really means it. Maybe this is where all those anthropomorphic cartoons come from—

I deal with this kind of behavior on a daily basis with my own offspring. *Try the old I'm-going-to-count-to-three trick,* I feel like whispering to her.

Finally, the last of the trio clambers up the trunk. We watch them. They watch us. Still no visible sign of their mother.

"They're coming down now," Fuller observes, although they seem to be staying put to me. He's heard their mom huff; it's a warning sound that means our encounter has entered a new phase.

"That's directed at us," he says as she huffs again. It sounds like someone trying to cover a cough. The first thing a bear wants to do is get her cubs up a tree, Fuller says. Then, if the coast is clear and she thinks she has time, she wants to get them down so they can leave the area.

We're not making things easy for her. We're hovering, not so close that we pose an immediate threat, but not far enough away that she can dismiss us either.

"She's going to back that huff up with a bluff charge," Fuller says, "if we don't leave soon." The cubs are sliding and slipping down the bark now. As they get closer to the ground, we're getting closer to the moment when 269 is going to come barreling down the slope at us, clacking her teeth. Bears can kick it up to thirty-five miles per hour, far faster than any human can run.[15] What was it we're supposed to do again? We can't climb a tree . . . we can't run . . . .

"I don't want to drive her out of these woods," Fuller

says, nodding toward the traffic noise that penetrates even here. He starts backing up slowly, and motions for me to follow. That's right—back up slowly and maintain eye contact. Show no fear. That's what you're supposed to do.

I have no problem keeping right at his elbow. I don't want to drive her out of this refuge either. But more than that, I don't really need to see what a bear looks like when she's clacking her teeth at you. That I can imagine all too well.

So far, we've been touring the neglected corners of the city, which is good habitat for bears. But people and bears share much closer quarters here, partly because bird feeders tend to be less common in industrial parks, and partly because bears, like possums and raccoons and foxes and other wild urbanites, are cavity dwellers. Human habitation is essentially a giant cavity, split into levels, with a tempting space, dry, spacious, and snug, right under the deck. We're not using it, so . . . .

This proximity to animals we kind of adore but also recognize could kill us generates lots of richly ironic material for stories. Ralph Taylor told me one: a team of researchers was searching for a radio-collared female during the early spring season to gather data on cub production. In this case, the telemetry wand took them first into a residential neighborhood. No big deal. They parked and got out of the truck. The signal was pointing toward a house, and it got stronger as they approached. They heard muted voices coming from the backyard. This is when they started to feel a little uncomfortable. "We're thinking, *where* is this thing?" Taylor recalled. He said they knew enough to call out first as they entered the side yard—you never know what kind of eccentric behavior might be going on in someone's backyard in bohemian Northampton. Sure enough, as they came around the corner they discovered a couple enjoying their hot tub on the back deck.

Meanwhile, the signal was getting stronger. It got stronger as they approached the back deck and explained what they were doing. In fact, it was strongest right where the couple was sitting in the bubbling water, because the bear was curled up in the crawlspace, about two feet beneath them. And she wasn't alone; she had three cubs with her.

I can only imagine the conversation between the biologists and the bathers, which must have been something along the lines of "I hate to disturb you folks, but I have reason to believe there's a bear right underneath your . . . ."

"You've never seen anybody get out of a hot tub that fast," Taylor joked.

Another story, this one a version of Goldilocks from Dave Fuller: an old man leaves his back door open so his old dog can go in and out. He comes up from the basement and he sees this brown thing in the kitchen. At first, he thinks his dog has been rolling in the dirt. Then he looks more closely and realizes that what's rummaging around in his kitchen isn't his dog after all. It's a bear, helping itself to whatever food is on the counter.

When Fuller and his team arrive on the scene, the bear is gone. But as they're standing in the driveway, who should appear but the bear, coming back for more of the old man's victuals. They chased it away, and like some kind of ursine apparition, it was never seen again.

Bears that get right up close. Bears that come inside. Bears that eat our food. These are stories about boundaries and transgression. Perfect fodder for fairy tales.

Fuller takes me up a road toward a "swampy redoubt," the Fitzgerald Lake Conservation Area, 625 acres that have always been inhabited by bears. When he was in grad school, this road was dirt.

"Now it's houses after houses," he muses. The places that bears once used as corridors and den sites are now the yards of dwellings built within the past five years or so. He points to a house sitting on a slope above the wetlands and low-lying woods along the roadside: that lawn was once the den site where 269, the mother with cubs, was born. Residential development is happening all over town—the fringes, the edges, the cornfields sold and turned into subdivisions—it all forces wild bears like 269 to migrate into the city, to shift from corn in the field to seed in the bird feeders.

Which isn't necessarily bad for them. As long as they stick to residential neighborhoods, they avoid hunters. If they wander into the woods or, worse, succumb to the temptation of the cornfields on the urban fringe, their days are probably numbered. Most of Fuller's stories about backyard bruins end at the barrel of a hunter's rifle, often in the city of Easthampton, which retains the gritty industrial-agricultural mix that is mostly a memory now in Northampton. People in Northampton don't want their neighbors to know they killed a bear. Not so in Easthampton.

"In Easthampton," Fuller notes, "you're less likely to be crucified in the newspaper for shooting a bear."

Hunting is one of those situations where all the cartoons and fairy tales make a difference in the real world; bears have a constituency, and that limits the way they can be managed. Since 1995, for instance, hunters can no longer use dogs to track and tree their charismatic quarry, which has limited the success of the hunt.[16] The state now issues several thousand permits a year, but only about 150 bears, mostly young males dispersing into new territory, get shot during the season. Massachusetts, according to Fuller, has kept harvest levels below 5 percent of the population for over two decades, during which time the bear population has been growing at 7 percent a year. That growth worries wildlife managers like Ralph Taylor, who shook his head when he contemplated the state's growing bear population. With the population at three thousand, as it is now, there have been no attacks. But what happens when the state population reaches ten thousand? How many bears can you have before conflict becomes inevitable?

In addition to a season that concludes just before deer season, there's a seventeen-day hunting season in September, specifically created to "appease" corn farmers, whose crops would otherwise sustain heavy losses. To find a bear in the heavily wooded terrain of the Berkshires, trained dogs would undoubtedly be helpful. But corn-fed bears are relatively easy to find. They leave plenty of evidence of their whereabouts.

A bear known as 280 met her end in Easthampton, gunned down in an old apple orchard. We visit a series of houses she liked to inhabit, the first a ranch with just a sliver of darkness showing under the lowest trim board of the porch, the next an upscale McMansion with just enough space under the front porch for her to squeeze into as a yearling, and then a contemporary place with a high deck, the space beneath now fronted with stone-studded masonry instead of the lattice she was able to bend aside. I feel as if I'm on a strange real estate tour in which we focus only on the underside amenities of each home.

Number 280 never used these places to give birth, Fuller says, but she often led her cubs to human habitation as soon as they could move around on their own. Possibly she was disturbed just enough by the tread of human feet above her head. The kids who lived in the ranch liked to shoot baskets in the driveway, a few feet from where she liked to rest her head. Imagine: a bear trying to snooze in her den, and not ten feet away the kids are chasing down jump shots. Didn't faze her. Didn't faze the owners of the house, either. They had some kind of vent through which they could peer into the crawlspace and check on her. They actually called Fuller to inquire if there might be a way to install a window there, so that they could observe her more easily if she gave birth to cubs.

Over the weekend, one of the radio-collared bruins got into trouble. The owners of a rural retreat at the edge of the city, complete with a gaggle of ducks, reported a medium-sized, scruffy bear with a collar had broken into their storage shed and tried to get into their house. Only one collared bear fit that description: 341, the teenager who denned in the junipers at the edge of the freeway.

To see if she's still hanging around the area, Fuller and I drive up a dirt road studded with mailboxes at regular intervals. Fuller knows the place well from his graduate work—it's always been heavily used bear habitat, but more recently it's been subdivided and transformed into an exurban enclave, the kind of place where people have long driveways and horse barns. When Fuller was doing research here, there were no houses on this stretch of road.

He pulls over at a wooden telephone pole. Although I wouldn't have noticed it, to Fuller it's like a community billboard announcing "Bear Turf!" It looks a bit like a chewed toothpick; the wood is weathered farther up, but at a certain point the splinters turn cedar red, exposing the resinous wood beneath.

"That's fresh," Fuller says, tracing the claw marks that run from his waist to just above our heads. He demonstrates how a bear will get up on its hind legs and shimmy its back against the wood, imbuing the post with its scent. If we had the olfactory aptitude of the typical bear, we'd know who the graffiti artist was, when she was last here, and her place in the social world.

Fuller plucks with his fingers and comes away with some wispy strands of black hair, an ursine calling card. He hands it to me. It's long and slightly wavy and very fine, more like Persian cat than dog. I wouldn't connect this with the soft plush of my kids' teddy bears, but then it wasn't the fur of the actual animal that gave rise to the cuddly imitation, it was a cartoon.

"Teddy" bears are a surprisingly recent part of the popular imagination; they originally embodied the exploits of President Teddy Roosevelt, who spent a great deal of his time at the dawn of the twentieth century stalking big game in the woods. One such episode found Roosevelt and his retinue in Mississippi, where, after a fruitless hunt that lasted five days, someone finally subdued a small bear and tied it to a tree for the president to shoot. Roosevelt refused to shoot it, and the moment was immortalized in a cartoon that showed him turning away from a cuddly little cub at the end of a rope. Stuffed bears and a children's story featuring "Teddy's bears" soon followed, and the fad took on a life of its own. Bears went from Goldilocks's anthropomorphized but still potentially ferocious antagonists to something my kids clutch in the dark to fend off nightmares. Quite a transformation indeed.[17]

Fuller examines the damp ground around the pole and spots something. Tracks. They're big and deep and fresh, the sign of something heavy trudging through the snowmelt and leaves to a path between some hemlocks. Like humans, bears have five toes and a long, tapered heel on their rear feet, and their tracks, especially if the claws aren't showing, look a bit as if a flat-footed and possibly inebriated human has been shambling through the mud.

What I see near our feet are some scuffed leaves, still filigreed with the white mold that spreads under snow, and some depressions in the mud. What Fuller sees is the recent passage of a big bear, probably a male of several hundred pounds, marking its territory. Most bears are active in the daytime, unless they've learned to be nocturnal in response to human activity. Males, particularly as the breeding season approaches, are almost exclusively diurnal. This big guy could have been through here fifteen minutes ago, for all we know. I'm not sure I want to be hot on his trail.

Fuller crouches and reads the leaves, following a meandering trial through the hemlocks, finding a few stray hairs caught in the bark of a tree. The trail leads away from the road, up a slight grade into thickets of mountain laurel, and as the ground dries out the sign gradually disappears. Through the woods we can see the roof of a house.

We make our way up the hill to the house with the ducks, but there's no radio signal from 341's collar. Even the new telephone poles here are frayed and gnawed and worked over, subsumed into a wild animal communication network. Number 341 may have gotten the message that a bigger bear was in the area, and left. We don't know where she's headed. The GPS unit around her neck sends out a signal every two hours, but the data get downloaded only once a month. What we have, in other words, are periodic glimpses into this parallel world. There's a lot happening between the signals. And then there are the bears with no collar at all.

7

Notes from a
Twenty-First-Century Rat Catcher

FACT: Approximately seventeen thousand native plant species inhabit the United States, and five thousand nonnative plants have escaped into native ecosystems. The "hotspots" for nonnative species in the United States are Florida, Hawaii, California, Louisiana, and the Great Lakes region.

———————

I t's a dank and dreary morning. The forecast is warning of flurries, and the sky looks like a bowl of congealed oatmeal. Not the nicest conditions for poking around the crawlspaces of Columbia. But the traps still have to be checked.

I'm in an SUV with Dan Phillips and his assistant Dave, and we're hauling a tool trailer to the first job of the day, in a downtown neighborhood not far from my house.

When you hear noises in the attic, Dan is the guy you call. He has a wildlife biology degree from Clemson, and he runs All Things Wild, a "nuisance wildlife removal" service. His business is exactly the kind of thing that keeps people awake at night. Scuttling feet. Fleshy thumps and scraping claws. And the thing that I, like most home-owners, fear most: what those in the trade call "D 'n' Ds." That's code for "dead animal removal and deodorization," a polite way of describing the stinking corpse sealed up somewhere in the walls of your house.

Dan Phillip's job, in other words, is on the frontlines of the struggle to coexist. Which is pretty much where I find myself. I'm trying to avoid killing things off. That's the whole point of certifying my backyard. But I don't know how. And in truth, there are times when instinct gets the better of me, times when if I actually saw a rat I would scream like a teenybopper, then clobber the sucker with a chair or a laptop or whatever came to hand.

"*Humane* removal?" Dan had responded somewhat skeptically on the phone before we met.

"Depends on what you mean by *humane.*"

In general, I'd say humane removal means extracting the offender with the least harm possible. But I'd like to know what he considers humane. How do you continue to love wildlife when you spend every day dealing with critters that have crossed the line?

The first house is in an older neighborhood with small lots and sprawling live oaks bubbling their roots around the sidewalk. It's a yellow brick structure with white craftsman molding around the eaves. I'm aware of the molding because Dan pointed it out as we pulled up, along with the crawlspace vents. The eaves and the crawlspace—that's where Dan's attention goes first. If you want to find out where the wildlife is getting in, he told me, you have to understand their life history, know their habits. You have to start thinking like they do.

He looks like someone who knows about wildlife. He's powerfully built, with narrow eyes and a heavy jaw and a pinch of snuff behind his lower lip, all of which combine to give him a quizzical expression, as if he's listening for something that normal people can't quite hear. He's dressed in the typical outdoorsman's uniform of heavy brown canvas, but the key to what he calls his "persona" is the slightly careworn felt hat pulled low on his forehead. It gives him a bit of the late "Crocodile Hunter" Steve Irwin's outback flair—he looks like someone who just can't get enough of all things creepy and crawly.

Although he's had his "Crocodile Hunter" moments, like the time he was "messing around" with a copperhead he'd found on the side of the road and it bit him on the hand, it isn't all just shtick: after graduating from Clemson, he worked as a hunting guide on a Texas ranch and as a field researcher on prairie dogs in Utah and South Dakota.

Dan and I ring the doorbell, peering in at a collection of empty vodka and tequila bottles in the kitchen windowsill. The residents are college kids who reported the problem before Christmas, and they've been gone most of the break. They have no idea what Dan caught while they were away.

Eventually, a sleepy young woman answers the door in a sweatshirt and shorts. I can't say she's glad to see the wildlife removal specialist at this hour. She follows Dan around the perimeter of the place as he recounts what he found. His first task, he tells her, was digging a dead possum out of one of the wells that led to a casement vent, which was buried in leaves. He then caught three more possums under the house. Two were on the small side. But he also caught one jumbo-sized male that probably weighed twenty pounds.

"You should've seen the head on that thing," he says, spreading his hands to the size of a watermelon. "That's what you heard scratching around under the floor."

His client nods, stifling a yawn.

After possums stopped appearing in his traps, he sealed up the crawlspace vents they were using to gain access, using a fine-gauge steel mesh and liquid nails. The crawlspace is now inaccessible, but that's only half the problem. He points to an obvious hole in the soffit board that runs along the roofline. It's about the size of the lid on a jam jar, and it's rough around the edges, as if it's been gnawed. Something has clearly been going in and out of there regularly, although the owner doesn't want to pay more to seal it off.

"You see that black smudge by the hole?" he says to me as we follow the woman back to the door so that she can cut him a check. "That's rats, most likely."

Rats are second on the property damage list. Squirrels

do the most damage; they have a penchant for gnawing, and for some reason they like the sizzle of electrical wiring between their teeth. Bats are further down because they don't chew holes to gain access to your attic. But having a quantity of their dung on your hands is no fun either.

On the way to our next house, Dan describes an office building that was harboring a colony of free-tailed bats. Not just a handful; we're talking hundreds of bats that would pour out of the attic in the evening from the small gaps between the cedar shakes. The guano in that attic was eight inches deep—they had to remove it with shovels. The office below smelled so strongly that the owner couldn't keep the place staffed. Solving the problem took three thousand dollars' worth of spray foam and an "excluder" that let the bats exit from one hole but prevented them from entering.

I ask him where the exiled bats went.

"Next door," he says, with a chuckle.

Our second stop is another college pad, not far from the part of town where nearly every doorway leads to a bar. These are some of the oldest neighborhoods in the city, and the houses grow in size and elegance as the streets climb the steep bluffs surrounding the university campus. Our destination is big and nondescript, a three-story building with a slouching front porch, ocher siding, and chocolate brown trim. I pass it almost every day on my bike route to campus without ever seeing it.

There have been reports of possums, rats, and squirrels romping around the house, but so far nothing has shown up in the traps. Dan and Dave and I stomp up on the porch and hammer on the door.

"Probably still sleeping," Dan says. "This guy can sleep through anything."

He fishes out a key and we unlock the door and troop inside to the foyer, where we pause, listening. Are the inhabitants all sleeping? Are they all at class?

This was clearly somebody's mansion at some point: the ceilings are at least twelve feet high in the parlor, and the floors have the deep walnut patina of a prized antique. A banister paneled in the same dark wood leads up to a landing, then on to the second floor.

The place doesn't smell like a mansion, however. It smells like *Animal House,* like a puddle of warm beer fermenting in the sun.

Dave tiptoes up the stairs with a ladder tucked under his arm, heading for the attic—the door is in the ceiling in one of the bedrooms. Dan and I tiptoe through the kitchen and down a set of twisting stairs into the crawlspace. I crouch under the floor joists, trying to keep my head out of the cobwebs as Dan's flashlight quickly reads the signs in this powdery netherworld. Nothing has disturbed the rat traps he's set, but something tripped the door to the possum trap he's wedged under the floor and baited with a can of sardines. He points to some traceries in the dust—a track. A cat, probably the neighbor's, has left tracks all around the cage. He curses softly. They've already caught that cat twice.

"Slept right on through," Dave says, joining us downstairs. The attic traps are empty, too.

Outside, it becomes clear why the animals noticed this habitation, even if I never did. The tenants don't pay any attention to what is going on outside, and the owners are never there. What was once the backyard has been turned into off-street parking surrounded by patches of scrub and a wobbly privacy fence. The patio is festooned with old beer cans brimming with wet cigarette butts. A single canvas fold-up chair sits forlornly next to a candle stub, the sole evidence that any of the human occupants have spent time out here contemplating the scenery.

It's the bear den by the parking lot all over again: the more time I spend in the backyard, the more I realize that most urban wildlife depends on neglect to survive. There's no conflict, because nobody cares.

Dan points to the eaves where two fascia boards, rippling with layers of old paint, meet. There's a hole about the size of a baseball right at the joint, and a black, greasy smudge extends beneath it. "Look at the size of that hole," he says. "Probably squirrels gnawing through there, then the smudge is where the rats have been coming in and out. That's hundred-year-old trim. You can't replace that."

As we head out to the truck, I ask what he would have done with a possum if he'd caught one. He grimaces, and I can tell this is an uncomfortable turn for so early in our acquaintance.

"Cervical dislocation," he says, and turns to spit at the base of a tree.

I must look puzzled. Cervical dislocation? Is that something to do with translocation? You know, moving the animals around?

"Break its neck," he says. He makes a snapping motion with his hand.

"Or shoot him."

He was trying to shock me.

"By the time people call us, they're ready to nuke 'em," Dave adds, closing the doors to the trailer.

I want to ask why they don't release them somewhere. After all, they're using a live trap. But I can tell I've hit a sore spot.

The discomfort sits with us in the truck. It's not that they want to kill wildlife, Dan offers. They are not allowed to release or move wildlife captured under nuisance wildlife circumstances. If diseased animals or "urbanized" animals are moved, the risk of moving that disease or problem to another place is real. Dan understands that an animal born in an attic is more likely to raise its young in an attic. When they catch a raccoon, for example, they prefer to take it to a wildlife rehabilitation center. But this is a business, and taking them to a rehab center involves the costs of employee time and fuel and a donation to the nonprofit rehab facility. Few clients want to pay an extra fee. When Dan takes an animal there, it's almost always on his own dime.

Riding in the truck listening to their stories, about the biggest rat they ever found, or the time a possum got into a wall and just kept going down and down until it got wedged in so tight it died, and the homeowner called because the body fluids were leaking out from under the trim boards, takes me back to my bird survey days with the US Fish and Wildlife Service. Crammed into a car at the end of a fieldwork day, my fellow wildlife lovers would tell stories about the badgers they saw or the coot eggs they found while they took turns pulling wood ticks off their clothes and dropping them on the glowing coil of the cigarette lighter. The same guys who caught jumping mice and kept them as pets, who kept snakes in a makeshift zoo of cardboard boxes and whooped when the serpents escaped into the living room furniture, who spent their days off slogging through swamps with binoculars in hopes of a rare bird sighting, would nevertheless watch gleefully as the tick scuttled toward the edge of the coil, then fizzled in a puff of foul-smelling smoke. The people who love animals, who are fascinated enough by them that they spend their lives seeking out their company, are often the same people whose work involves killing them.

I think back to the interview I had before that field season with Fish and Wildlife. The service had two possible jobs, one going out to North Dakota to work on black-footed ferrets, the other to Minnesota to survey birds. *How did I feel about killing things?* the director asked. I'd have to kill a lot of prairie dogs to feed the ferrets—was that a problem? I genuflected and generally looked uncomfortable while saying I was fine with it. I rationalized the process pretty easily: this is an endangered species we're trying to save, and it's not like there are other options on the menu. Black-footed ferrets eat prairie dogs; that's what they evolved to do. Someone has to kill the rodents to feed the ferrets, or we won't have any ferrets. But when it came down to it, could I actually kill one? I was offered the bird job, so I never had to find out. I'm guessing it would've been a problem.

"Everybody has their fluffy animal," Dan allows. "I guess you could say otters are that for me." One time, he was hired to do a beaver removal. He set a trap by the lodge, and when he came back it wasn't a beaver in the trap with its back broken; it was an otter.

"I didn't like having to drown that animal, but that's just what I had to do."

We sit without talking for a few minutes. Dan checks his voice mail.

"If I had enough money," he muses, "I'd buy a parcel

of land and set up a rehab center for the animals I catch. Might do that one day, even though it probably wouldn't pay for itself."

We turn into a new subdivision with spacious landscaped yards and brick multilevel homes. Dave points out a squirrel—it's at the edge of someone's roof, trying to force its way into an electrical coupling. Dan points out a wedge-shaped gap at the corner of someone's eaves—squirrels again, squeezing their way inside.

They've developed an eye for it. In brand-new neighborhoods, they see nothing but mice. It takes a few years for the shrubs and small trees to start producing seeds. That's when the squirrels enter the neighborhood. When the shrub layer matures and the trees reach some stature, then the possums arrive. By the time you reach the stage of my neighborhood, you've got the whole range of possibilities, and problems, on your hands.

"People say, 'Well, why me?' I say it's nothing to do with cleanliness," Dan says, after pointing out yet another squirrel attempting a break-in and entry.

"Look, your house is just a big, hollow tree to them."

The house in question is a two-story brick place with a large lawn and a few stubby crepe myrtles arranged tastefully in front of the windows. It's near the end of a cul-de-sac, with some woods at the far end of the lawn.

"This guy is kind of making us look bad," Dan says.

They've been checking this trap for weeks, and so far the squirrel has eluded capture.

We get two ladders from the side of the trailer. Dan and Dave coax them up rung by rung until they're almost fully extended. Then they prop them against the roofline and give the base a good shake. Thirty feet to climb. Dave starts for his corner; Dan heads for another. Then he comes back down to cut some flashing. They're going to be putting up 270 feet of steel replacement flashing behind the gutters on this place.

"Can you climb a ladder?" he inquires.

No way, my instinct replies. Tight underground spaces make me uncomfortable, but my terror of heights is disabling.

Nevertheless, I nod and give the ladder a shake. Then I clank up the aluminum rungs until I'm feeling the air ripple through my clothes. Dan looks small and amused way down below. I push my hand under the asphalt shingles. There's aluminum flashing back there, but it's too flimsy and the squirrels have just pushed it down to expose the construction gap behind it. It doesn't seem that it should be that easy to get from the outside world of inclement weather to the inside world of carpets and kitchen cabinets.

Trapping is only a small part of the total cost of wildlife removal; exclusion is the humane side of the equation, and it's what Dan and Dave mostly get paid to do. They spend the bulk of their time in a tool belt loaded with black urethane spray foam, wire cutters, and a percussion drill, either crawling around under the house or perched on a ladder at the eaves. The bigger the house, the more complicated the rooflines, and the harder it is to do their work.

"People don't realize how dangerous and difficult it is to close off these places," Dan calls up to me. I realize it. I'd like to get down off this thirty-foot perch, thank you very much. He points to a length of fascia trim that runs perpendicular to the front door. See that? The only access to that roofline is by the pitched roof above the door. They're going to have to stack three connected ladders to reach that spot, bracing and leveling the base of the ladder and then connecting the segments together until they look like half a rollercoaster run.

I climb down. The ladder flexes and sways ever so slightly, just enough to make my stomach flutter. This is one job I would gladly pay anybody else to do.

Dave, meanwhile, has made his way up to the corner of the eaves. He slides his hand in past the gutter and into the space beyond.

"Got him," he says.

Down comes the body with a fleshy thunk. A male squirrel, eyes wedged tight, a faint red tinge around his muzzle.

"Coming or going?"

"Going."

Where the squirrel was headed when he hit the trap

matters. If he was trying to get in, then their job is probably done. If he was going out, however, there may be another way of getting inside.

"Must've stepped around it," Dan says. "Or maybe he was already in there."

You can't tell if an animal is inside when you're setting a trap, he explains. They'll squeeze right down into the tiniest hole while you tromp around the attic looking for them. You'll swear they're gone, but they're right there looking at you.

A squirrel trapped in an attic isn't going to just curl up and die—he's going to chew his way out of there. That's why you never close up a place completely until you're sure all the animals are gone. And the most convincing way to do that is to catch them in a lethal trap.

A squirrel trap looks like a giant metal spider, its arched fangs loose and jangly until it's set. There's no wooden platform. Instead, the jaws sit like a cage around the spring, forcing the squirrel to step on the trigger in the middle. When it does, the cage snaps down on the animal's torso, squeezing the life out of it.

There are live traps for squirrels, smaller versions of the trap-door cages they use for possums. But would I consider it humane, Dan wanted to know, to have a squirrel go crazy inside one? Possums are different, he said. Everything about them is slow, and they can handle sitting in a cage with no place to go. But a squirrel—a squirrel can't take that kind of confinement. And it might have to spend hours, or even an entire day like that, since he's got twenty-five open accounts at any one time. The whole time, that creature would be tearing itself up in there. Is that humane?

I allowed that such an experience was probably not ideal, and I didn't have any better options to offer. Later, Dan would show me an excluder they keep in the trailer. It would be possible to construct an excluder, he said, that would allow squirrels out but keep them from coming back in. But that approach doesn't work as well — the animal isn't going to give up on the nice, cozy home he's been enjoying; he's going to look for another way inside, and his teeth are harder than most of the materials he's likely to encounter in our walls. Most clients don't like the idea that the animal is still out there looking for a way in, and they don't want to foot the extra cost.

He calls the homeowner when we get back in the truck.

"How have the noises been?"

"Actually, they stopped about two days ago," I hear the guy say on speakerphone.

"That's 'cause we caught it."

"Great!"

This is what the clients of All Things Wild pay for: they pay to have someone else do the dirty work, to deal with animals they don't want to see or hear or smell. They pay for someone else to clean up droppings, to go spelunking beneath their homes and scaling the vertiginous heights of their eaves. But the real service Dan provides is dealing with the death of the animal. The client gets home from work, and the dead squirrel is gone. How it died and the evidence of its passing need never trouble the client's conscience. I'd be tempted to hire someone like this myself. Get rid of the rats and the possums. And those damn squirrels, too. Call me when they're gone, and don't give me too much detail. Out of sight, out of mind.

In the back of the trailer, lying on top of the "coon" cages, is a small stack of dead squirrels and a dead rat, all plucked from traps the day before, all facing the same way, their grimacing mouths pointed toward the doors. I ask about the rat, and Dan picks it up barehanded. It's stiff and flattened, as if carved from wood. A black rat: I can tell from all the pics I've seen online, the way the back arches up toward the lengthy tail, although the fur on this one is a mix of muted brown hues. I mention the tail, and Dan holds it out—definitely longer than the body.

So this is what my nemesis looks like, the visitor crawling around in our walls. It's not so intimidating, not particularly diabolical or toothsome. Of course, our visitor could have been the brown variety, too, which would have been heftier.

Dan says the whole thing about roof rats liking the attic and Norwegians liking the crawlspace is overblown—they get everywhere, depending on the time of year. In the summer, the attic is so hot it's kind of a dead zone;

nothing wants to be up there except bats. But in the spring it's a warm and inviting place. Female raccoons are especially on the lookout for warm places to raise their young; they spend most of the year living in street drains, but for a few weeks each year they clamber into attics to nest.[1]

Dan has a soft spot for raccoons. He once raised a female for eight months, "before she got to be too much for most people to handle." Although they appear almost pudgy, a raccoon's stocky build conceals surprising strength. When you set a raccoon cage, you have to make sure there's nothing nearby, because a trapped raccoon will seize anything it can reach and tear it apart in a frantic effort to escape. They also bite, of course, and since they carry rabies, a raccoon bite is serious even if the wound itself is minor.

Dan has been bitten. He got a call about raccoons in the attic, and when he got there he found that the babies had knocked the valance from a bathroom fan and were peering down from the ceiling.[2] When he went to grab one, it nipped him on the hand. The injection site for rabies treatment is the buttock, the gluteus maximus being the only muscle big enough for a needle of that thickness. The immunoglobulin is like molasses, and it leaves a knot like a golfball in the flesh. Dan had to get a course of injections, and he couldn't sit down for three hours after every one. Yet he doesn't hold a grudge against members of the *Procyon lotor* family.

He asks if I want to hold the dead rat.

No, thanks, I say, even though I know this is how you confront a phobia, by hefting the animal in your hand, feeling the fur and the whiskers brush against your skin, getting so close that the source of your discomfort no longer holds any power.

By the end of the day, we've baited a lot of possum traps, peeling back the lids on tins of herring and sardines and potted meat—possums *love* potted meat, Dave says. We've dipped a little plastic wand in attractant and dangled it from the back of the cage. Dan gave me a whiff of that greasy brown paste from a glass jar; the putrid mix of death, dung, and putrefaction nearly knocked me over.

That's not the worst. At one place, Dave opened the crawlspace door and squirmed his shoulders through it, then pulled out a trap baited with a tin of herring filets. The bait didn't look like fish anymore, however. The oily chunks were bristling with three-inch strands of black mold; they looked like a patch of scalp exhumed from a grave.

Dan held up the tin, carefully, so that the amber oil didn't spill on his hand.

"Now this is the kind of stuff I don't like to breathe," he said. "We deal with so much gross stuff all the time that I just laugh at it. In fact, I've seen this mold. Never this long. But this is the mold you see growing on possum poop. It's either this black mold or a white mold that you see. Makes sense that you'd see it in this cage, I guess."

The mold that grows on possum poop. A champion specimen, no less. We all laughed about it, although what was running through my mind was the possibility of zoonotic disease. This black fungal pelt we could see, but what we couldn't see were the spores and microbes and egg masses floating around in the dust under there. Imagine that chunk of fish as a specimen of our lungs.

Our tour of Columbia's crawlspaces turned up plenty of other stuff I wouldn't care to touch. Dave has a practiced eye for carrion. In one pungently musty crawlspace, he plucked something furry from the dust, the kind of thing I wouldn't go near without a hazmat suit. At first he guessed squirrel tail—it's a common practice for possums, apparently, to drag the carcass of a road-killed squirrel back to the crawlspace, leaving behind only the fluffy tail. This turned out to be something else: a mummified baby possum, its head compacted against its body so that it looked like something you'd peel off the bottom of your shoe.

"I don't do as much as I should," Dan allowed, when I asked about wearing a respiratory mask.

"Histoplasmosis and toxoplasmosis—I think I've probably been exposed to all of them at some point. I've got a pretty strong immune system, I guess. I just don't get sick. Don't get colds or anything."

"He gave his dog tapeworm," Dave chimed in. They explained the life cycle of a tapeworm, how it has the flea as an intermediary. When the dog feels the flea bite, it will often nip and swallow the flea, ingesting the worm's eggs in the bargain. And where do the fleas come from? The trailer. Lots of fleas in the trailer. They have to douse it regularly with disinfectant, although even that won't get rid of raccoon roundworm eggs. Those eggs, they told me, can withstand temperatures of 140 degrees. If you want to make sure a cage is free of them, you have to run a blowtorch over it.

Was I grossed out yet? Yes. But wait, there's more. In humans, roundworms go for different organs than they do in their normal host. They show up in your eyes and your liver and your brain. I could tell the guys were relishing this.[3]

"He also gave his dog the mange," Dave said.

Dan nodded sheepishly.

"Girlfriend got it, too."

"Caught these cute little foxes," he explained. "We were cuddling them and taking pictures of ourselves with them. Sure enough, we got this rash . . . ."

The rash "itched like hell" for a while, but since the mite can't reproduce on humans it subsided eventually. The long-suffering dog he had to take to the vet, however.

Baiting a trap is a bit like the first installment of a fish story. You don't end the story with *I threw out my line;* you end it with what you caught.

I get a call two days later. Dan and Dave are headed to the traps we set in Camden, a small satellite city known for its horse farms. The owner has reported some activity in the trap.

The tidy house is powder blue stucco, set back in what looks a lot like my yard—wild untrimmed trees, a "lawn" of sand and leaves. The ground is spongy with mole tunnels.

Dan and Dave were expecting to catch something here. On first inspection, the perimeter looked pretty tight. But then Dave crawled under the deck and shone a flashlight back at the house, and sure enough, a crawlspace vent had been knocked out, leaving a nice, wide hole into the crawlspace. The next vent had also been removed to make way for a duct that led to an appliance inside. Last year, the owner told us, he noticed a smell, and wound up digging a dead possum out from the corner over by the HVAC unit—it was winter, but it still smelled something awful. The varmints were getting in by digging under the steel sheath around the HVAC unit, then following the big duct inside the wall.

Dave and I go around the house while Dan is on the phone with someone who has squirrels in the attic. He's explaining that there are two separate charges, one for removing the animal and one for excluding them from the premises. They'll do an inspection that afternoon.

There's the steel cube of the HVAC, still glistening with dew.

There's the back deck.

And—

"Potted meat," Dave says. "Gets 'em every time."

The possum is on the small side, much smaller than a cat, its fur pale and its tail thick and hairless and surprisingly short. When it sees our shadows bend across the cage, it panics and recoils into itself. It's trembling. Dave says it's a myth that the creatures play dead when they sense a threat—he never sees them do that in a trap. They're just slow all around.[4]

What I notice most is the way the liquid brown eyes are set close together beneath the brow so they peer down over the bridge of a hairless pink nose. The animal's lips are pulled back to expose its gum line, which is also a bright and fleshy pink. The teeth are white needle points. The possum has licked out most of the potted meat. And it's also licked all the nasty, smelly brown goo from the dangling plastic scent wand.

Dan comes back and hoists the cage. The animal hisses at him and bares its teeth. The other trap under the house is empty, but in the back of the trailer there's another possum from a different part of town, in a cage wedged beneath some water snake cages. This one is about the same size as the newcomer, but the long hairs over its pale coat are black, making it look as if it has been rubbed in coal dust.

They're bound for execution, which gives the proceedings a melancholy air—I somehow want a better end to the story than their demise. Like translocation. Why not take them a few miles down the road and drop them off in a patch of woods?

Dan shakes his head. He's already explained; this is a business. As a licensed wildlife control specialist, he can't just release trapped nuisance animals wherever he likes; they could spread disease, they could come right back, they could annoy someone else. If people want to pay him to use excluders instead of traps, that's great. But most clients are paying him to make the problem go away for good, not come ambling back down the garden path. They don't want to see these animals again.

If you know the animals are gone, then get busy and seal up the gaps before they come back. Apply black urethane foam, install steel mesh, and you've saved yourself and the wild things a lot of aggravation and angst. That's the take-away message from my time with All Things Wild.

So why don't I do it? I buy the materials, and even write "crawlspace" at the top of a "To Do" list. The problem is this: as much as I want to do the right thing, I do not want to go under the house. I know there are plenty of people for whom this job would be no big deal. I'm not one of them. I don't like heights, and I don't like small, confined spaces that smell of the grave and make me feel as if I'm being buried alive. I've seen enough black mold and petrified corpses, thank you. As the weeks turn into months, "crawlspace" gets underlined and circled, finally disappearing altogether. Out of sight, out of mind. Then one night, the completely predictable happens. We've had a night out at the movies, which is not unheard of around our place but still uncommon enough that it feels both liberating and nerve-racking all at once. Although our babysitter has completed her degree in early child education and is working on a graduate teaching certificate, we keep the cellphone on vibrate. Just in case.

Of course, when she calls, we don't hear it. We don't know anything is amiss until we get home, when she tells us she heard something. It sounded like someone trying to break into the house—a banging, scrabbling sound as if he were trying to pry open a window. She was scared enough to call us, and when that didn't work, she called the neighbors. Our neighbor came over and went around the house, but he didn't see anything.

When she points to where the noise was coming from, I nod knowingly. *It sounded almost like it was in the wall,* she says, tapping the place where the old coal-stove chimney is hidden behind drywall.

I say it could just have been my son kicking the wall in his sleep; he does make that thumping sound occasionally. But I know that's wishful thinking. The grace period has expired, and I'm responsible for whatever suffering is about to ensue.[5]

When we had the possums in the trailer, I confessed to Dan that I'd seen the moldy evidence of possums before—in our attic, not far from the evidence of rats. The white mold variety, suggesting that some time had passed since their last visit. Dan and Dave talked me through the steps of rigging up an excluder, even showed me a tube made out of canvas that looked a bit like something a pastry chef would use. If I really want to have possums in the yard but not in the house, I could try something like this.

Now that I have an animal under there, however, I understand the perspective of the homeowner who just wants it gone. I feel invaded, and the excluder comes with difficult-to-answer questions: Where exactly are the animals gaining access? Are you sure? Are there other weak points in your home's perimeter they might exploit? And a caution: if you don't set it up properly, you run the risk of trapping the animal under there, where it will go into a frenzy trying to get out. If a desperate possum wedges its way deep into your walls trying to find an escape route and fails? Then you have the body fluids leaking under the trim boards and soaking into the carpet.

With a trap, however, you don't have to worry about whether you've found the only entry point or inadvertently locked the critter inside. You trap until there are no more animals to worry about. Then you seal up the holes. It's logical, I've seen it in action, and I know it works.

I buy a stainless steel Safeguard possum trap just like the one the professionals use. I also purchase little tins of potted meat, although I decide to forgo that brown fecal-smelling paste they use as an attractant. Potted meat smells bad enough.

The possum trap is far easier to set than a rat trap; just make sure the bait is on the far end so that the creature has to cross the touch plate to get a taste, then push the door up and make sure the little hook catches on the bar. All set. The instructions say that a "skillful trapper" will wipe away his own smell, but I don't worry about that. If this thing has an aversion to my scent, why is it trying to get inside my house?

As dusk falls, I crouch by the crawlspace door, right next to the HVAC unit. It's warm and the windows are open, and I can hear the chirps of the lovebirds we're pet-sitting while my son's preschool is on break. They're in a big cage in the living room, scattering birdseed and bird poop all over the towels we've put on the floor. It's a strange juxtaposition of the wild and the tame.

You may have wondered by now why we don't have any pets. I grew up in a house full of pets, with cats curled up in laundry baskets, a terrier that bolted for the front door every time it opened, gerbils that spun their creaky wheel all night long, even a pet rabbit that my aunt won at the state fair. I remember them all fondly. My grand-mother had a beagle who would curl up in my closet at night, and occasionally I would get down from my bed and curl up next to her—I didn't mind the occasional flea jumping along my arm. But for now, we've got more than enough cleaning and feeding and potty training and walking to the park on our hands.

In goes the cage, right by the door. I'm not ready to go any further into that eerie horror movie world.

Is that the hollow clinking of a tin can I hear coming from under the floor of our bedroom, like a cat eating Whiskas straight from the can? I sit up in bed, looking around, a startled diurnal creature trying to make sense of the midnight landscape. Could it be?

The cage is positioned right beneath the alarm clock, which means that every time there's a noise I wind up verifying how long I've been awake. One hour, ten minutes. One hour, fourteen minutes. Two hours, fifteen minutes . . . .

Something is definitely under there. I can hear the zing that the cage makes when it's rattled or bumped, but noises seem to be coming from up in the wall, too. Maybe there's more than one? Maybe I didn't set the trap correctly, and the thing is enjoying a feast. Potted meat— how delicious! It all feels a bit like an Edgar Allan Poe story, the one where the heart of a murdered man is beating under the floorboards, driving the narrator insane. I crush a pillow over my head.

When I venture outside with a flashlight in the morning, the squirrels are bouncing through the treetops, the cardinals and wrens are chortling away, and the only sign of the macabre is the turkey vulture riding the thermals overhead, on the lookout for roadkill.

I pull on leather gloves and squat down on my haunches. As the plywood door makes its usual dull pop, like the plastic lid on a can of mixed nuts, the cage starts rattling on the other side.

A face. A woeful possum face with dark, liquid eyes and a fleshy pink wedge of nose, squeezed into the furthest corner of the cage but still illuminated by the rectangular shaft of morning light.

It isn't the cutest ball of fur I've ever seen. More like a balled-up bath towel someone left out in the rain. There's a fresh pink scar beneath one eye, and its lower lip looks raw along the gum line from where it's been worrying the steel bars. It shows me all of its glistening white fangs, then tries desperately to claw its way out through the bottom of the cage. When I reach inside for the handles on top of the cage, it growls, kind of like an angry cat, then rears back hissing with its mouth open.

The good news: possums don't normally transmit rabies. Their body temperature is so low, Dan claimed, that the microbe can't hack it. I may have to deal with all kinds of fungus and worms and bacteria taking root in my flesh, but if I make a wrong move, at least I won't have to get the rabies shots in my buttocks.

When I pull the cage out from under the house, the kids are watching. How will they reconcile this snarling prisoner with the fluffy friends that populate their inside world? They want to know everything, of course. What is it? What's wrong with it? Why is it in the cage? Why am I carrying it? What am I going to do with it? Where am I putting it? Why am I taking it away? They're question-generating machines.

I drape a sheet over the cage and put it in the shade while I empty the back of the station wagon. The possum continues to hiss and snarl and claw at the bars.

The questions keep coming.

We drive three miles to a swamp, the possum and I, through neighborhoods and stoplights and finally to the industrial edge of the city where the river meanders along through floodplains. We pass a big, dead raccoon along the way. There's a sewage treatment plant nearby, and a private school, but no housing for more than a mile on both sides of the road, just crop fields and tupelo swamp. I drive with the windows down. The possum has a smell, like a wet, panting dog.

What I'm doing is frowned upon by just about everything I've read. I checked with Harvin Brock, captain of law enforcement for the state's Department of Natural Resources: he said he wasn't aware of any statute making it illegal to transport an animal away from my property, nor was it against the law to livetrap a nuisance animal without a "depredation" permit, as long as the animal is within one hundred yards of my house. But it is strenuously discouraged, for good reason. Wildlife officers deal with seventy animals a month in our county that are suffering from disease, usually either rabies or distemper. If you transport an animal, you're taking along whatever diseases that animal might be carrying, too, spreading disease to uninfected populations. Brock's advice was familiar: destroy the animal and bury it on your property. Later, he emailed the language in the state statute covering depredation permits, which included the phrase: "An animal captured pursuant to this subsection must be destroyed or with a department permit may be relocated." In other words, what I'm doing is indeed illegal, even if the law is not enforced.

Why didn't I do the exclusion work when I had the chance?

I pull over. The tinkling sound of blackbirds singing comes in through the window, along with the roar of traffic on the nearby highway. Black, shiny turtles cluster on the logs floating in the green duckweed stew. I keep expecting one of the logs to blink—it looks like perfect alligator habitat.

I set the cage down on the other side of the road, where a tilled field stretches out beyond the roadside trees to the semis zooming down the highway for Charleston. I've been warned that possums will often refuse to leave the cage or take a few steps and refuse to move any further, overwhelmed by the sensory overload of their new location. But this one bolts out into the dry leaves, down the embankment, and into the brush, her tail stretched out behind like an index finger.

I watch as she follows her nose around from tree to tree, at one point climbing ten feet up a trunk, reading the invisible signatures of the local inhabitants. I say "she" because her abdomen is clearly distended in a pouch—there must be a clutch of young in there, still too small to cling to her back. No wonder she was hungry.

She scares up a cottontail and backpedals to a halt, rocking her head to grab the scent, peering desperately into this bright and bewildering landscape. Thrashers swoop in to see what's happening and start scratching in the leaves in her wake. She passes a hole at the base of a tree with piles of fresh clay around it—maybe a groundhog, or it could be a fox. . . . In the distance I can hear the freeway, see the trucks roaring under a green sign. I hope she doesn't wander that way.

Will she know how to survive out here? When Iqbal Malik translocated monkeys from the urban precincts of Vrindavan, her team always provisioned the troop until they figured out how to survive outside the city.[6] Same for zoo-reared tamarins released in Brazil, same for the urban monkeys at the Asola refuge. Urban animals aren't going to do much better than most of us in the middle of the wild. Throw us out of a helicopter into some remote jungle, and in all likelihood we'd never be seen again, having starved or poisoned ourselves or died of thirst and infection or been devoured by something. No wonder the village at the edge of the Asola sanctuary had a problem with monkeys: the monkeys were just doing what we would do, heading back to the habitat they know.

If I had to guess what this possum was doing with her nose to the ground, I'd say she was looking for the trace of a familiar scent. And once she finds it, she'll start heading back more or less the way we came in the car, getting closer and closer to the streets and yards she and I both know well. She'll either make it back to the neighborhood or die trying.[7]

I don't want to catch her again. Or any of her kind. I'd like to retire the trap altogether. What you realize, as soon as you see that face behind bars, is that this really is a last resort for anyone who cares about the suffering of animals.

If I could crouch, that would be one thing. If there was an actual door, that would work. But slithering in the powdery dust looking for dung? Isn't there some way I could weasel my way out of this part? If I hadn't set myself up for this, if I hadn't said I'd personally explore the limits of backyard coexistence, I'd immediately hand this job over to Dan. I don't care what it costs, I'd tell him. Just don't make me go under there and inspect your work.

Once the potted meat has been sitting untouched under the house for several days and I know the coast is clear, it's time to begin.

The easy part is the crawlspace vents. These are open

slits about the same width as a brick turned on its side, and they are spaced in decorative groups of three all the way around the base of the house. They aren't wide enough for an adult possum to squeeze through, probably, but they're just right for rats. The skinks and anoles love them—and since they're good for rodents they're probably attractive to serpents as well. Who knows what slithers into that musty shade at the sound of a footstep?

All I have to do is sit in the sun and cut some quarter-inch mesh to the right size with tin snips and then use liquid nails to fix it to the bricks. I do it in stages, so that whatever is under there has time to escape. Crawling under the house to seal off holes is bad enough. Crawling under there to retrieve a "D 'n' D"? That's a nightmare I'd prefer not to contemplate.

The time arrives for my immersion in the urban wild. I gear up with headlamp, kneepads, gloves, ventilator mask, and protective glasses and squeeze through the door, sliding along a sheet of unfurled plastic. I'm trying to see this world as Dan and Dave would see it. "You'll see hair if it's possums getting through there," Dave had told me. "It'll look like a perm from the eighties—kind of a curl to it." He'd made a curlicue in the air with his finger.

Dan had advised me to focus on the HVAC. That's probably the culprit, he'd said. Sure enough, the foil-clad main vent is surrounded by heaps of broken brick left behind by the contractors who installed the system, decades ago. This was their idea of sealing off the wall? They might as well have added a "Rooms for Rent" sign. Clear out the rubble. Get out the steel mesh and the black urethane foam. Seal the borders into inviolable barriers. Our space. Their space. I don't look for glowing eyes or scat or hair in my headlamp beam. I don't focus on the plumes of dust and wonder what might be floating around in them. Dan told me I needed to think like an animal, but I don't want to do that. Not under here.

I retire the trap for a week or so, until I see a big male squirrel hopping to the lounge chair with the fuzzy little orb of a peach clenched in his jaws. His path is the same as last year: bound into the shrubby trees, scale the telephone pole, then scamper across the roof of the neighbor's garage. Same old, same old.

This year, however, is going to be different. I'm hazing. I'm putting that possum trap right under the peach, and I'm baiting it with a little platter of peanut butter mixed with golden oat crunch, and I'm sprinkling the interior with peanuts and raw almonds. Yes, almonds. If you like peach pits, you'll love our almonds.

Hazing is part of the animal damage control officer's repertoire—these days, the USDA spends a lot of time and money developing new ways to scare the wits out of varmints, especially birds near airports, instead of just killing them.[8] These methods take the scarecrow idea to a whole new level; we're talking fireworks and sonic booms, drones that swoop like falcons, even a pigeon eviction strategy Dan described, which entails running electrified mesh along the eaves where they like to roost. In South Carolina, the chief target is vultures, which roost in communal flocks, drenching the rooftops and cars below with digested carrion. To discourage these guys, the USDA recommends hanging an "effigy," a dead vulture preserved by a taxidermist and hung upside down from a visible spot in a nearby tree. Talk about grim lawn ornaments.[9]

Is terrifying an animal humane? Again, it's a question of options. After a commercial plane struck a goose and went down in the Hudson River, the authorities decided that something had to be done with the Canada geese that flock between the green pastures of Brooklyn's Prospect Park and JFK Airport. They decided hazing wasn't enough and began shooting them by the thousands.[10] Maybe I've become desensitized, but the squirrels and I have a problem, and I've tried resolving it amicably. I need to communicate more firmly. Hazing beats killing.

Setting the trigger so that the lightest brush will snap it shut, I feel a bit like the witch in the old Grimm fairy tale, luring Hansel and Gretel into her stew pot with sweet morsels plucked from her house made of candy.

At first, nothing. The squirrels won't go near the cage or the trees. The trap probably still smells of possum.

But when I get home on the second day, there's movement in there.

A male. It looks smaller than last summer's nemesis, although it's hard to tell because it's ricocheting off the sides of the cage in a kind of super-speed version of the zigzag squirrels sometimes do in the road when your car is bearing down on them. I think about what Dan said about squirrels in a cage—would it be more humane to kill it instantly? Or would the most humane thing be to give up on food production altogether?

I'm dealing with critters that are eating food I want to eat, which seems like a very different situation from keeping an animal out of my house. If I have to use a cage to keep my house free of wildlife, so be it. If I have to use a snap trap, so be it. If I have to go crawling around in the horrible burrow under the house to seal the animals out, I guess I can make myself do that.

But trapping an animal so I can taste a peach—I'm not sure how that fruit is going to taste, honestly. Taste itself is a kind of alchemy; the tongue is a blunt instrument, refined by our olfactory ability to find meaning in vapors and gases. And this amalgam of different sensations is dredged in the redolent seasonings of memory, such that a taste of peach conjures more than itself; it brings back stories. If you're Proust, that's a great thing. If you bite into a peach and it brings back scenes of animal fear and suffering, well . . . .

It can be done. You can probably argue that it has to be done. Grape, blueberry, and apple growers in the seven states where most of these crops are grown reported forty-one million dollars in losses to wildlife in 1998.[11] Coyotes and woodchucks, pigeons and starlings, blackbirds and rats—we shoot, poison, and trap these animals by the millions every year. That's part of what we eat, although we don't see it on the label of the corn chips cooked in sunflower oil. It's only when you try growing food yourself that you realize how intense this struggle for the harvest really is and how difficult it is to resolve.

He's not dead, I tell myself. He's not happy, but at least he's not dead.

I take one of the kids' paintbrushes and dip it in a can of exterior paint. Then I approach the cage. The squirrel does everything he can to keep his tail between us, but eventually I dab some white on his back and tug open the door. Up he goes. From a branch beside my neighbor's roof I can hear him making a soft crowing sound, as if he's calming himself down out loud.

I feel better. Maybe this hazing idea will work. Maybe that sound is a warning to his clan. If I can just keep them scared enough to leave the peaches alone for a few weeks, we'll be fine. The squirrels and I have no problems for eleven months of the year. We can get through this.

Two hours later there's a white-striped squirrel in the cage.

"You can have either squirrels or peaches," Nicola tells me as she breezes out the door to pick up the kids from school, leaving me alone with the burden of my pastoral dream.

If the experiment had ended here, my fall from hopeful and naive wildlife enthusiast to mournful, self-recriminating spider would have been complete. But I persevere, mostly because I don't know what else to do. And it sort of works. After two visits to the cage, the striped squirrels seem to get the message. Stay away from those fruit trees. Find something else to eat. I've managed to communicate, via the usual channels of fear and instinct, the boundaries of our territory. That's how things often get done in the natural world.

Help arrives, too, from unexpected quarters. My daughter receives a pop-up pink play castle with all the Disney heroines posing on the sides. They're smiling, but there's something unsettling about those enormous, coquettish eyes and gleaming white teeth, especially if you're a squirrel. Rapunzel seems to be particularly menacing; she's half-glancing over her shoulder at a pet chameleon, which makes her look a bit like a golden-tressed feline waiting to pounce. When the tent is up, I discover, the squirrels stay out, especially when I add half a dozen of the kids' bowling pins to the branches of the fruit trees. They're designed to look like candy-striped aliens, and they stare through the leaves with giant yellow eyes, like a flock of owls.

The behavior modification lasts long enough that I actually get to harvest a handful of small, bug-pocked, and black spot–afflicted nectarines. The kids wrinkle up their faces and say they're gross. But objectively, after I've peeled off the mottled skin and cut away the plum curculio grub tunnels, what's left tastes pretty good. And the suffering of squirrels? I can taste that, too.

8

The Bees of Brooklyn

FACT: Managed European honeybees pollinate an estimated $14.5 billion worth of crops each year in the United States. Other "wild" pollinators service approximately $3 billion worth of crops.

My son likes things that buzz. Most of his toys are animated in some way, and often his wooden toy box will begin buzzing or babbling as some action figure at the bottom of the pile suddenly decides to come to life.

Earlier this spring, he liked bees. Nicola took him to see the film *Queen of the Sun,* which makes the case that honeybees are a critical part of our food system, and yet instead of treating them well, we've been exploiting them as industrial livestock, shipping them cross-country on semis, replacing their honey stores with corn syrup, leaving a trail of dead bees in our wake.[1]

Brook came home demanding that we do something to save the bees. Like putting up a hive in our backyard. Just like the people in the film who had friendly bees crawling all over their naked torsos. Then we could harvest our own honey!

I had my reservations. The only way to situate the hive properly in a sunny location with ten feet of open space in front for landing purposes would be to prop it against the privacy fence our neighbors put up. I could have asked if they'd mind having forty thousand bees less than an inch from their lawn, but I already knew how they felt about ant nests.

I also knew that Brook likes to poke things with sticks. He's passionate about swords and light sabers and delights in jabbing me in the ribs or swatting me from behind. I could just imagine him approaching the hive with his glowing blue light saber, his little sister peering over his shoulder. He'd reach out with the plastic wand, tap lightly, and the whole hive would erupt in a cloud of retribution.

"When can we get our bee hives, Daddy?" Brook kept pitching me whenever we went outside to play in the yard, usually with sticks.

Then he got stung for the first time.

We were hiking in the mountains outside of Asheville, North Carolina. It was great. We'd gone only about a quarter of a mile, but I'd already waded into a small stream and turned over stones to show the kids crayfish and salamanders and all the other creepy crawlies dwelling underneath. The kids weren't whining about how far it was, they weren't asking to be carried, the sun was out and dappling the glossy rhododendron leaves. They were charging ahead; I was dawdling behind, enjoying the view.

I heard Brook scream. Not the I-fell-down-and-it-hurts-wail but the scream of immediate peril. In a heartbeat, I was up the hill and around the bend, where I found him clutching his leg, his face scorched with pain, terror, and bewilderment.

"It bit me," he sobbed, over and over again. His sister, Beatrice, was terrified and sobbing, too; she'd tripped over a root and skinned her knee.

Up ahead, it turned out, was a yellow jacket nest. Right next to the trail, but nearly invisible, just a small hole in the ground.

No warning, just violence.

My immediate thought was, "What if he's allergic?" We had no Benadryl on us or in the car, and we were in the middle of the woods. I hated bees then, and by bees, I meant honeybees, bumblebees, wasps, and yellow jackets, the whole stinging horde.

I picked Brook up and hustled him back down the trail to the stream, where I plunged him into a pool of cold water. He'd been stung twice, just below the knee.

As it turned out, the stings didn't swell all that much, possibly because he had no antibodies to the venom in his system.[2] We splashed water on his knee, and I explained the difference between a bite and a sting.

In the aftermath of this incident, Brook would freeze in terror every time he saw a bee-sized insect zip across the yard, and I found myself explaining that bees and wasps aren't really interested in us. They only get angry when they feel threatened or their nest is threatened. Leave them alone, and they'll leave you alone.

It took even longer for me to regain my own sense of the distinction between honeybees and yellow jackets. The problem is that these members of the *Vespula* and *Apis* clans overlap in terms of life history: they're both venomous, both striped in shades of yellow and black, and, most important, both social nesters. I didn't plan to fixate on venom here, thereby reinforcing everybody's phobias and doing a disservice to those who spend a lot of time and energy combating invertebrate stereotypes. Not all social bee species sting; before African honeybees arrived in South America, honey was harvested from indigenous species that didn't defend their nest with venom.[3] Most solitary wasps are innocuous; I've never had a problem with the two-inch-long cicada killers dragging their bulky prey to a burrow in our flower beds, and I've even considered purchasing a little mail-order packet of parasitic wasps to deal with some of the pests in the veggie patch.

But, you know, if you're talking about creatures you might encounter in your yard, you pretty much have to cover the risk of encountering something poisonous, even if that risk has been blown out of all proportion. Venom is a vestige of wildness that's basically archaic in an urban context, more likely to disqualify you from city life than help you defend against a predatory attack. Ask my mother how long a copperhead is likely to last in her North Carolina yard, especially after one bit her Yorkie in the face last summer, requiring two thousand dollars of antivenin. Her answer: about as long as it takes to fetch a shovel and chop its head off.

Our relationship with the social nesters of the wasp family is also pretty hostile. Setting aside their role in the broader ecological scheme of things, we have no compelling reason to want them around the house, and we interact with them by accident unless we're blasting their nest with our own synthetic venom.

Our relationship with honeybees, on the other hand, is paradoxical and difficult to categorize. They're both sweetness *and* sting, wild *and* domesticated, a nonnative species that's nevertheless vital to our ecosystem as we know it. The field bees in an urban hive free-range through the city, gathering pollen from gardens and roadsides and parks, then returning to the nest provided for them by their keeper. They're a free-range experiment already under way in some of the biggest, most densely populated cities in the world, including London and Paris.

In New York, honeybees had been lumped in with

yellow jackets for years, under the category of creatures with venomous stingers, menacing fangs, predatory appetites, and/or the capacity to grow into sewer-dwelling reptilian giants. Alligators, wasps, tigers, and honeybees, in other words, were all illegal to keep as pets or livestock.

The threat of fines never stopped a few intrepid apiarists from keeping "secret hives" tucked away on undisclosed rooftops. In 2010, however, under pressure from the growing urban farming and community garden movement, the city changed its codes. It's now legal to free-range your bees in the five boroughs, and although the community of beekeepers is still small enough that everyone seems to know each other, hundreds of newcomers are trying their hand at it. Based on the number of people involved in various clubs, Brooklyn beekeeper Tim O'Neal estimates there are now about a thousand hives in the five boroughs of New York, and more are on the way, although most have not registered with city authorities. That's a lot of wildlife to have free-ranging through the windswept plateaus of the built environment in search of nectar and pollen.

O'Neal is a recent college grad from Ohio's farm country, tall and rangy, his sandy hair swept like a bird wing across the bridge of his glasses. His checked flannel shirt is tucked into a pair of distressed jeans, which is pretty much the unofficial uniform for urban farmers these days. But what sets Tim apart from the majority of Brooklyn's backyard biodynamic farmers—sets him apart from newbies like me, in other words—is that he's been keeping bees for fourteen years now, since he was in his early teens. He came to beekeeping before its recent bump in urban popularity, back when it was still the province of rural farmers and an idiosyncratic, passionate handful of hobbyists. Now he's riding the wave, teaching introductory classes in beekeeping and working as the beekeeper for various organizations, including Red Hook Community Farm, where I've come to see him in action at their Added Value harvest festival.

I'd known him about five minutes before his fist came down to smash one of the yellow jackets prospecting around the old honeycomb-encrusted wooden frames he'd put out for display on a folding table. Chitinous and tough, refusing to go down without a fight, the yellow jacket countered by jabbing its stinger into the meat of Tim's palm, which prompted a small grunt and a final series of table-rattling body slams.

"They're robbers," he explained, plucking the mashed corpse gingerly between his finger and thumb as a gaggle of farm visitors drifted close to see. All summer long, he said, the larvae in the yellow jacket nest have been giving out little drops of honeydew to encourage the adults to look after them. Now it's fall, the colony has stopped producing young, and the adults are in sugar withdrawal. They're desperate and ornery, and they'll invade a beehive and fight to the death to get their sugar fix.[4]

We stand behind the table and watch people gravitate toward the patch of autumn sunshine where a Puerto Rican salsa band is warming up. Tim has set up an observation hive on one corner, and the honeycombed frame inside is swarming with frantic workers and the occasional bubble-eyed drone. Worker bees are female, and they do all the hive's work, collecting nectar and pollen, processing and storing honey, tending to the young and defending the hive from intruders. The male drones loaf around the hive and wait, hoping for the chance to breed with a virgin queen from another hive. At the end of the season, when the hive is conserving resources, many can be found sitting forlornly on the ledge outside the entrance to the hive. Their sell-by-date expired; they've been ejected and left to starve.[5]

We have a long history of anthropomorphizing bees, finding in their social structure and behavior some reflection of our own civilization, particularly our cities.[6] The more I've learned about bees, however, the less humanistic their priorities seem. We humans tend to prize the individual, but the colony is a rigid collective, and in that kind of system the individual is expendable. When a worker bee stings, her abdomen is torn apart, and she dies. When a drone mates with the queen, his abdomen is ripped apart, and he dies. When a new queen emerges from her natal cell, the first thing she does is go around to her sisters who haven't emerged yet and kill them off. Even the queen is not above the brutal and dispassionate logic of the hive. An aging queen will often lay the eggs that will become her successor, after which a host of workers will sometimes smother her to death in the hot, tight clasp of their bodies.[7]

The bees in here are a mix of genetics, Tim says, tracking the path of individual bees through the glass. When a virgin queen takes her one and only mating flight, she draws a crowd of drones, not from her own hive, but from any managed or feral hives that may be in the vicinity. She then mates with several drones, ensuring that the fertilized eggs she produces will have differing parentage from the father's side. A few of these bees have darker, almost charcoal abdomens, which is characteristic of several domesticated stocks such as Germans and Carniolans. They're better equipped to tough out a northern winter but also have an irascible reputation. The creamy blond ones look more like Italians, known for their docility. Most beginners start with Italians, since nobody likes to get stung.[8]

Then there are the feral bees. Darker usually, acclimated to life in the city, prized by some, avoided by others. It's possible to get your hands on a feral colony in the spring, when a successful hive will split and send out a "hiving" swarm in search of a new abode. If you show up with the appropriate receptacle when a tree limb or parking meter is coated in wild bees, you can scoop them up and release them into your unoccupied hive.[9] A feral queen has urban survival traits to pass on to her workers, and as a result you're likely to get more honey. But you'd better have a high tolerance for bee venom.

"There's probably some Africanized genetics in here, too," Tim observes without a trace of "killer bee" hysteria. The hives at Added Value were stocked with nucleus hives (minicolonies) from Florida, where "Africanized" genetics are a bit more ubiquitous. Beginners do not start with Africanized bees, which have been hybridizing their way north from Brazil since a handful of queens were mistakenly released in the 1950s.[10] They've made their way through the southeastern United States, where most queen bees are raised for sale, following the mild climate zones north along the Eastern seaboard. Africanized bees don't look any different from bees of European stock, but they behave very differently. When you evolve with honey badgers and other marauders who view your nest as a piñata stuffed with calories, as African honeybees did, you develop an itchy trigger finger. Africanized colonies, Tim reports, actually sound different from a normal hive; they buzz collectively at a slightly higher pitch.

Tim has found that the bees in this colony are more easily perturbed than your average hive, just a tad more likely to get worked up and start stinging. I'm surprised he's so blasé, since he happens to be allergic to bee stings. He's already been stung once this morning getting the frame into the observation hive, he says, showing me the puffiness in his knuckle by flexing it back and forth. No biggie. He's already popped a Benadryl, and he keeps an EpiPen with him, just in case.

He's set out three kinds of honey for sale. One is dark as a pint of stout, while the second is a pale, translucent gold. These two are the pride and joy of the urban beekeeper, the distilled efflorescence of this place. Honey offers a record of what was blooming where and when; it offers a reckoning of whether the nectar from daffodil bulbs and Bradford pear trees and goldenrod fields and hanging baskets was abundant or scant. The bees have a map of the city as seasonal greenscape: this is the result.

The pale honey with a floral taste is a reflection of the border between Oceanside, on Long Island, and Far Rockaway, in Queens, in springtime. The dark honey, thick as molasses, glinting amber when I hold it up to the sun, was just harvested a couple weeks ago by one of Tim's friends. The flowers of fall, goldenrod, aster, mums, apparently have more minerals and antioxidants in their nectar. Both varieties are raw and unfiltered, so all the pollen and enzymes are still floating around intact. Tim isn't sold on the idea that honey can cure hay fever: he works for a university hospital, doing immunological research on the AIDS virus, and he tends to think that our immune response to pollen is more complicated than that. But it can't hurt.

"There's wax in it," he tells a couple who are pushing their son in a stroller. "There may be a bee leg or two. I consider that protein."

Then there's the third honey, the showstopper, the one that seems to halt people in their tracks and lure them to the table. Raw, unfiltered, and red as a stop sign. Red Hook honey, circa last summer, propped up in a test tube on a little reclaimed pine display stand. Polished with beeswax, of course.

Honey is the record of a place in time, and in this case, that place is in flux, a fascinating mix of pastoral and industrial, old and new. Red Hook Community Farm sits in what was until recently a semiabandoned industrial wasteland across the bay from the Newark Airport, surrounded by narrow cobbled streets, brown fields, warehouses, and factories, a handful of which are still in business. This ambitious project, which provides produce as well as hands-on horticultural education for neighborhood teens, sits on nearly three acres of asphalt that was previously a playing field for dockworkers. Beneath all the tidy raised beds of tomatoes and kale, beneath the compost piles and the sapling fruit trees and the weedy area where the bees gather in a shimmering aurora around their hive, the asphalt is still there.[11] And beneath the asphalt, judging by the low and flat character of the land, there's excavated dirt, piled on top of what was once marsh and oyster beds. Across the street, brighter than the cloud-scudded autumn sky, stretches the cobalt and canary facade of IKEA.

For seven decades, this corner of the city has been home to a factory whose business is creating food additives. Back when this was all smokestacks and soot and trucks, nobody was around to notice if a little of this or that seeped out and spilled. Nobody cared, especially if what you were spilling wasn't PCB-laced hydraulic fluid but sugar syrup, the kind that goes into various food products. So you happen to spill a little maraschino cherry juice on the floor of the plant, so what?

Then the city legalizes beekeeping, and the beekeepers start colonizing the shores of Red Hook. During that first summer, they begin to notice that their honey has a weird red tint to it. In fact, when the sun strikes their bees as they return to the hive, they glow like laser pointers or tracer bullets. This isn't normal. It isn't happening elsewhere in the city.[12]

Tim got involved when the source was still a mystery. A number of apiary veterans were on the case: it was the kind of biochemical detective story that attracts a certain kind of people to beekeeping in the first place, not the sweet taste of honey itself but the complex, idiosyncratic relationship of keeper and hive.

At first, Tim suspected transmission fluid from the nearby bus depot, since transmission fluid contains ethylene glocol, a sweet (but poisonous) substance that is often dyed red. Spots of something are common in an urban hive: he's found spots of vivid blue in his Fort Greene hives, the result of somebody spilling Gatorade in a parking lot or dropping a half-eaten blue raspberry slushy on the ground.

A couple of tainted cells—that's easy to remove before processing the honey. But this red dye is spread like a stain through entire hives, contaminating the entire harvest. He tasted it—it didn't taste like honey. It tasted like Karo syrup, thin and cloying with an unpleasant, metallic aftertaste. Some hives just had a smear of it, just a patch here and there of red honeycomb, but as the team of beekeeper sleuths got closer to the source, the hives turned crimson. Finally, they zeroed in on the factory, tucked away in the industrial anonymity of a scruffy warehouse district.

No screens on the windows of the plant. Trucks sloshing corn syrup on the ground, leaving puddles where the newcomers to the neighborhood arrived in multitudes to lap it up. Judging by the number of contaminated supers in the hives, Tim suspects the bees transported several hundred pounds of syrup from the factory over the course of the summer.

This "news of the weird" story became a local media sensation, and the health department got involved. Now there are screens on the factory windows, and the owner has started work on a new plant that will presumably keep bees and corn syrup from mixing. There will be no more red honey from Red Hook.

People are attracted to the color red. They gravitate to the table because they spot these vials of red goodness and they want a taste. They're seeing a fantasia of superbly ripe apple and crisp watermelon rather than a concentration of the dyes that make kids crazy and give rats cancer in high doses.

"This is what happens when honeybees get into a maraschino cherry factory," Tim says, as the visitors zero in on the red stuff. "It's fast food for bees. It's fast and easy and not very good for you. Like McDonald's."

"Does it taste like maraschino cherries?" someone asks hopefully.

"No, it tastes like Karo, actually. It tastes like corn syrup."

Who wants to hear that about the pinnacle of their ice cream sundae? There's disappointment in the air.

"You can taste it if you want," Tim says skeptically. "But I wouldn't recommend it."

"How about making a red velvet cake with it?" one guy insists. "Or what about a red mead?"

Tim scoffs at the idea. Why would you want that when you have this wonderful raw and unfiltered stuff for sale right over here? This red stuff is really bad for you, and for bees. Every red honey hive he knows of died this past winter.

In my view, the whole conversation is perilously close to exposing what it is we're really eating when we drizzle a dollop of honey. We're eating something that a multitude of insects has regurgitated from their enzyme-rich honey crops, then spent a great deal of time and energy masticating with their jaws, transforming the flowers' complex sugars into fructose and glucose, sharing it around with their siphonlike tongues. Honey mixed with water will ferment and spoil; to prevent this from happening, the bees evaporate down the moisture content by forming a wind tunnel with their wings. We're eating a substance, in other words, in which insects have performed all the tasks that a maple syrup maker will perform with tubes and pails and long-simmering vats. That's pretty amazing. But it also means we're eating something that has spent a lot of time inside bugs.[13]

I'm even less enticed by the idea of eating unfiltered insect regurgitations in an urban context—if these guys are concentrating red dye number 40, what else is in the mix? If honey is a reflection of a given place, then my first thought is I want the honey from the hinterlands, not the nectar of the brown fields.

As Tim points out, however, the agricultural landscape is not necessarily chemical-free. Growing up in Ohio, he witnessed the effect of pesticides on his hives. Suddenly, the bees would just disappear, and down the road he'd find little signs on the edge of a farmer's field, warning people that it had just been sprayed. Research has shown that the pollen and nectar bees bring back to the hive are contaminated with a variety of pesticides. Bees have demonstrated the ability to recognize the contaminated material and wall it off in the hive rather than consuming it themselves, but low-level residues still make their way into honey along with the chemicals beekeepers use themselves to ward off diseases in the hive.[14]

One of the reasons peregrine falcons fare better in the city is that the urban food chain isn't as heavily contaminated with agricultural chemicals: a pigeon fattening on bread crumbs isn't accumulating as high a pesticide load as a duck feeding in a runoff ditch. The same is probably true if you're gathering and concentrating the nectar of urban blooms instead of dodging the white plume behind a yellow plane in some rural crop field.

It's not that honey is worse for you than other foods but rather that the red dye offers us a glimpse of what is widespread but normally invisible in our food system. You are not just what you eat but where it comes from. Choose wisely.

Not everybody wants a taste of red honey. A teacher wanders up: she's the principal at a nearby charter school. Their science teacher used to keep bees upstate, and they'd like to add a hive to their back garden. Maybe Tim could come and offer a demonstration. Fellow beekeepers pass by, eager to share their experiences of last winter's disasters. One guy says he checked his hives during a February thaw, and they were huddled together in a tight buzzing ball. Then he got up on the roof in April and saw a handful of bees hovering around the entrance.

"Robber bees," Tim interjects, nodding grimly. "After the honey."

The hive was eerily silent, but the bees hadn't absconded. They were still there, freeze-dried and dead, clustered in a petrified swarm.

"It was a really bad winter," Tim consoles him. "A lot of the bees in the city died."

They talk shop about various challenges, like "bald brood," which may be caused by wax moths that chew away the walls of the cells in which larval bees are developing, pocking the comb with exposed larvae. Or it may be that the bees themselves chew the caps of the cells in an attempt to rid them of parasites. Honeybees in general are having a tough time these days, so there's plenty to talk about. Tiny mites cluster in the workers' lungs, sapping their strength and making it hard to breathe, making them vulnerable to fungal and viral infections. Add in the various chemical exposures bees face in their forays across the countryside, and you have the makings for the epidemic that has come to be known as "colony collapse disorder."[15] The hive appears to be functioning normally one week, and then suddenly the field bees are gone, as if they all went out to forage one morning and just dropped out of the sky for good, leaving their honey stores and immature bees and even the queen behind. Most beekeepers have come to rely on miticides and fungicides and antibiotics to keep their colonies alive, but these chemical treatments affect the health of the bees, too. You won't find synthetic miticides in Tim's hives, however. He's helped start a New York branch of the group Backwards Bees, for beekeepers who want to manage their hives without chemicals.[16]

By late afternoon, the agitated bees in the observation

hive are getting tired. If at first the air around the hive seemed to crackle with vibrating energy, things are definitely waning now, like a flashlight that's been left on too long. It's time to put the frame back in the hive.

Up to this point, the stinging capability of bees has been theoretical: I'm pretty sure I'm not allergic, and since the standard for human tolerance of bee venom is ten stings per pound of bodyweight, I'd have to get nailed close to two thousand times before I dropped dead.[17] Veterans say you get used to a sting here and there. No biggie.

But I don't really want to get stung. Not even once if I can avoid it. I know what it feels like, and I know, deep down and viscerally, that I don't like it. The bees' defense strategy is functioning perfectly as far as I'm concerned.

We don traditional beekeeping gear. Tim has a white jacket with elastic straps that go over his bare hands and keep the sleeves down against his wrists, and a broad-brimmed white hat with a drape of mesh. I have a similar hat with a white drape that comes down over my shoulders and cinches tight around my waist. Why white? Because darker colors remind bees of predators they don't like, and that makes them angry. Black, for example, they associate with bears, their ancient adversaries.[18]

That's great. My coat is bear-pelt black, and underneath I'm wearing a brown shirt. I cinch the waist cord tighter, until it feels like a tourniquet. Tim tells me to push up my sleeves so they're tight against my forearms.

The thing is to not have any place the bees can burrow. They like to burrow into a seam or up a sleeve and then sting when they get pinched. My throat is dry.

"Come closer," Tim says, beckoning. "You can't see anything from way out there!"

He opens up the smoker, which looks like a galvanized camp coffee pot attached to a bellows, and gets it going with a wad of wooden shavings and newspaper. As he works the bellows, a thin tendril of wood smoke, the smell of a nice, warm hearth on a chilly night, wavers skyward.

The hive is basically a stack of wooden boxes called supers, each filled with hanging wooden frames, like an inverted filing cabinet. The bees fill these frames with honeycomb, which can be plucked individually for inspection by the keeper. In the middle is a "queen excluder," a screen that allows workers to pass through to the upper layers but keeps the queen laying eggs in what is known as the "brood box" near the base. The bigger and more productive the colony, the more wooden boxes stacked on top to make room for honey storage. This one is stacked five segments high.[19]

When Tim lifts the lid off the top super, the bees scramble out, zooming around in tight agitated spirals. Boom! He's stung in the meat of his hand again. Instead of fussing about it, however, he grabs the smoker and lays a thick plume along the seams of the exposed stack. When a bee stings, it releases an alarm pheromone that transforms the agitated group into an angry mob. But this signal can be trumped by the smell of an even greater crisis: fire. Bees react to wood smoke as if their house were burning down, diving back into the hive to gorge themselves on honey in preparation for an emergency relocation.[20]

Some of the exposed house bees do seem to be crawling around the supers rather than launching into the air. But not all of them. A couple dozen or so are crawling across Tim's white back like letters trying to form sentences. And they're coming at me, too. I have them crawling across the mesh of my face, so close they're blurry. They're creeping along the mesh above my waist and coming down my sleeves until I shake them away. They look like they're prospecting, looking for folds and creases, for the sensitive places where they can squeeze in and get the most bang for their venom. Africanized bees are said to concentrate their fury on the face, that target-rich constellation of sensitive organs and orifices. The USDA warns against trying to escape them by jumping in water—the swarm will wait for you to emerge for a breath, and they'll be on your face and down your throat before you can fill your lungs. People have drowned this way, in a broth of dying bees.[21]

Tim lifts the glass off the observation hive, and now these indignant and slightly bewildered bees are also swarming around us, too.

"You can come closer," he says. He scoops up a handful of bees from the observation hive and dumps them into the supers. He cups another handful, and since I'm still hovering on the periphery, he comes to me with a handful of bees.

"See," he says, displaying the simmering ball in the palm of his hand.

"Bees are a liquid."

"That's amazing," I admit, wondering if the hand that he's now cupping upside down so the bees hang from his palm in a seething glob is the same hand that just got stung.

"That's swarming behavior, right? Isn't that what they do before they sting?"

"It's actually called *festooning*," Tim explains. This is what bees do when they're trying to close a fissure in the hive or hang in a swarm from a bough. They link legs, forming long chains.[22]

"I just love doing this, by the way," he adds as he strides through the weeds to where a couple of mothers are picking out pumpkins with their toddlers.

"Bees are actually a liquid," he announces to them, holding out the bees.

The visitors look a bit perplexed.

He comes back. The bees are still sitting in his hand. Not stinging him, apparently. He hasn't flinched the whole time.

He proffers them, unflexing his fingers slightly so the clump sits high in his hand.

Do I want to try it?

If I could just get over my fear of getting stung, I'd be happy to hold that vibrating concentration of life in my hand. But the thing about bees, the thing that distinguishes them from free-ranging livestock like goats or sheep, is that they retain that indelible stamp of wildness. You can't be certain you won't get stung, even with the most serene colony of Italian bees. You're working at the boundary of the wild and the tame.

Tim refastens the tension straps around the hive to keep it from blowing over, and as we head toward the stalls, the bees detach themselves from our clothing one by one. I've missed my chance.

The hive is the domesticated side of the story. The wild side is where the field bees go when they leave the home we humans have provided for them. Zooming skyward, they join what is essentially a wild throng of invertebrates whose free-ranging habits we know next to nothing about. There are 800 species of bees east of the Mississippi, for example, and about 230 species inhabit New York. The bulk of biodiversity of the city, in other words, is found on this remarkable but generally unnoticed part of the ecological spectrum.[23]

"Ninety percent of animals on Earth are invertebrates. And we know very little about most of them," Liz Johnson, who manages the Metropolitan Biodiversity Program for the Center for Biodiversity Conservation, told me. As a prime example she offers Central Park, which is right across the street from her office in the American Museum of Natural History. A few years ago, the program set out to catalog what was crawling around those acres. Their surface leaf and soil samples turned up a full complement of invertebrate species, many of them nonnative and unfamiliar even to experts who have worked on soil invertebrates for years. One scientist agreed to bring a particularly intriguing specimen of centipede to a world meeting of myriapodologists, who eventually reached the conclusion that this species had never been described by science. Right across the street from a temple of scientific knowledge, in other words, an unknown, probably nonnative species was making a living in the leaf litter while thousands of urbanites strolled past unaware.[24]

"There's biodiversity everywhere, including in the city," Johnson emphasized. "There are new things to discover right on the doorstep."

This summer saw more of the same: a new species of sweat bee, aptly named *Lasioglossum gotham,* was collected by one of the museum's scientists at the Brooklyn Botanic Garden.[25] Only 6 percent of the city's bees nest in hives; this newly discovered one nests in bare patches of dirt while others tunnel into the pith of hollow plant stems to overwinter. The unkempt corners of the urban landscape make good bee habitat, Johnson told me. If you want to encourage more invertebrate diversity, leave bare patches in your lawn. Leave brown dead stems from last year's herbaceous border standing, and don't rake up all your leaves. That sounds like my backyard management regime.

I'm certainly not going to discover a new species during my own expedition into the city, although I know more about bees than I once did. Yes, I know what a carpenter bee looks like now, but I wouldn't know a new species of sweat bee if it was sipping salt from the tip of my nose. We're talking about an insect that's about the size of a twist of black tea; would I even know it was a bee instead of a wasp or a fly? Bear in mind that distinguishing most of these species requires a microscope at the very least. It took DNA analysis to confirm the unique identity of *Lasioglossum gotham*.

Even if I can't identify them all, I would like to know where the pollinators go, and I'd like to explore the city as a beescape. Back when feral bee colonies were commonplace in the woods, a reasonable living could be made tracing bees back to their hives and relieving them of their honey. Honey hunters roamed the colonial woodlands, "flouring" bees so they gleamed brightly in flight, then "lining" their flight path back to the hive.[26] I want to head in the opposite direction: I know where the honeybees arrive with their nectar and pollen, but where are they foraging? Where do they go when they're outside our control?

To answer questions like these, Liz Johnson's program

joined forces with the city's Greenbelt Native Plant Center to create the Great Pollinator Project. The idea was to enlist "citizen scientists" in gathering data about where the city's bees tend to go and what they do when they get there. For several years, bee watchers stood vigil over floriferous nooks and parks in the five boroughs, identifying several categories of bee species and recording visits to certain species of flower, such as goldenrod and mountain mint. These citizen scientists gathered a substantial quantity of data. They submitted more than fifteen hundred reports, and although the data analysis hasn't been completed, they identified certain areas of the city where foraging bees tend to congregate.

The High Line is one such place. Once upon a time, the west side of Manhattan along the Hudson River thrummed with industrial noise. Warehouses and factories bustled with immigrant workers, ships straddled the docks and wharves, and trains rolled over it all on an elevated line that brought cars right into the meatpacking plants to unload. By the late 1970s, however, most of the factories had closed up, abandoning the train line to the wild pioneers of the urban jungle, which we commonly call weeds. Not for nothing those frilly puffs of airborne seeds, those tough kernels meant to pass through the digestive tracts of European house sparrows. Goldenrod showed up. Sumac. Rank, tough, invasive grasses, all taking root in the accumulated dust and grit that had settled over the decades along the tracks. Feral bees were undoubtedly foraging here, too.[27]

It's a gray and blustery morning as I head down into the meatpacking district to get a look at the new High Line, which opened as a public park a few years ago and doubled in size last summer to more than a mile of elevated, linear parkland. Shimmery new condo buildings seem to hover like disco balls above the sooty brick of the old warehouses. I climb a flight of metal stairs and emerge above a parking lot full of sedans. A billboard-sized art installation blots out the street view with a misty mountain scene, jagged snow-dusted peaks, distant forest vistas, no human evidence of any kind. *Full Moon@The North Sea,* shot by Darren Almond in the remote Huangshan Mountains of China, intensifying the juxtaposition of nature and culture, wild and tame.

Despite the weather, a stream of camera-toting tourists flows down this winding, narrow canyon rich with microhabitats. The tracks are about twenty feet wide, wide enough for vegetation on both sides. Along one stretch, the elevation seems to heighten the exposure, the wind scouring the path with brackish spume licked up from the river, and then, in the lee of a condo tower, the heathery green of late summer is still in bloom.

Whatever nostalgia I feel for the old ruins disappears quickly once I'm surrounded by the habitat that has replaced it. I've spent a lot of time trying to optimize the habitat in my own yard, creating different structural layers and microhabitats, trying to keep plants in bloom across three seasons, and I have to marvel at how imaginatively those constraints have been dealt with here. This could have been just turf studded now and again with a few petunia-flecked planters. Or nothing, no vegetation at all, just gravel with a street view. Instead, the people who envisioned this place tried to stay true to what was here before: the "Gansevoort Woodland," for example, seeks to re-create the sizable trees that had taken root in a narrow section of track where the soil deepened.[28]

The features on the backyard wildlife certification checklist are all here: water, food, places to nest, places to feed. In one stretch, water trickles under benches set up for human basking, and miniature cattails and sedges overlook the harbor.

I spend some time on a bench, partly because it's out of the wind, thinking about specialists. Liz Johnson had said that the reason there are so many more bee species outside the city is because many are specialists, and they require habitats that just don't exist in the urban environment. Take marshland, for example. Although most of the city was built on salt marsh, not much of that remains in Manhattan, or any of the other boroughs, for that matter. And yet here, in the water feature, we have a tiny fragment of that lost specialist habitat. Is it too little for a specialized marsh dweller to find, or use?

I also wonder about the touchstones for this kind of

ecosystem. I've already invoked the metaphor of a stream-bed, and a shoreline offers a similar stretch of linear riparian habitat. But neither is elevated, suspended in the sky. What kinds of wildlife can inhabit this novel ecosystem, this narrow ribbon of greenery that sits high above the traffic, a terrestrial habitat with no on-ramp for terrestrial species? Do we think of it as a terrace garden, an outpost of green embedded in a cliff face? If you come looking for wildlife, what do you find?

For certain pollinators at least, this is a fantasyland. Most of the plants are either in bloom or heavy with seedpods and berries. Even the trees shake berries and catkins in the wind: there's sassafras and buckeye, viburnum and black cherry, willow and birch. I've been told the plantings feature vast patches of mountain mint, a nectar-rich favorite for bees whose season has now passed. The bee balm is also fading, and the purple coneflowers are brown and stiff, but the Canada asters are at their peak, thousands of purple buttons toppling over into glowing wands of goldenrod. Look closely at their orange hearts and the fringes look glazed, like wet eyelashes. Yellow patches of coreopsis, blue caps of gentian, some remnant sprigs of knapweed and sage, some black-eyed Susan blooms among the already ransacked seed heads. Here and there, creamy orange honeybees cling to the wind-tossed blossoms, as if they've been shipwrecked.

When the midday sun melts through the curdled sky, I get a sense of the pollinator potential here. Bumblebees pitch themselves at the goldenrod, dislodging green bottle flies and brown wasps. Honeybees clamber through the asters. House sparrows skulk beneath the grass, tugging seeds from the grass stems and squabbling. They're so close I can hear their bills crunch and crackle and pop, like a freshly poured bowl of cereal.

The new section ends in a chain-link fence, surrounded by unreconstructed warehouses and the sights and smells of industry. On the other side of the fence lies the past, the old wilderness. Different species of bunch grass nod in the wind, punctuated by a few sprigs of faded goldenrod, but mostly the line is bare, like the side of a high plains highway. It feels even more barren after the gardens I've passed through on the way. None of what I've seen is an authentic reflection of unmediated nature; the plants are out of season, their roots suspended fifty feet in the air by a steel frame. And yet the park teems with life. A single monarch butterfly, late for a migrant, weaves along the path, rises over the fence, and keeps going, headed for the river.

While the High Line's linear structure highlights the contradictions of urban ecology, Central Park takes shape around the idea of a retreat, a withdrawal from the fretful roar of competing sensory experiences.[29] It's an 843-acre rectangle, surrounded by some of the most densely inhabited territory on the planet, yet big enough and old enough that the interior feels far away from the frenzy of the street. Walking the High Line, you inevitably feel a bit like a voyeur. You're so close to the windows of the apartments that the bedrooms and kitchens feel like dioramas in a museum of human domesticity. In Central Park, however, you feel as if you are escaping into the woods, an experience borne out by the wildlife that surrounds you.

Five minutes inside the south side entrance, past the pedicab drivers lounging by the ice cream stand, I spot my first neotropical migrant: a ruby-crowned kinglet gleaning the lower boughs of a mature linden tree. The contrast with the High Line has to do with size and shape, but also with the maturity of the tree cover. This greenspace has long been on the map for avid birders, who come here religiously to record the rise and fall of migrant populations. I spent hours on the High Line, and the only native birds I saw were the mockingbirds jousting amid some wind-sheltered willows. I did spot gulls coasting overhead and pigeons nodding from the edge of a rooftop, but they weren't using the High Line as habitat.

I climb up on a massive rock outcrop by a busy playground. From here, through the canopy of sycamores and oaks and tulip poplars, I can hear the tinny, wind-up toy cacophony of what must be a huge flock of icterids. Grackles, iridescent and jaunty, combing the lawn between some smaller rock formations. Somebody decides to cut through the grass, and the flock ripples into flight, rising like the folds of a black shroud and revealing another, less flighty species still marching through the grass. It's starlings, waddling in small, quiet clusters, pecking the soil between grass blades, some of them already in their spangled winter plumage. As I cross the lawn, they bounce a bit of distance away and keep feeding.

Central Park probably looked pretty much the same in 1890, when Eugene Schieffelin arrived with his starling flock. As I imagine it, he stands in a secluded corner, surrounded by trees. The muted chatter of the birds becomes more urgent and quizzical as he lifts the fabric covers from their cages, one by one. They can see the sky framed by the canopy, and they can sense that something is going to happen. Maybe Schieffelin quotes a bit of Shakespeare, a kind benediction from one of the plays that favors birdsong (it wouldn't be the lines from *Henry IV*, since that quotation refers to a starling trained to irritate people with its chatter). With a flourish he opens the first door, and the continent's first starlings emerge into freedom.[30]

Standing in the middle of the flock, surrounded by the legacy of that fateful moment, I'm alarmed by how disconcertingly similar his ambitions were to mine. What he wanted, broadly speaking, was to create a richer experience of biodiversity in the city, and although he tried and failed to reconstitute the entire Shakespearean aviary in New York, he did manage to bring most of the human population into everyday contact with wildlife. I like seeing an abundance of birds doing their work amid millions of people. Abundance, plenitude, profusion—that's a rare experience these days, at least when it comes to vertebrate species.

But the birds didn't stay here in Central Park, unfortunately. Can any species that thrives within the city ultimately be contained within its borders? That probably depends on the particulars of the city and the species. For starlings, the moat of Long Island Sound was no obstacle; neither were the other boroughs' matrix of buildings and streets. They spread their Shakespearean irritation across the country, descending by the thousands on feedlots and downtown buildings, crossing the threshold between abundance and pestilence. Nothing we do makes a dent in their numbers.

Just across the path from the grackle and starling horde lies Hallett's Preserve, four acres of forest that's fenced to keep humans out. Nobody has raked over here, and leaf litter carpets the soil, suppressing the grass. The starlings appear to avoid this corner—they evolved to peck and scratch in sheep-dotted fields. Squirrels cadge acorns gathered from the canopy of a massive oak, the first wild mammals I've seen all day. Overhead, blue jays sip from a key hole in the trunk of a tree. White-crowned sparrows scuff through the leaves under the shrubs. I can barely hear the intimate notes of these nearby birds over the seething noise of the grackles.

Near a pool of sluggish brown water, I see something olive flit between the undergrowth, then burst into a loud rollicking trill—a common yellowthroat, black mask and yellow throat bulging with song. *Witchitee, witchitee, witchiteee....*

As I'm leaving, it occurs to me that I haven't seen a single bee. There's nothing for them to pollinate in this corner of the park: no asters, no goldenrod beneath these mature trees. The flower beds are ready for winter. This austerity is in keeping with the underlying ecology—at this latitude, the flora should be wrapping things up, and the bee colonies should be winding down into slumber. Any bee I see still roaming around is pushing its luck, pushing against the boundaries of the climate. It should know better.

Across town, however, about a mile or so as the bee flies, there's still pollen and nectar to be had. The High Line proposes a vision of urban habitat that depends more on microclimate than latitude. That's the fundamental question of urban wildlife gardening: Are you trying to simulate nature as it would have been before humans arrived, or are you making the most of the facts on the ground, the novelty of the built environment?

When you leave Central Park, you confront the geometry of stone and glass that at first feels like the walls of a container. Then the surface begins to develop texture, lines of balconies, windowsills, turrets, rooftops. Multifaceted. Permeable. All this will never be Central Park, but it could be some version of the High Line. It's all potential habitat.

9

Zoopolis

FACT: Wildlife trafficking is the third largest illegal trade in the world after drugs and weapons. In Brazil, an estimated forty million animals are taken from the wild every year. Only one in ten of these animals survives long enough to be sold.

I've been struggling with the meaning of biodiversity as I putter around our autumnal garden, planting perennials I bought at an end-of-season sale, bee balm, asters, and purple coneflowers, all native to this continent perhaps but not this city. Providing food, water, cover, and places to raise young, it seems to me, is a way to directly address the diversity of habitat, with the hope that species richness will increase in response. Given the host of creatures that have shown up by now, I'd say this hope has been realized.

What's still troubling me about my yard, however, is the portrait of urbanization I described at the start, the one in which Michael McKinney describes urbanization as a leading cause of biotic homogenization. "The problem for biodiversity conservation," he argues, is that despite "high species richness in urbanizing areas, including the importation of non-native species, global biodiversity continues to decline. This pattern of local enrichment but global decline is a crucial one for conservation biology because it may divert public attention away from the more global problem of global species decline."[1]

My yard may be rich in species, in other words, but that diversity ultimately comes at the expense of the total diversity of the planet. My backyard efforts are the equivalent of fiddling while Rome burns. Other studies have questioned this view, notably one based on research in the city of Baltimore, which found a surprising degree of habitat diversity in the city, with abundant native and nonnative species arranged in distinct rather than homogenized populations. "Ninety-five percent of the exotic plant species in riparian areas within Baltimore were neither broadly nor invasively distributed," the study found, "but instead were only locally abundant." The same held true for starlings, pigeons, and house sparrows.[2]

Nevertheless, I haven't been able to dismiss McKinney's point, because he's right to some extent about my yard. The language on my sign doesn't directly address the global biodiversity crisis, and what I'm doing with my hybrid perennials is increasing local diversity with species you might find anywhere. Across town, the zoo is addressing global species decline directly by breeding rare species and maintaining metapopulations, but their efforts and mine don't intersect.

Maybe because it's football season, I've started appreciating the power of wild animals as secular symbols. Since we don't have several thousand years of religious tradition to serve as the foundation for coexistence here in Columbia, what about that bestiary cavorting on the sidelines? Why doesn't Columbia, South Carolina, have an official animal? In fact, why can't I name the official animal of any American city? Picking an official city animal seems like an obvious extension of the sign: if you're a stakeholder in terms of habitat, doesn't it make sense to have a stake in the species that roam there, too?

Our city has no mascot, no creature that says something about who we Midlands urbanites are and how we live. Teams adopt animals—my own university embraces the Gamecock, a screeching, razor-clawed rooster (until last year, keeping chickens in the city was illegal, primarily because officials feared it might encourage cockfighting). States have their official animal rosters, too. Even the gray squirrel, to my surprise, is a symbol: of North Carolina and Kentucky, not Charlotte and Louisville. Our state animal is the white-tailed deer, a designation that may bring a smile to hunters' faces but undoubtedly makes many suburban gardeners grit their teeth. Which is a good indication that the state animal, bathed in the glow of rural goodwill, isn't a good default option for the city.

You have to be careful, of course, because the symbolic gesture has literal repercussions. And once you've established the symbol in the hearts and minds of the populace, it's hard to take it back. Laws and regulations struggle to counteract the power of metaphor: devotees of Lord Hanuman, for example, aren't about to stop feeding monkeys just because the government frowns on the practice. More tragically, consider the plight of the tiger and the rhino, victims of their own symbolic potency. How do you convince people that the symbol is not meant to be taken literally, that a pinch of tiger penis or rhino horn will do nothing for human virility? How do you ensure that the reverence people obviously feel results in protecting live animals in the wild rather than in consuming tidbits of the dead? You need a metaphoric sense of ownership balanced by the recognition that these are wild animals, not household pets.

An organization called Rare specializes in this kind of work. Their Pride Campaigns use commercial marketing tactics to create a sense of protective ownership for unique local species. Every campaign has a mascot, a friendly face to rally around, even if it's a "crawfish." Kids want their pictures taken with the creature; mayors want their pictures taken, too. Gradually, the cultural norms shift toward awareness and protection. The approach has proven very successful: the first Pride Campaign, developed by Rare's current global ambassador, Paul Butler, and officials at the Saint Lucia Forestry Department, when Butler was a recent college grad in 1977, saved the Saint Lucia parrot from extinction by transforming the bird into a folk hero. As with many of the creatures in Rare's growing menagerie, the parrot mascot has become an enduring symbol of island identity, and it still appears in costume at festivals.

We don't have to live with the symbolic animal to love it. Think of nearby Clemson, South Carolina, home of the Tigers football team, whose symbol is the track of the big cat. What are the conservation possibilities of that kind of symbolic identification with an endangered animal whose habitat is thousands of miles away? Does it matter if the big cats don't live here? Several zoos already have promotional agreements with their state motor vehicles department, allowing drivers to purchase a special license plate with a picture of a charismatic wild animal. The Pennsylvania Zoological Council, for example, has collaborated with the state of Pennsylvania to offer a "Save Wild Animals" license plate with a picture of an Amur tiger, one of the rarest big cats in the wild. Some of the proceeds go to the state's zoos for conservation and education work. As these license plate efforts suggest, in the age of the metapopulation, you may need this kind of flexible identification to combat global species decline.

I started looking for cities that had adopted a particular animal as their own. And I found an intriguing possibility in the Brazilian city of Belo Horizonte, where the black-tufted marmoset, *Callithrix penicillata*, has been named the city's official animal after a citywide popularity contest in which the marmoset's chief rival was a South American species of opossum. It wasn't much of a competition: this opossum bears a broad charcoal stripe running from ears to tail, leading many to confuse it with a skunk, since the Portuguese word for both animals is *gambá*. Black-tufted marmosets, on the other hand, are kitten-sized and charismatic: with their floppy, striped tail, these primates look like Dr. Seuss sketched them in pencil and forgot to color them in.

These urban adapters have learned to thrive in the city. They're actually quite common in remote forests, too, but they've managed to adapt to the company of millions of human residents, scrambling along power lines and roosting in city parks. They're free-ranging, in other words, even coming down to cadge tidbits of food from their caged cousins at the city zoo. Like practically every other urban creature, however, they get into a fair bit of trouble, too.

The habits of urban black-tufted marmosets would probably be unknown outside of Brazil were it not for the work of Robert Young and the team of graduate students he has assembled at the Pontifical Catholic University of Minas Gerais. The whole notion that animals in the city might offer valuable research opportunities seems somewhat counterintuitive in a country like Brazil. Belo Horizonte sits in the middle of two of the biologically richest regions on the planet—the Atlantic Forest and the Brazilian Cerrado. There are literally hundreds of species—not just invertebrates but charismatic mega-fauna—about which next to nothing is known. In many cases, they can be found right outside the city limits. Ocelots prowl the hills above the city: why not study them? When your country has vast regions brimming with opportunities for study, like the Amazon and the Pantanal (the Brazilian equivalent of the Everglades), why bother with animals in the city?

As it turns out, once you look more closely at these animals and their behaviors, all sorts of fascinating questions arise. You can learn about how wild animals cope with the stress of the urban environment. You can discover how city dwellers respond to the animal they've chosen as their mascot. And you can take these lessons about how wild animals and humans interact and make use of them, particularly in creating better habitats for captive animals in zoos and research facilities.[3] Seeing this officially urban animal make its way through the concrete jungle seemed like the perfect chance to take the measure of the free-range fantasy I'd harbored at the start of this experiment.

When I arrive in Belo Horizonte at the start of Brazil's rainy season, the city's two soccer teams are getting set to play each other, an event the residents apparently take very seriously. Think official symbols are frivolous? Try telling that to Brazilian *futebol* fans.

"If you go out after seven, don't wear blue or black," Robert Young warns me on our way to a *feijoada*, a restaurant that serves a buffet of rustic Brazilian fare. "You don't want to get shot on your first night here." Someone could be gunned down tonight for wearing the wrong colors, he tells me.

Although he originally hails from Scotland, to me he looks indistinguishable from the compact, vaguely European, futebol-jerseyed multitudes ambling down the street. He's wearing a rugby jersey whose silvery white and blue must represent some neutral party, and his silver hair is trimmed short, setting off his faintly tanned complexion. Sunglasses cover his greenish eyes. After a decade here, he knows how to blend into the urban habitat. It occurs to me that normally the way a biologist dresses for the field would be irrelevant—a field station isn't a catwalk, and the animals don't judge anybody's fashion sense. But here, paying attention to what you wear is a grim necessity, a street-smart form of crypsis.

Unlike my host, I'm wrapped in an orange Gore-Tex rain parka and clomping along in my hiking boots, looking every bit the lanky, lumbering prey item who can't even keep his eyes on the street because the treetops are full of birds he's never seen before. I tell Rob I can't wait to get my binoculars out of my baggage so I can ogle some of these avian novelties.

"I wouldn't do that," Rob says, and I can tell he's thinking, *This guy has no clue.*

He advises me to keep cameras, binoculars, watches—all of the usual tourist paraphernalia—out of sight. And stay inside after dark, too. The murder rate in Brazil is four times that in the United States, and then there's the quicknappings and the muggings and the burglaries. Haven't people warned me about this?

Well, kind of, yes. The State Department website was brusque and clear: watch out.[4] But the tourist guides I perused rationalized these threats. Given the length of time you're in the country, they argued, and the places you're likely to visit, your personal risk is relatively small.

It's not that I've never experienced the menacing side of urban life. American cities used to be like this—drug violence spilling out of the poorest neighborhoods into the mainstream, gunfire claiming victims with alarming regularity. But cities exist in time, and times change. Witness the changes in New York. The period when Central Park was off-limits after dark, when you had to be on guard when you walked certain streets, has apparently given way to a less menacing urban zeitgeist. A *New York Times* article published this year calls attention to a new phenomenon brought about by the city's falling crime rate: New Yorkers, not clueless visitors like me but actual residents, are using Central Park at night. They're walking and strolling and jogging long after darkness falls, something they would never have done in an earlier era.[5]

I've given a lot of thought to what this Brazilian city has to offer wildlife, but I haven't considered the way human history and politics might shape where people live and how they behave toward each other. Nor have I considered the influence of fear, risk, and socioeconomic status on urban ecology, how concerns about personal safety might ultimately wind up affecting the habitat and behavior of wild animals. If parks are no-go areas for *Homo sapiens* after dark, then dusk may be the cue for wildlife to emerge. Some studies of the sprawling city of Phoenix showed that plant and bird diversity varied with socioeconomic status, with wealthy areas showing higher diversity. In fact, researchers recorded several species of bird in parks in wealthy areas that were absent from parks in less affluent areas.[6]

I did arrive in Brazil with certain impressions: when I was a teenager, I saw the film *Pixote,* about the life of Brazilian street kids, and more recently I'd watched *City of God,* about the terrible violence in Brazil's poorest neighborhoods, the *favelas.*[7] But all this seemed like an exoskeleton the country had recently shucked off in favor of something bright and new: Wasn't Brazil, like India, on this amazing upward trajectory, with millions of urban poor people rising into the prosperous middle class? Times change, and what happened in Central Park could happen in Brazilian cities, too.

Before my flight, I'd happened upon a small item on the international news page of an American paper: SWAT teams in Rio de Janeiro had entered Rocinha, a sprawling favela that was essentially ruled by drug cartels. The area was once off-limits to police and nonresidents alike, but with both the World Cup and the Olympics coming in the next few years, the country has embarked on a "pacification" campaign, staging military-style invasions of these areas to clear out the gangs and establish permanent police stations. These efforts have been controversial, and the gangs have been fighting back: in 2009 they shot down a military helicopter.[8]

There are favelas in Belo Horizonte, too. You can see their lights twinkling along the jagged brow of the surrounding hills, their rooftops spilling down the creases, a testament not only to the tenacity of the residents but also to their desperation. When waves of immigrants arrived from the rural hinterlands and Brazil's major cities began to swell, these unplanned, unauthorized villages took shape in places that were deemed too steep, too prone to mudslides, too far from electric lines and sewers to be fit for human habitation.

The result is disconcerting for an American accustomed to the geography of suburbanization. Here the gated community sits right across from the favela, and they both sit right on the border of the city nature park. Great views from up there. Lots of wildlife. But you'd better watch yourself.

Compared to the customary drone of my neighborhood, Belo Horizonte is a vortex of noise. I'm riding in the back of a car while one of Rob's former graduate students, Marina Duarte, pilots us toward the municipal park, a forty-acre patch of greenery in the midst of squealing buses, honking horns, hissing air brakes, and thundering planes. The tension in the air is palpable—everybody around us is trying to get to work, and they're squeezing into lanes and zipping through yellow lights and cutting each other off.

For us, this atmosphere isn't pleasant, and I dare say that on some deep somatic level it isn't healthy for us, either. We're trying to keep up a conversation in English, Marina, her former research assistant Luis, and I, but the discombobulating randomness of the soundscape keeps us from really communicating. Which was precisely the point of Marina's research here: to study the impact of the city's acoustic landscape on the behavior of the marmosets that live right in the thick of it.[9] The city poses a number of challenges to creatures that evolved under different circumstances, some of them obvious, some of them less apparent to us but nevertheless critical to some species' survival. Light pollution, for example, isn't a life-or-death matter for a diurnal species like us, and one could argue that well-lit public spaces help us survive a city's more menacing districts. If you're a nocturnal creature, however, getting waylaid by a porch light on your way to mate is potentially fatal, for you and your kind.

Noise pollution isn't a deal breaker for us either: although studies have suggested that high levels of ambient noise can impact our physical well-being in a variety of ways, we have our soundproofed windows and our noise-canceling headphones to help us cope. If we can't hear each other on our cellphones, we can always turn up the volume or roll up the window of the cab.

Black-tufted marmosets, on the other hand, live in family groups, and the way they keep tabs on one another and warn each other of impending doom is through a repertoire of high-pitched chirps and rolling trills. In the forest, where they evolved, they'd be competing with birdsong and the sigh of the wind through the leaves, but here they have to deal with a never-ending thunderstorm of anthropogenic noise. Sometimes it's automobile traffic. Sometimes it's the hubbub of human voices and music. Every Sunday the major thoroughfare that runs past the park is shut to cars for the Hippy Fair, a kind of artsy flea market where big crowds gather. The crowds enjoy the park as well, and thus the noise shifts from the roadways on the perimeter to the playground and the benches in the park's interior.

Marina's fellow researchers looked at spectrograms of a bus squealing to a halt to pick up passengers: the frequency patterns matched up almost perfectly with the "phee" calls marmosets produce to keep in touch long distance. Which means that urban marmosets have to deal with two challenges to their survival: they have to cope with high ambient noise levels that make it hard to hear one another, and they have to recognize that a lot of what sounds like marmoset chatter is actually just traffic noise.[10]

If they couldn't adapt to these environmental stresses, you wouldn't find a family group living in a single tree in one of the city's school playgrounds or entertaining the passengers at a downtown bus station. According to Rob, there's even some evidence that the park's marmosets have adjusted the range of their vocalizations so that they don't overlap with the buses. But Marina's study also suggests that the group moves in response to noise; they avoid the edges of the park during high traffic volumes and seek out secluded corners during the fair. In fact, the marmosets will give up the chance to cadge tidbits from tourists, and put themselves at greater risk of predation, just to find a place where they can hear one another.

On the morning we visit, the contrast between the bustle outside the gates and the calm, damp shade of the greenery is heightened by our arrival on a maintenance day, when the park is closed to visitors. Broom-wielding teams are cleaning up the aftermath of the Hippy Fair, but otherwise the paths and playgrounds are empty.

We follow the park's naturalist, Andrea Oliveira, along the park's winding paths, past massive fig trees whose roots dangle down into the earth like matted hair, through bamboo thickets and rows of towering palms. My companions all know the layout of the park in intimate detail. Andrea has worked here for years, and Marina once worked here, too. Luis and Marina have spent hours mapping the GPS coordinates of each tree and measuring noise levels with parabolic microphones. They all know the difference between the high-pitched titter and "phee" of a marmoset and the sounds of various species of birds trying to make themselves heard, like the feline squall of the *alma de gato*, or cat's soul, a cuckoolike bird we spot creeping through the dead leaves of a palm.

Near the playground, Marina reaches up to show me some pits gouged into the bark of an overhanging bough. Most of them have healed over, but one is dark and moist with oozing gum. One of the reasons marmosets can adapt to a variety of habitats comes down to this: yes, they can eat apples, cotton candy, and peanuts, and they can pounce on the occasional bird. But they also have the ability to gather nourishment from the sap and gum of common trees, a dietary flexibility that means they won't go hungry in the city.

They do, however, have plenty to fear in this park. Andrea points to a scattering of kibble on the concrete, evidence of human support for another of the park's charismatic, free-ranging denizens: cats. Brazilians, my companions agree, are mostly dog people. But this park, for whatever reason, has gained the reputation as a friendly destination for unwanted felines over the past twenty years. Some erstwhile owners actually come back and feed their former pets, but even if they don't, there are plenty of other dedicated cat fanciers to scatter dried food around the benches.

Once you look, you see them everywhere, drowsing in the sunshine, tongue-bathing themselves, blinking in post-breakfast satisfaction. Estimates of their number range as high as two hundred, with more arriving daily. Many have big, round holes in one ear, a sign that they've been trapped and spayed and then released by a local animal welfare group. But this population control effort can't keep up with the flood of new arrivals. There are plenty of kittens in the mix.

They don't look particularly ferocious or even aware of what's going on around them. Various thrush species are bouncing along the sidewalks and rummaging in the fallen leaves, and the cats pay them no heed. Nevertheless, these predators control what happens in the park from the ground all the way up into the canopy. There used to be squirrels here, Andrea says, but she hasn't seen one in years. They spent too much time foraging on the ground.

The marmosets have managed to adapt to life in a cattery. Small primates are at their most vulnerable when they're on the ground without a tree nearby and when they're asleep. The former they avoid; treeless expanses like parking lots and playing fields are essentially no-go zones. The latter is more problematic—unless they choose their sleep site carefully, they may never wake up. Marina and her team have discovered that the municipal park family deals with this predicament by selecting a handful of sleep trees from the nearly four thousand specimens in the park. They aren't the trees that look like good candidates to me. The enormous figs, for example, look like fortresses to me, full of shadowy places to hide. No good from a marmoset's point of view: any tree with low branches, or pendulous roots, gives the cats an easy way up into the canopy. If you want to keep them out, you need a tall main stem without any low branches, so that it can be accessed only by moving through the canopy. The bark can be smooth, or even better, it can be covered with thorns, as if ringed with concertina wire. In all, of the 275 tree species in the park, only thorny native palms, two eucalyptus, and a single fig fit the bill. The team never observed a cat on the prowl in any of them.[11]

When we finally spot the family, they're on the ground, in the danger zone.

"There they are," Marina says in a stage whisper, hustling toward a plaza framed by a bare metal trellis.

I see something on the ground, something small, dark, and long tailed, and my first thought is squirrel. That's a squirrel. Then cat. That's a cat, a fluffy little cat. I have no image stored in my mind's eye, no reference point for creatures like these in an urban setting.

But what about that hunched posture? And the length of that tail? And most of all the way they tilt their head, fixing us with an unblinking, hyperalert, protohuman face? Squirrels have dark eyes fixed to either side of their muzzle, giving them a broad field of view, but the eyes of a marmoset are amber, with the pupils centered over their snubbed nose, like ours. When they look at you, they look *at* you. Then they look elsewhere, up, down, and sideways, the constant downside of having your eyes close together in a predatory world.

There are three of them, wrestling with an underripe mango.

Juveniles, Marina says.

We probably seem a bit too keen, our fascination almost predatory in its intensity. When we get close, they leave the half-gnawed fruit and retreat, first inching up the poles of the trellis, then bounding reluctantly into a dense clump of bamboo surrounded by benches. They're used to being approached by eager hands and faces. Another study conducted in the park, which took visitor behavior as its subject matter, observed people photographing or "trying to make physical contact with" the marmosets four times an hour on the average afternoon.[12] I don't think these people had seen anything like the photo Marina sent me, of a bloody-mawed marmoset dragging a parakeet carcass up a tree trunk.

The adults are calling from the branches of a nearby tree, high-pitched chirps and trills that I might easily mistake for the twittering of unfamiliar birds. But the juveniles seem to be biding their time. They're risk takers, these youngsters. That's how primate society is often organized, with a breeding pair of adults at the center and those on the verge of adulthood testing the limits of the social fabric, lingering at the edge of the group, hoping to make contact with a potential mate or find an open niche in another group.

In a park full of predators, risky behavior can get you killed. Marina's team saw cats kill three juveniles in the park over a four-month period, and two more cat-related deaths were reported in the months before the start of the study.

Eventually, the juveniles get bored or realize we aren't going to cough up any treats. They clamber into the canopy and disappear. And once they disappear, the distinctive mottling of their fur makes perfect sense. Pressed against the bark of the branches, half-obscured already by the dappled shade of the leaves, they're gone.

About as close as I've come to wildlife trafficking so far is scooping up a comatose lizard and transporting it to my house. Or is that wildlife rescue? You take something into captivity, even with the best of intentions, and then the creature wakes up, and whoa, you have a wild animal on your hands. Now what? As for "Dr. Lizardi," as we've named our only pet, a glass aquarium with a heat lamp and a ready supply of crickets seems to suit him (or her).

In Brazil, however, the same scenario is a huge problem. Imagine you're traveling outside the city, and you see what seems to be a sweet and docile little primate for sale on the side of the road, a marmoset in a tiny wooden cage. It's illegal to own an animal like this, but in rural areas the roadside stands offer a wide selection of the country's rich biodiversity for sale.

All the way home the creature keeps to itself, allowing you to pick it up and stroke its head, more ragdoll than wild animal. But fast forward a day or two: whatever drug the traffickers gave their captive has worn off, and now it's bouncing off the walls, biting the hand that feeds it, destroying the furniture.

You can't keep this creature. And you can't take it back where it came from, because you don't know where that is. If you encourage people to identify with animals, a scenario like this will keep you awake at night.

In cities such as Belo Horizonte and Rio, green space beckons on the fringe of the downtown. Why not just take a quiet stroll in the park one evening and let the creature go back into nature? Doesn't that seem like the kindest gesture, under the circumstances, rather than killing it and burying it in your yard, as I was told to do with the possum I caught? In addition to cats, the municipal park gets its share of wildlife releases, including marmosets. Last year, Marina told me, the family group here included what appeared to be a hybrid of Geoffrey's marmoset, another common pet trade species with a puffy white face. Nobody knows how this particular animal turned up in the park, but hybrids between the two marmoset species are not an uncommon sight.

Although possessing a wild animal is illegal, you can turn your erstwhile pet over to the Environmental Police or to the Brazilian Institute for the Environment and Renewable Natural Resources (IBAMA) without penalty. As a result, these agencies are inundated with animals, both those they seize and those they receive voluntarily, some common, some critically endangered.

Because they struggle to keep up with the constant flood of creatures, IBAMA has been forced to find private animal shelters to take on the overflow. One such center is located on the outskirts of the city, which I visit with Camila Texiera, a doctoral student in urban ecology at the federal university who completed her master's work with Robert Young.

To understand the ecology of the city, Camila studies "callouts," the incident reports of the officers whose job is to respond to wildlife-related problems. When you analyze years of these reports, what emerges is a portrait of the challenges posed by urban life. The reports gathered for a previous study tallied over three hundred incidents with marmosets, or more than one per week. Two-thirds were of marmosets causing trouble; the rest were a catalog of common injuries: marmosets wounded by cats and dogs, electrocuted by power lines, or simply falling out of trees onto the unforgiving concrete.[13]

Many of the complaints, according to interviews conducted with the officers involved, came from people who had been feeding the marmosets, only to become unnerved by their increasingly demanding guests. If you feed a family of marmosets from your breakfast table, they may come to expect a daily handout. And if they don't get it one morning, don't be surprised if they come looking for it . . . inside your kitchen. The creature that starts out an official mascot can still become a pest.[14]

As we walk inside the walled compound that houses the Criadouro Científico, our first view is of a pen housing nearly a dozen red-legged seriemas, stilt-legged birds of the plains about the size of a heron that are sprinting stiff-legged up the walls of their pen with ear-splitting whinnies. Although they can fly, these terrestrial birds wind up here because they often suffer broken legs after colliding with cars.

One seriema hobbles around on an artificial leg that Marco, the rehabilitation center's founder, designed. He's a veterinary surgeon with a practice in the city, a soft-spoken man with gentle eyes and a hint of silver in his trimmed beard. This used to be his weekend retreat, he says, but the animals kind of took over. No more swimming pool; now this is the house of the animals. Although IBAMA has certified the place as a wildlife rehabilitation center, Marco foots the bill for the keepers and the food.

He shows us the sunny toucan pens, then the macaw cages, where he advises me not to stand too close: the highly intelligent birds have a way of showing their distaste for strangers that involves projectile streaming of unpleasant white substances. The birds waddle down their perch for a look at me, stretching their long, gaudy wings. Highly sought after for the pet trade, the three macaw species have all done well here, pairing off and producing additional cohorts of bobble-headed chicks in the nest boxes at the back of their cages.

We take in glossy black curassows, toucanets, parakeets, and blackbirds, each with their own peculiar trafficking story. In some species, only the males sing profusely or are spectacularly colored, and thus the trafficked population is almost entirely male, with no chance for breeding. The green-winged saltator, for example, is an otherwise nondescript bird whose song is so highly prized that it is often used in competitions with cash prizes. Saltators and other spectacular singers captured in the wild can fetch two hundred dollars; a proven winner can be worth fifty thousand. Marco holds up the cage of his own favorite, a seven-colored tanager, glowing like a gemstone in the drab setting of its cage. Some birds have had their wings clipped to stubs to keep them from flapping around. One parakeet is blind, probably from cigarette burns used to make it more docile. Marco says the traffickers will sometimes break the breastbone of an animal so the pain will keep it quiet.

These animals are essentially victims of a love for wildlife gone bad. If the blind parakeet had benefited from one of Rare's rebranding programs, there's a good chance it wouldn't be here. A mascot, when properly developed, is a communal resource. The public protects the welfare of individual animals without claiming them as their individual property. Marco's charges, in contrast, have suffered from the notion that the qualities we appreciate in wild animals can be extracted from their proper context in the wild and sold as commodities.

"This is an endangered one," Marco says repeatedly, holding up cages with small green parrots or a single flitting songbird. "This one is also. And this one." There's a songbird from Patagonia with an olive-yellow crest, a "yellow cardinal," nearly extinct in the wild from trapping for the pet trade, and only a handful known to be in captivity. Marco would like to try breeding them, but there isn't enough known about their mating behavior in the wild. Two hyacinth macaws, their plumage so intensely cobalt they look as if they've been rendered in pixels rather than natural pigments, perch on his arm. Both happen to be female. Endangered, but unable to breed. Charisma is a volatile commodity.

At the far end, in the last quadrangle that workmen are in the process of converting to even more cages and pens, stands a small horse that was terribly burned in a fire, its pale cream fur still patchy around pink scar tissue. I wonder where casualties like these will go when the last cages here are full.

When Camila and I arrive at IBAMA's offices, just off a busy downtown street, they're working on a marmoset that arrived yesterday afternoon. This is what the injured subjects of Camila's "callout" study look like in the flesh, a tiny creature cupped in a technician's palm, its eyelids clamped shut and mouth ajar. It was picked up on the street somewhere in the city, and it's been having seizures ever since, tremors running through its reedy torso.

Daniel Vilela, who directs the triage center, thinks it may have been electrocuted by a transformer while scrambling along a power line. Or it may have fallen out of a tree and smacked its head. Or it may be infected with the herpes virus that gives people cold sores but usually kills marmosets. At the city zoo, the wild population was nearly wiped out at one point by people taking bites of their apple or banana and then handing the marmosets a dose of fruit laced with the herpes virus. The infected marmosets developed a disfiguring rash of cold sores all over their faces—the zoo put up images of the victims to discourage feeding—before dying of the disease.

Whatever the cause, things don't look good. The tech is trying to get the sedated marmoset to swallow whitish liquid from a syringe, but it dribbles out the corner of its mouth onto a spread of newspapers. There's a freezer nearby—inside are the bagged specimens of those that didn't make it.

The triage center is an open-air gallery of cage-filled rooms surrounding an interior courtyard. One room is devoted to mammals. Here the injured marmosets recuperate, developing into new social groups before being released on the outskirts of the city. A group of three, all captured individually, greet us with a shrill shimmer of noise, pressing their white-splotched foreheads to the wire to look into our faces and gauge our intentions. Are we here with food or some sort of medical procedure?

They seem healthy enough. Although the mortality rate for injured animals is quite high, according to Vilela the overall mortality rate for animals brought to this center is only 15 percent. That seems low compared to wildlife centers I've visited in the United States but is probably due to the sheer number of healthy confiscated birds coming through every day. Many of the small mammals brought to wildlife centers in the United States suffer from distemper, a fatal and incurable disease that isn't commonly seen here.

The rest of the place is overrun with confiscated animals—in the center of the courtyard, which is not much bigger than a parking space, dozens of red-and-yellow-headed *jabuti* tortoises clamber over one another, piling up like battered cars. A crowd of aquatic turtles bob in a murky green pool. Parrots and songbirds fill the surrounding galleries of cages with a cacophony of shrieks and cackles and chirps. The smell is as powerful as the noise, a mix of bleach and the sharp ammonia of bird waste, sweetened by the scent of ripe papaya and mango from the pile of peels in the prep kitchen.

This facility is supposed to be temporary housing, but the vast number of animals arriving every day makes placing them in shelters like the one run by Marco nearly impossible. Outside in the parking lot, there's a heap of wicker and wood cages, all trampled into pieces so that they can't be used again. It looks like a collection that would take years to build, a pet store's worth of caging. In actuality, it's just a few days' worth.

Fifty animals arrive here every day. On Mondays, Vilela says, they get three hundred, and the three keepers and volunteers "go crazy" trying to find space for them. Twelve thousand arrive every year. The vast majority are songbirds, and the native adults wind up staying in the triage center only briefly before being released outside the city. Babies are given to volunteers willing to undertake the round-the-clock feeding routine. Some animals that can't be released, such as macaws, go to zoos or to centers like the one Marco runs. There's no problem finding takers for charismatic and rare species like hyacinth macaws, but it's hard to find space and funding for something that's common and not very cute, like an overgrown pet turtle.

The torrent of confiscated animals doesn't stop, even when the center is ostensibly closed. The intake area is supposed to be shut for renovation. Part of the concrete floor is torn up, and workmen are moving through with paintbrushes and various tools. But while we're watching the injured marmoset treatment, an environmental police officer arrives—he's got cages of confiscated birds, and he insists that he needs to drop them off. Vilela sends him away. Yet when we return from the tour, a worn wooden box has appeared inside the door, its captives chirping from each of the dozen little cells. They're *sabia*, a common, rufous-bellied thrush species I saw in the municipal park. Brazil's national bird.

Every day since my arrival, I've been gazing longingly at the green scrim of hills draped in rainy season mist on the edge of the city: Mangabeiras Municipal Park, one of the largest urban parks in Latin America. The diversity of species here is particularly rich; along the steep, eroded lines of these mountains, the coastal rain forest known as the Mata Atlantica merges with the scrubby savannah of the *cerrado*, fusing two of the world's biodiversity hotspots. This is the city's version of Central Park or Golden Gate Park, a place that plays host to concerts and various festivals, yes, but also serves as a quiet corner where humans, like marmosets, can take refuge from the noisy soundscape down below. I'm hoping I can finally break out my binoculars and the hefty bird guide that seemed to take up a third of my carry-on luggage.

Of course, the park is still right on the edge of town, which means that it borders both the middle-class neighborhood of Mangabeiras, where Camila grew up, and the vast favela that clings to the slopes at the park's edge.

The well-to-do live up here, too, their modernist glass castles edging the vertiginous and scenic drop at the top of the winding park road. As we passed a row of trophy homes, Rob motioned for Camila to pull over—he'd spotted a burrowing owl perched on a boulder across the street, its nest a few steps away from a fire hydrant.

The park feels deceptively safe. We pay a guard at the entrance and park in an enormous, nearly empty lot with a fountain and a snack bar and bathrooms. There are information signs and maps, everything you'd expect from a modern experience of nature: the scenic beauty, the comforts, the protection of resources and visitors alike.

Rob, however, has offered a more macabre version of the park. One of his undergraduates was conducting a research project here, he told me, when she stumbled across something unpleasant—a freshly buried corpse. She wasn't alone at the time; for safety reasons, the park had provided her with a guard. But they were unarmed. Terrified that whoever had disposed of the body would come back at any moment, the research team beat a hasty retreat.

Another time, one of his colleagues who studies owls was out at night with a research team on the edge of the park, driving around in a jeep that was painted in camouflage. Suddenly, they heard gunfire. In the same moment, they noticed that the bullets were pinging the leaves and dirt all around them, like something out of a movie. A gang had mistaken them for the police and had opened fire with AK-47s.

Another colleague was studying frogs, which tend to reveal themselves by singing at night. If you want to collect data on them, in other words, your best chance is under the cover of darkness. This colleague and another researcher crossed paths one night with an armed assailant who tied them up and left them while he went to fetch the rest of his gang. The two managed to free themselves and escape, fortunately, but it's enough to send a chill down my spine.

Back home, when I was reading the article about marmoset sleeping sites, I'd been struck by an odd phrase: "For personal safety reasons, it is possible to study [the marmosets] only between 0800 and 1800 h."[15] A study of sleeping habits that ends at six in the evening? I'd thought. Although marmosets are diurnal creatures and retire soon after sunset, I wondered why you wouldn't keep watching when it actually got dark and some of their potential predators started to prowl. Now I understand.

As soon as we step out of the car, we spot an animal about the size of a terrier trotting along the steps of an outdoor amphitheater, pausing occasionally to snuffle a candy wrapper. It looks a bit like a raccoon that's been stretched like a piece of taffy between snout and tail, long and thin and low to the ground, with a slender trowel of a nose and a faint black mask.

A coati, a relative of the raccoon, paying us no heed.

"They love trash," Rob says.

We scramble along behind it, passing a sign with a

beaming coati cartoon figure instructing visitors that these are wild animals that must never be approached or fed human food.

"This female is clearly lactating," Rob observes. We can see the rows of her swollen teats. But where are her offspring? Males are solitary, but females usually join forces to herd their young along. We watch her jump to the top of a lidless steel trash bin—definitely not coati-proof—and after a quick glance at us, slide down inside until only her brushy ringed tail is protruding.

I ask Rob why there aren't more coatis in the city proper. I mean, if you're feeding a yen for garbage, why not head down to where the real action is? Why don't coatis behave like their cousins, the raccoons? I don't think I've ever lived in a place that didn't have raccoons, but their behavior differs from coatis in one key respect: most of what they do, they do under the cloak of darkness. Coatis, in contrast, are diurnal; they forage during the day, which means they're more likely to come into contact with people and their pet dogs. In the city, you can't really trot down the street in broad daylight, snuffling around for chips and earthworms and bulbs. Too many stray dogs running loose, Rob says. Too much traffic.

We venture down a path into the forest, and we don't get far before we find one of the twenty-five groups of marmosets that live in the park. Or, more accurately, they find us. The understory starts to sway and shake, and suddenly half a dozen miniature action figures are coming down to the bricks of a small plaza to beg from us. A begging dog wags its tail and watches your face intently; a begging marmoset sits upright on its haunches with its arms out and its palms upturned imploringly. Their attention is riveted on you, and yet they remain deferential, rarely making eye contact. It feels as if someone has trained them in the interspecies language of supplication.

We have nothing to give them, but just as the juveniles are beginning to heed the *phee* calls of the retreating adults, who should appear on the path but the begging animal's version of manna from heaven: a family with two pink-clad young girls, one in a stroller. Do animals stereotype us? Probably. Suddenly the whole place comes alive. Here come the marmosets. Here come the coatis, a whole mob of moms and pint-sized youngsters tussling with each other and probing the soil with their snouts. Here come the rusty guans, pheasant-sized birds that hunt and peck along the ground.

The marmosets park themselves right in front of the stroller. They know, and as a parent I know, that bite-sized morsels are tucked away in there somewhere. Animal crackers, maybe? The marmosets inch closer.

"People like marmosets so much because they're small and cuddly," Rob says. "If we had capuchin monkeys here, I don't think there'd be as much tolerance of them."

Or rhesus monkeys, I think. If these were rhesus monkeys encircling us, I'd be terrified.

Just then the child in the stroller shrieks and kicks. Nobody has offered any food, and one of the audacious juveniles has crossed the line—it may even have tugged the girl's pant leg. The mother bends down and comforts the girl while the marmosets take the hint and retreat into the forest.

We continue up the path and emerge from the rain forest into the scrub typical of the cerrado. The path is deserted except for a family of guans shepherding their fluffy chicks along the edge. We watch an adult pluck a seed and squeeze it into the beak of a chick. "Altruism," Camila says, while Rob takes some photos. It's rare to see chicks this young in the wild. Guans turn secretive during the breeding season; they usually disappear for a month, then reappear with more mature offspring at their side.

From here the contours of the favela are clearly visible further along the ridge. It all looks picturesque from a distance, but as Rob's stories attest, in an urban park you can't pretend that the natural history exists in separation from the social history. Camila's current research looks at the relationship between socioeconomic status and callouts, which is a way of describing how the city's official mascot plays across the divisions of class and ethnicity. As we head back to the lot, I wonder if something like the black-tufted marmoset brings the city's people together or if the divisions are too deep for an animal to matter.

The highway that leads from the airport into the center of Rio is, according to Rob, known as the "Gaza Strip." There are two favelas on either side of the road, and rival gangs are known to shoot at each other over the top of the streaming traffic.

Am I glad to be in the know? It certainly complicates the otherwise stunning view. The famous statue of Christ the Redeemer rises in epic grandeur from the steep green mountains of the Tijuca forest, and I can see it, gleaming like an ivory candle set in an exposed dome of granite, as the taxi streaks through the hazy evening light of the supposed danger zone. Across the bay, another mountain range rises above the city of Niteroi, corrugated by time into a jagged series of stone spires and obelisks. A nature lover's dream, and yet the disparity between rich and poor, the turmoil of drugs and guns, weighs on my mind.

Maybe Rob is just paranoid, and I'm just an anxious traveler. Maybe I'm just alert to the signs of heightened security that seem to be everywhere, like the guard in the booth who waves us up the steep, cobbled residential street to my bed and breakfast and the automatic metal gate we pull through to enter the drive.

The historic mansion is tucked beneath an ancient,

bromeliad-studded mango tree. It was built to house the founder of the tramline that takes tourists on a winding tour through the Tijuca forests to the stone footing of the Christ statue. What I liked about it was that it backed onto the forest, with marmosets and monkeys and toucans visiting the grounds daily. The views from the veranda are spectacular, casting across a sweeping valley to the twinkling lights of a favela on the opposing ridge.

I lie awake, listening to the thumping base of some *tropicalia*-inflected hip-hop, shouts of people having a good time, dogs barking in alarm: there's a party going on in the favela next door. What's brought me here? Not the dance parties or the tasty capirinhas or the beaches of Ipanema. I'm here to track down one of the black-tufted marmoset's cousins, an endangered species that has been discovered on the exurban fringe of the city. An endangered species that also happens to be potentially invasive.

By this time, the contours of the story feel familiar. A veterinarian who kept a private zoo as a hobby passed away in Niteroi, leaving behind fifteen small primates with shaggy black fur and coppery manes. Only 6,500 golden-headed lion tamarins, or GHLTs, as biologists like to refer to them, still inhabit tiny fragments of the Atlantic rain forest in the northern Brazilian state of Bahia, which lies hundreds of miles and several impassable river drainages from Niteroi. The heirs, not knowing what to do with their charges and probably aware that there might be legal ramifications for possessing an endangered species, decided to do the animals a favor by releasing them into those jagged hills I saw from the airport road.[16]

In 2002, residents of Niteroi observed them in just two or three groups, but a population explosion was already under way. By 2009, when a census was undertaken, there were fifteen groups with more than a hundred individuals, foraging in neighborhoods and roosting in the city's protected forests.[17]

One of the reasons these tamarins are doing so well here, scientists suspect, is because the local residents are feeding them. The benefits they receive in terms of calories outweigh the risks they take with roads and power lines, at least so far.

For an endangered species population to grow tenfold in less than a decade seems like a conservation success story. You might think anything you could do to boost their number in the wild would be a good thing. The bigger the metapopulation, the more tamarins you have in different locations, and the less chance you have of the species going extinct through some local catastrophe. Why not have tamarins free-ranging around the city's green spaces? Why not have the local residents take a bigger role in caring for them? Wouldn't that mean more habitat, more tamarins, more people with a stake in their survival . . . .

If only things were that simple.

There's another conservation success story to consider

here, one of the greatest in conservation history, in fact: the golden lion tamarin. The golden lion tamarin, or GLT, is the only primate species whose fortunes have improved enough to be downlisted from Critically Endangered on the *IUCN Red List of Threatened Species* to Endangered.[18] Amid a human population explosion, widespread deforestation, and urban sprawl along Brazil's Atlantic coast, human beings have managed to turn things around for this tiny primate. It's a relative triumph to be sure, since the fate of the species remains tenuous. But it's good news in a time when we have too little to cheer about.

Look at a map of golden lion tamarin populations, and what you'll see is a constellation of green dots spread in a rough semicircle northeast of Rio, most around an hour's drive from the city. One of these dots is less than twenty miles from the burgeoning population of nonnatives.[19]

For GHLTs, those twenty miles still constitute a formidable obstacle course. The greenery of Niteroi's protected hills is misleading; beyond them, major highways thunder through cattle pastures and densely populated towns with nary a tree in sight, mile after mile of sprawl. Tamarins don't do well under such circumstances—that's why they're endangered, because development has replaced their native forest with roads and fields and housing developments.

Nevertheless, biologists are worried that some resourceful individuals might thread the needle and arrive in the habitat already occupied by golden lion tamarins. And there's always the chance some sympathetic homeowner will decide to deal with a nuisance tamarin by transporting it to the nearest forest in the back of their car, just as I did with the possum under our house.

Nobody really knows what might happen if the two species were to meet. Nobody anticipated that a creature with a tenuous hold on life would suddenly become an invasive species. The two species have been known to hybridize in captivity, but in the wild it's also possible that they would compete for limited nest cavities and food. The nonnatives might also introduce diseases they picked up along the way.

Conservationists aren't willing to take that chance. Led by the Brazilian primatologist Cecilia Kierulff, a team will soon undertake the delicate task of trapping and relocating an endangered species in the urban wild.

Luring the animals into a cage is a fairly straightforward process, particularly for animals that already associate humans with food. Bananas work well for attracting tamarins, according to Leonardo Oliveira, who studies GHLTs in their native habitat. And although there is always a risk of mortality, he told me, he's never seen one injured.

But to trap in a residential area, you need the support, if not the permission, of the human inhabitants. Otherwise, traps tend to spring shut with nothing inside or disappear entirely. That support is far from certain here, which isn't surprising. The conservation community has spent decades convincing people that wild tamarins are a blessing to have around. Now, however, the message is getting complicated. One species of tamarin belongs; the other is a charismatic interloper that must be removed. And to further confuse matters, the tamarin that belongs here isn't actually here. You're not replacing one tamarin with another, at least not yet.

"Some people call them 'my monkeys,'" Kierulff told me from her home in São Paulo, describing the people she'd encountered while surveying for GHLTs in Rio's exurbs.

"They don't want us to take them."

Her task will be to convince the locals that their "monkeys" will be better off elsewhere. The team plans to trap the tamarins in family groups, quarantine them to ensure that they are free of disease, and eventually transfer them to a ten-thousand-acre preserve within their native range. This forest currently has no resident tamarins, an indication of just how rare this species is in the wild. Kierulff expects the entire process to last three years, because the team will continue to monitor the translocated population after their release. That postrelease monitoring has proven crucial to success with golden lion tamarin reintroduction. In fact, one of the many ironies here is that the painstaking effort to figure out what reintroduced GLTs need to thrive now offers scientists a detailed model for how to translocate their invasive cousins.[20]

Everybody knows where the golden lion tamarins are. The private preserves have become popular ecotourist destinations, and if you show up, the star attractions are usually quite obliging. But the nonnatives aren't on any tourist map, and they aren't easy for an outsider, especially an outsider whose command of Portuguese is basically limited to smiling inanely and muttering things like *Sorry* and *Speak English?* to find. The aerial photos in my possession show pale puzzles of dense urban development extending deep into the interior, the borders of one satellite city blurring into another. But right in the midst of this sprawl, two fingers of green forest seem to reach down the steep slopes of the mountains toward the coast. One is a state park. The other is a regional park. The tamarins are in between there . . . somewhere.

I've enlisted help to find them. The hotel owner's son, Diogo Valença, grew up in one of the beachside communities of Niteroi and has agreed to be my guide. I like Diogo; he's a brawny young guy who plays guitar in a rock band and speaks excellent English, having spent time Miami and Los Angeles. He likes to punctuate his sentences with "man," as in, "Hey, man, why don't you hike the tram tracks up to the Christ statue?"

When I did as he suggested on my first morning in Rio, I found myself at first elated—I was climbing steadily through the forest, watching blue morpho and glasswing butterflies loop along in front, my binos at the ready. Then I reached the first bridge, where the tracks extend over a ravine. On either side of the tracks were planks, dark with rain and slick with moss. A single line of metal pipe, meant to serve as a railing, keeled toward the drop below, which was probably well over a hundred feet. Suppressing a rising sense of vertigo, I took about twenty careful steps across the creaking boards before I noticed three things almost simultaneously—first, that several of the boards ahead had foot-sized gaping holes in them; second, that the "railing" in my hand was the kind of flimsy thing that Wile E. Coyote was always left holding in midair before he whistled down to the base of a cliff; and third, that the metal-on-metal screeches descending from above could mean only one thing—the tram was coming.

I scuttled back to the edge of the bridge and stood on the gravel as the somnolent faces of the tourists swished past, imagining myself halfway across, pressing myself against that rickety railing, peering down into the abyss as the tracks shuddered beneath me. And if the rotting boards had disintegrated beneath my feet or that rusty metal rail had given way?

I found a path through the ravine instead. But who made the path? The answer became clear as I emerged into the parking lot for what appeared to be an abandoned tram station or hotel, a big, white stucco building with a spacious front porch planted right on the edge of the tracks. The windows were boarded over and covered with graffiti, but the plywood had been pulled from one of the doors, and people were coming in and out and getting back into delivery trucks or hopping on bikes and disappearing down a dirt track toward what was apparently one of the favelas that looked so pretty from the veranda of my hotel. I had arrived at exactly the kind of place Rob had warned me to avoid.

Squatting on her heels in front of the place was a woman in a futebol jersey with the withered, heavy-lidded expression of an addict. She lifted her gaze as I climbed out onto the road, and suddenly her face creased in an incredulous and coy smile, as if she couldn't quite believe her good fortune.

She hailed me in Portuguese. She looked younger up close, her frizzy, amber-tinted hair flattened back from her forehead, her arms thin and brown.

When I shrugged apologetically she tried again, in English.

"You have a cigarette?"

"Sorry," I said, and hurried up the tracks, hoping I could get out of sight before anybody else spotted me and imagining what Rob would say about my foolishness.

When I finally got back to the hotel, I told Diogo about my anxious encounter with the first bridge and how I'd been unable to summon the courage to cross a second, which snaked along the edge of a precipice with a deep ravine beneath, the planks pocked with unlucky footsteps all along the edge. It looked as if it went on forever.

"I was in the middle of that second bridge one time and the tram starts coming," he confessed, laughing heartily. "I get to the side and I'm hanging onto the rail and looking down. Oh, man, my heart is going boom, boom, boom!" He thumped his chest for emphasis.

"Scary, man!"

I also told him about the monkeys I'd seen coming back down the tracks. A group of capuchins, not the rare native species that can only be found deep in the Tijuca forest, but the introduced variety, tawny brown with a stiff black tuft rising vertically above their faces like a tonsure. These urban capuchins are probably hybrids of at least two species from elsewhere on the continent, an example of what scientists fear could happen with tamarins.

The capuchin troop appeared to have been visiting a house party on the side of the tracks, salsa booming, people kicking a soccer ball around, food smells sizzling from an outdoor kitchen. When I spotted them, however, half the group was crossing the tracks via tree limb, and the rest were halfway up a jackfruit tree, tearing into the white pasta pulp of the fruit, which is the size of a watermelon and sheathed in a leathery, spike-encrusted peel. Originally from Asia, jackfruit has colonized many disturbed areas in Rio's forests, aided no doubt by capuchins. The seeds, which are the size of a bird's egg, pattered like hail all around the base of the tree, another example of nonnative synergy.

According to Rob, these guys are the South American equivalent of rhesus monkeys, home-invading urban terrorists. What I witnessed, however, was a surprising degree of sympatric calm. Joining the group at the communal jackfruit was a single squirrel monkey, another species introduced here by the pet trade. Not much bigger than a marmoset and far smaller than even the juvenile capuchins, the squirrel monkey had strikingly yellow fur on its arms, the result of rubbing itself with handfuls of urine. Not a habit I'd like in a pet. Squirrel monkeys thrive in a wide variety of lowland forest habitats, dining on fruit and insects and the occasional bird, much like marmosets.

Rather than drive this delicate creature away, the capuchins treated it with a surprising degree of decorum. I watched as one of the juveniles, fed up with waiting for the squirrel monkey to move along the trunk, reached up and pinched it on the bottom. Not enough to hurt. Just enough to say, *hey, can you move here, I'm trying to get to the buffet.* The squirrel monkey shifted aside, and the capuchin squeezed past. There was no screaming. No retaliation. This mutual tolerance is well documented; in their native habitat, these two species travel together for protection. What's interesting is that these descendants of captive animals have managed to maintain the practice here.[21]

Our first foray into the hills above Niteroi ends with a pedestrian waving our little sedan off—the steep and winding road ahead is good only for all-terrain vehicles, especially during the rainy season. We'd just spent the better part of an hour searching for this very road in a busy commercial district. You see something on Google maps, tidy lines superimposed on a grainy satellite image, and you think, okay, no problem. Then you ground truth and discover that online topography doesn't look nearly as rough and pitted as the real thing. Back down into the haphazardly marked city we go!

Eventually, we find our way up the other side of the ridge, where the walled compounds of the wealthy end in a rambling dirt road shaded with bamboo and jackfruit trees. Here, hard by the boundaries of the state park, residents live in exurban seclusion. We've finally reached that patch of green on the Google map.

It looks like a jungle version of the small town in Massachusetts where I grew up. A heavy black power cable stitches the sky over the washboarded dirt road. Each house is set within a parcel of several tangled acres, the kind of development Brazilians refer to as a *sítio*, a weekend retreat, a hobby farm.

Several of these retreats are almost palatial, but the place on the corner is a humble collection of cottages and sheds terraced into a hillside above a trickling stream. Laundry hangs from a line. Young kids are playing under the watchful eye of their grandmothers and the family dogs.

Diogo asks the older women if they've seen the "micos," not the *mico estrelas,* the nonnative black-tufted marmosets that have been introduced here, or the other introduced species, the *mico comum,* the common marmoset with the white tufts around its ears. What about the *mico leão da cara dourada?* The one with the golden face?

"Oh, yes, yes," they say, which is about the extent of my understanding of the conversation. They gesture to the woods across the street, where there's an elevated platform for garbage collection attached to the power line pole. Diogo translates.

"They come from there all the time. Every day they come. They travel on the power lines."

The woman with thick glasses and neatly fastened hair feeds them all the time. She likes them. But her sister doesn't like them so much because they come into the house. In our neighborhood in Columbia, all houses have screens. But here, people seem to like their windows open. Despite the risk of contracting dengue fever from a mosquito species that prefers to lurk indoors, I haven't seen a single screen. The breakfast room in my hotel has spacious open windows, and I can easily imagine a tamarin climbing in to sample the fruit bowl.

I ask the women if they've seen the tamarins today. In their native habitat, the group would probably travel over a mile in their daily foraging for food. But in a residential neighborhood, they might stick closer to their known food sources, as free-range tamarins do at the zoo. Could the wires above the road be their circuit from house to house?

We park near a sign that lays out lots for sale and set out on foot around the circle. There are primates in the vicinity: a group of black-tufted marmosets scrambling along the power line in front of somebody's hobby farm. Just like the squirrels back home. The group considers us from the mossy boughs of an old tree, tilting their heads to examine us while a stocky, old dog stands guard at the end of the driveway below. I'm hoping for a flash of copper mane; like squirrel monkeys and capuchins, it's not uncommon for the tamarins and this species of marmoset to form mixed groups in their native ranges. Even though they're foraging for the same kinds of food, more eyes means more protection from predators, especially raptors like the caracara we saw perched on top of a telephone pole just down the road.[22]

"They'd come down," Diogo says, "if we gave them a banana." That's the international currency of human-primate relations, the banana, good for currying favor with macaques, marmosets, and, we hope, tamarins. Unfortunately, we're rather poor in the banana department— I just ate mine, leaving us with one left over from lunch.

We pass a man raking leaves who says he just saw the tamarins. Yes, he's sure they were tamarins, not mico estrela. Yes, they had the golden faces. They were just here. They like that big jackfruit tree across the street.

This affinity for jackfruit, according to Leonardo Oliveira, is a key distinction between GHLTs and their golden cousins. He studies GHLTs inhabiting what is known as *cabruca,* shade-grown cacao plantations along northern Brazil's Cocoa Coast, in which farmers clear the understory for their crop but leave an overstory of native trees to provide shade. These are disturbed forests, often lacking complex layers of habitat, yet the tamarins have managed to adapt, thanks in part to the calories provided by this Asian import.[23]

We pass a father and son trundling a washing machine down the road on a handcart. Yes, they, too, have seen the tamarins. Just down there, they say, there was a film crew shooting footage of them. Last week. Just down there in that bamboo.

They seem to be ambivalent about the animals' presence. They understand they're endangered, they say, but five years ago, before the first tamarins appeared, they regularly saw birds nesting in their yard that have since disappeared. Spectacular birds, like the seven-colored tanager, birds they miss. The tamarins find everything, the father says, pawing the air tamarin-style, as if he's combing through thick vegetation for bugs and frogs and nestlings.

Down the hill, a banana plantation runs in a narrow strip along the road, with a steep forested ridge above. Across the road is another house, half hidden by a massive clump of timber bamboo.

I'm about to say something to Diogo about the incongruity of parked cars and endangered primates when I see a figure scamper across the road into the brush. My first thought is just as before: a cat. A black cat. What's that cat doing out here? Then I'm running with my binoculars slapping my chest. And Diogo is sprinting ahead and yelling, "It's them! It's them! The micos!" He's gesturing wildly toward the banana trees, which are flapping their floppy leaves as the tamarins try to flee. Their alarm calls sound . . . alarming, like the piercing last cry of a rabbit squeezed in the jaws of a predator.

Caught on the wrong side of the road, the last member of the group perches high in the swaying culms of bamboo, searching frantically for a way to get around us. As it clambers higher, we spot the reason it's traveling more slowly—two tiny infants cling to its back. They're each about the size of a chipmunk, with the brushy stubble of a black-and-tan Yorkshire terrier pup. Tamarins usually give birth to twins, then share the responsibility for carting the youngsters around. This adult we've cornered could be their father or their older sibling or their mother.

To see these animals in the wild is rare. To see one scrambling along the edge of someone's yard is disconcerting and heartening all at once, casting doubt on easy assumptions about the frailty of endangered species and their inability to tolerate human contact. One myth that is gradually giving way is that endangered species must be inherently unable to coexist with humans. In the case of tamarins, the assumption that these animals require pristine old-growth forest has shifted in response to research, which has shown that even relatively young forests can offer certain advantages for these animals.[24] Some endangered species can apparently do just fine with people around, especially if those people are feeding them.

Diogo peels his banana and wades into the roadside brush. Behind the bamboo sits a tile-roofed garage shading what appears to be a rusty tractor and various piles of odds and ends. I'm not paying any attention to what's in there and whether it might be valuable, but somebody is. I hear him shout. In Portuguese, so I have no idea what he's saying. He's further up the driveway, presumably inside the house.

Diogo pays him no heed. He's turned into the tamarin whisperer, a chunk of banana held high, a stream of comforting nonsense pouring out of his mouth. The tamarin remains unconvinced by all this attention, poised to leap. But where? Its family is calling frantically from the ridge beyond the bananas now, but how can it reach them? It calls back; we can see its tiny lower jaw flicker like the needle on a sewing machine.

Whoever is in the house shouts something again, his husky baritone sounding more and more peevish. Diogo pushes deeper, urging the tamarin to trust him.

It seems interested. It follows every move of the banana, as if maybe, if it were high enough, it might . . . .

Diogo takes another step, reaching, stretching, then crashing down into the ditch that's hidden beneath the lush vegetation. Dead branches snap and crackle like gunfire beneath his feet.

The next thing I hear is footsteps; someone's running down the driveway. With a bellowing roar, an old man charges into the road. He's shirtless, his tanned skin collecting in loose folds above his shorts, his hair wild around his bald crown, a pair of thick, misty bifocals riding down his nose.

What rivets my attention instantly, however, is the machete. A hefty blade, dark with use, is cocked over the guy's head, as if he's about to chop our heads off.

I'm closest.

He gallops about three steps toward me, pigeon-toed in his flip-flops, before he really sees me. Binoculars. Mini cam, index finger still pressing the record button. Sun hat, the kind with the flattering nylon neck drape that no self-respecting Carioca would be caught dead in.

He skids to a halt. He's panting, stiff with adrenaline, his glasses fogged so thick his eyes look like they're floating in half-rinsed cups of skim milk.

The machete wavers, then slides to his waist.

I haven't had time to move or even raise my hands in terror. With my rudimentary Portuguese failing me, I pivot and point emphatically at Diogo.

I hear Diogo say something reassuring about micos and Americans. It's probably good that I don't speak

Portuguese at this point, because I imagine there's probably a bit of sympathetic back and forth about the crazy things we crazy tourists insist on doing. Or maybe the old man is a friend of the tamarins. Maybe he feeds them under the roof of that garage—that's why they keep showing up here.

I don't get the sense he wants to be questioned by us. I'm beginning to suspect we woke him from a nap.

"Tudo bem," he proclaims, and heads back to the house.

Our quarry has taken advantage of the incident to get beyond us, hastening along through the branches to a bough that reaches over the road. We watch it shimmy across, then spring into the vegetation beyond, working its way along a path that doesn't touch the ground.

I have to keep reminding myself that these are endangered animals, that unlike the squirrels in my yard, these creatures aren't abundant everywhere. We've seen how resourceful they are. We've seen them on the ground. Seen them cross a road. Not a busy four-lane highway filled with traffic, but still a road. Maybe they could indeed find a way to make it to the golden lion tamarin preserve. Maybe those fears are justified.

One day soon, the researchers will come with baited traps, and these tamarins will be on their way back to their native haunts. As I watch this one disappear with its precious cargo, I wonder what this place will feel like when they're gone. Will this exurban habitat feel empty without them? There's been some talk of reintroducing golden lion tamarins here after the current inhabitants are gone, but many of the biologists I spoke with doubt that would be worth the investment of time and money. Ultimately, this area is still just a small island of habitat, cut off from other populations, clearly affected by human habitation. Rio's backyard, not endangered species habitat. Better to spend limited resources on improving existing preserves.

This view assumes that conservation costs a lot and has to be handled by professionals, especially when it comes to endangered species. What I see here, however, is conservation that costs nothing. Nobody's paid to monitor this endangered species or provision them. Nobody's paid to manage them. These endangered animals are as wild as the squirrels and cardinals on the bird feeder in my front yard, as wild as the rhesus in Delhi, as wild as the black bears rambling around the yards of Northampton. Not as wild as they might be elsewhere, but not tame either. The complications and contradictions are almost paralyzing, but I've come to appreciate the power of our affinity for wildlife, of our desire for an immediate, positive relationship. If you can harness that power, then you can make a real difference.

Epilogue
On the Doorstep

FACT: Peregrine falcons nest on bridges, window ledges, rooftops, and clock towers. Fourteen pairs currently nest in New York City. Twenty pairs nest in London.

———

It's spring again. Surveying my own backyard, I see the stirrings of coexistence. The peaches are blushing, the Carolina wrens are nesting in our mailbox, and the squirrels are scraping holes in the lawn in search of buried acorns. The crawlspace, happily, is comfortingly quiet.

Our yard is continuing to evolve: the trees we planted have gained some girth, and the shrubs have spread out beneath them. You'd never know much of it was recently asphalt. As the plantings leaf out and bloom, I hope the sign looks less like an excuse and more like inspiration.

The National Wildlife Federation's certification process has changed since I filled out the checklist. The question about invasive species is gone. According to David Mizejewski, the group added that question when the certification process went online in 2005. However, they could see from their website traffic that many potential gardeners working their way through the checklist stopped when they reached the "sustainable gardening practices" section and never finished, perhaps because it was intimidating or confusing or too advanced a concept for a beginning wildlife gardener. Because the organization wants the program to be as inclusive as possible, they removed this barrier to participation. "The truth is everyone has exotic plants in their yard," Mizejewski said, "myself included. The goal is not to weed out 90 percent of the people we're trying to reach." It's not just the best yards, he said, or the ones with the biggest budgets. Even a balcony can be certified habitat.

Like everyone I've met, I'm still exploring what it means to coexist. I haven't found the perfect answer for how to share food and shelter with wildlife, nor have I managed to get them to raise their young in designated spots. But I've reached the point at which I'm aware of the complexity of coexistence, where I'm beginning to see that it's a process, a relationship built on trial and error, on keen observation. And it strikes me that this is how you go about putting down roots in a place—it doesn't happen all at once, with a single harvest, with a peal of harmonious bells. It's hard, ongoing work: if it were easy to coexist with other species, we'd be doing it already.

It's challenging to find ways to grow your own fruit and have squirrels in your backyard, too, but that's what makes it interesting, this evolution of a culture of coexistence.

I spoke with Rare's Paul Butler after I got back from Brazil, and I broached the idea of trying to create a mascot for an urban population eager to make a difference. Could you somehow connect the in situ wildlife population with the ex situ population of wildlife enthusiasts, maybe by having the wildlife equivalent of the sister city movement? Could we have a local bird we cared about and an endangered bird from somewhere far away that we also adopted as our own? Butler liked that idea. His home, on the coast of Kent in England, displays its sister city affiliations right when you come into town. Why not do the same with wildlife? We brainstormed some possibilities. You could have a Baltimore oriole and a critically endangered Montserrat oriole, for example, which was nearly wiped out by recent volcanic eruptions.[1] Something unique and charismatic at home, and something equally compelling abroad. One penny from all the people in Baltimore would probably pay for the conservation efforts on Montserrat for a year. Why not?

We tried to come up with a candidate for Columbia, something unique, preferably with eyes facing forward so people think it's cute. We'd want something without any negative baggage, something that already featured prominently in a local story or legend. We could have a competition between schools to identify candidates, and then have the city vote to choose between the finalists. You could have the zoo get involved in collecting donations.

When I mentioned the Carolina wren, he ran with it. There are endangered wrens all over the world. I thought about the pair raising their young in the mailbox on the wall next to our front door. How they refused all the nest boxes I built for them, how they like to flutter inside the house if we leave a door open for a few minutes. Small but brave, loud and curious. I thought about what stories my kids might tell about them. It's a start. One potential candidate, one step toward creating a movement.

Notes

Chapter 1. Certified

Headnote: Mark W. Schwartz, Nicole L. Jurjavcic, and Joshua M. O'Brien, "Conservation's Disenfranchised Urban Poor," *BioScience* 52 (2002): 602.

1. Douglas B. Inkley, Amanda C. Staudt, and Mark Damian Duda, "Imagining the Future: Humans, Wildlife, and Global Climate Change," in *Wildlife and Society: The Science of Human Dimensions,* ed. Michael J. Manfredo et al. (Washington, DC: Island Press, 2009), 202–214.

2. National Wildlife Federation, "Certify Your Habitat," http://www.nwf.org/Get-Outside/Outdoor-Activities/Garden-for-Wildlife/Certify-Your-Wildlife-Garden.aspx.

3. Gift, *Weed,* 81–82.

4. McKinney, "Urbanization," 247.

5. Earley, *Looking for Longleaf,* 32–45.

6. Kenneth Dodd, *North American Box Turtles: A Natural History* (Norman: University of Oklahoma Press, 2002).

Chapter 2. Zoos Without Bars

Headnote: Kenn Kaufmann, "Birding That Counts," *Audubon,* November 1, 2011, 14–15.

1. Mullan, *Zoo Culture*; Croke, *Modern Ark*; Jonathan D. Ballou et al., "History, Management and Conservation Role of the Captive Lion Tamarin Populations," in Kleiman and Rylands, *Lion Tamarins*, 95–114; Golden Lion Tamarin Management Committee, "Husbandry Protocol for Golden Lion Tamarins (*Leontopithecus rosalia rosalia*)," revised 2006, http://www.nagonline.net/HUSBANDRY/husbandry_chapters.htm#T.

2. Centers for Disease Control and Prevention, "Lyme Disease—United States, 2003–2005," *Morbidity and Mortality Weekly Report* 56 (2007): 573–576; UN-Habitat, "Overview and Key Findings," *State of the World's Cities* (London: Earthscan, 2008), x–xi; Clark E. Adams, Kieran J. Lindsey, and Sara J. Ash, *Urban Wildlife Management* (Boca Raton, FL: CRC Press, 2006), 1; DeStefano, *Coyote*, 11–15; Ruediger Wittig et al., "What Should an Ideal City Look Like from an Ecological View? Ecological Demands on the Future City," in *Urban Ecology: An International Perspective on the Interaction Between Humans and Nature*, ed. John M. Marzluff et al. (New York: Springer, 2008), 691–698.

3. Kristina Cawthon Lang, "Primate Factsheets: Vervet (*Chlorocebus*) Taxonomy, Morphology, and Ecology," Primate Info Net, Wisconsin Primate Research Center Library, last modified 2006, http://pin.primate.wisc.edu/factsheets/entry/vervet; Laurance Fedigan and Linda M. Fedigan, "*Cercopithecus aethiops*: A Review of Field Studies," in *A Primate Radiation: Evolutionary Biology of the African Guenons*, ed. Annie Guatier-Hion et al. (Cambridge: Cambridge University Press, 1988), 389–411; Michael J. S. Harrison, "Optimal Foraging Strategies in the Diet of the Green Monkey, *Cercopithecus sabaeus*, at Mt. Assirik, Senegal," *International Journal of Primatology* 5 (1984): 435–471; Fedigan and Fedigan, *Cercopithecus aethiops*, 404, 398.

4. Woodrow W. Denham, *West Indian Green Monkeys: Problems in Historical Biogeography* (Basel: Karger, 1987).

5. A. M. Boulton, J. A. Horrocks, and Jean Baulu, "The Barbados Vervet Monkey (*Cercopithecus aethiops sabaeus*): Changes in Population Size and Crop Damage, 1980–1994," *International Journal of Primatology* 17 (1996): 831–844.

6. Mike Schindler, "At Dania's 'Monkey Farm,' Chimps Fight for Your Life," *Miami Daily News*, Apr. 21, 1946.

7. *Wheels Across Africa (Part 1)*, 13 min., Wilding Picture Productions, ca. 1936.

8. *The Dania Monkey Story*, dir. Dale Minnich, 45 min., 1992.

9. Associated Press, "Monkeys Threatened by Airport Expansion," *Boca Raton News*, Sept. 19, 1983; "Airport Orders an End to Monkeying Around," *Lakeland Ledger*, Sept. 21, 1983; Minnich, *Dania Monkey Story*.

10. Linda D. Wolfe, "Rhesus Macaques: A Comparative Study of Two Sites, Jaipur, India, and Silver Springs, Florida," in *Primates Face to Face: The Conservation Implications of Human-NonHuman Primate Interconnections*, eds. Augustin Fuentes and Linda D. Wolfe (Cambridge: Cambridge University Press, 2002), 325–326; Kristen Jensen et al., "B-Virus and Free-Ranging Macaques, Puerto Rico," *Emerging Infectious Diseases* 10, no. 3 (2004), doi: 10.3201/eid1003. 030257.

11. De Waal, *Ape*, 129.

12. Associated Press, "Residents Go Ape Over Plan to Nab Monkeys," *Sarasota Herald-Tribune*, June 25, 1993.

13. George M. Linz et al., "European Starlings: A Review of an Invasive Species with Far-Reaching Impacts," in *Managing Vertebrate Invasive Species: Proceedings of an International Symposium*, ed. Gary W. Witmer et al. (Fort Collins, CO: USDA APHIS Wildlife Services, National Wildlife Research Center, 2007); Baskin, *Plague of Rats*, 35–36; Todd, *Tinkering with Eden*, 135–138.

14. Harriet Ritvo, "The Order of Nature: Constructing the Collections of Victorian Zoos," in *New Worlds, New Animals: From Menagerie to Zoological Park in the Nineteenth Century*, ed. R. J. Hoage and William A. Deiss (Baltimore: Johns Hopkins University Press, 1996), 43–50; Nigel Rothfels, *Savages and Beasts: The Birth of the Modern Zoo* (Baltimore: Johns Hopkins University Press, 2008); K. Myers et al., "The Rabbit in Australia," in *The European Rabbit: The History and Biology of a Successful Colonizer*, ed. H. V. Thompson and C. M. King (Oxford: Oxford University Press, 1994), 108–157.

15. David Pimentel, Rodolfo Zuniga, and Doug Morrison, "Update on the Environmental and Economic Costs Associated with Alien-Invasive Species in the United States," *Ecological Economics* 52 (2005): 273–288.

16. Robert J. Young, *Environmental Enrichment for Captive Animals* (London: Wiley-Blackwell, 2003); Hancocks, *Different Nature*, 77–78; Croke, *Modern Ark;* DeBlieu, *Meant to Be Wild.*

Chapter 3. Little Eden

Headnote: National Agricultural Statistics Service, "U.S. Wildlife Damage," USDA, 2002, usda01.library. cornell.edu/usda/current/uswd/uswd-05-03-2002.pdf; National Agricultural Statistics Service, "Fruit Wildlife Damage," USDA, 1999, usda01.library.cornell.edu/usda/nass/fwd/wild0599.pdf.

1. Masumoto, *Epitaph for a Peach,* x–xi.

2. Michael Pollan, *The Botany of Desire: A Plant's-Eye View of the World* (New York: Random House, 2002), 43–57.

3. Gift, *Weed.*

4. Rosenzweig and Blackmar, *Park and People;* John Kieran, *A Natural History of New York* (1959; reprint ed., New York: Fordham University Press, 1982).

5. Twigs Way and Mike Brown, *Digging for Victory: Gardens and Gardening in Wartime Britain* (London: Sabrestorm, 2010); The Royal Parks, "Allotments," http://www.royalparks.org.uk/about/allotments.cfm.

6. David Quammen, "Thinking About Earthworms," in *The Flight of the Iguana: A Sidelong View of Science and Nature* (New York: Scribner, 1988), 10–16; Nico Eisenhauer et al., "Invasion of a Deciduous Forest by Earthworms: Changes in Soil Chemistry, Microflora, Microarthropods, and Vegetation," *Soil Biology and Biochemistry* 39 (2007): 1099–1110.

7. Aldo Leopold, *A Sand County Almanac* (1949; reprint ed., Oxford: Oxford University Press, 1989), 181–187.

8. Eric Mader et al., *Alternative Pollinators: Native Bees* (National Sustainable Agriculture Information Service, 2010), http://www.attra.ncat.org/attra-pub/nativebee.html.

9. Stephen B. Bambara and Michael Waldvogel, "Carpenter Bees," Department of Entomology Insect Notes, North Carolina State University, updated July 2009, http://www.ces.ncsu.edu/depts/ent/notes/Urban/carpenterbees.htm.

10. Louise Huxley, "The Grey Squirrel Review: Profile of an Invasive Alien Species, Grey Squirrel (*Sciurus carolinensis*)," *European Squirrel Initiative* (2003): 16–17; A. Okubo et al., "On the Spatial Spread of the Grey Squirrel in Britain," *Proceedings of the Royal Society London B* 238 (1989): 113–125.

11. David Quammen, "The Face of a Spider," in *Flight of the Iguana*, 3–9.

12. Holmes, *Suburban Safari*, 69–78.

13. Randall Lockwood, "Anthropomorphism Is Not a Four-Letter Word," in *Perceptions of Animals in American Culture*, ed. R. J. Hoage (Washington, DC: Smithsonian Institution Press, 1989), 41–56.

Chapter 4. The *"Monkey Menace"*

Headnote: Mewa Singh et al., "Action Plan for the Control of Commensal, Non-Human Primates in Public Places," IUCN SSC Primate Specialist Group, 2005, http://www.southasianprimatenet work.org/pdf/Action%20Plan%20Monkey%20Manners.pdf.

1. R. Witte, D. Diesing, and M. Gödde, "Urbanophob-Urbanoneutral-*Urbanophil:* Das Verhalten der Arten gegenüber dem Lebensraum Stadt," *Flora* 177 (1985): 265–282; McKinney, "Urbanization," 249–250.

2. John E. Fa and R. Lind, "Population Management and Viability of the Gibraltar Barbary Macaques," in *Evolution and Ecology of Macaque Societies*, ed. John E. Fa and Donald G. Lindburg (Cambridge: Cambridge University Press, 1996), 235–262.

3. R. S. Moore, K. A. I. Nekaris, and C. Eschmann, "Habitat Use by Western Purple-Faced Langurs *Trachypithecus vetulus nestor* (Colobinae) in a Fragmented Suburban Landscape," *Endangered Species Research* 12 (2010): 227–234.

4. Aman Sharma, "Delhi's Roads Are the Deadliest," *India Today,* February 23, 2010.

5. "Losing Delhi Ridge," *YouTube* video, 1:37, posted by *Hindustan Times Media,* February 15, 2008, http://www.youtube.com/watch?v=2pEAkAPKGPA&feature=player_embedded.

6. Linda D. Wolfe, "Rhesus Macaques: A Comparative Study of

Two Sites, Jaipur, Indian, and Silver Springs, Florida," in Fuentes and Wolfe, *Primates Face to Face*, 311–315.

7. Indrani Basu, "Hired Langoor Bites Man in East Delhi," *Times of India*, October 25, 2010.

8. R. A. Hinde and T. E. Rowell, "Communication by Postures and Facial Expressions in the Rhesus Monkey (*Macaca mulatta*)," *Proceedings of the Zoological Society of London* 138 (1962): 1–21.

9. James Vlahos, "Howl," *Outside Magazine Online*, January 28, 2009, http://www.outsideonline.com/outdoor-adventure/nature/Howl.html?page=all; Dean Nelson, "Monkey Catchers on Guard for Barack Obama's India Visit," *Telegraph*, November 1, 2010.

10. Charles H. Southwick and M. Farooq Siddiqi, "India's Rhesus Populations: Protectionism Versus Conservation Management," in *Monkeys on the Edge: Ecology and Management of Long-Tailed Macaques and Their Interface with Humans*, ed. Michael D. Gumert, Agustín Fuentes, and Lisa Jones-Engel (Cambridge: Cambridge University Press, 2011), 275–292.

11. Charles H. Southwick and M. Farooq Siddiqi, "Primate Commensalisms: The Rhesus Monkey in India," *Revue d'Écologie: La Terre et la Vie* 49 (1994): 223–231.

12. Iqbal Malik, "Consequences of Export and Trapping of Monkeys," *Primate Report* 34 (1992): 5–11.

13. Tom A. Waite et al., "Sanctuary in the City: Urban Monkeys Buffered Against Catastrophic Die-Off During ENSO-Related Drought," *EcoHealth* 4 (2007): 278–286.

14. "Monkey Menace: Delhi Deputy Mayor S. S. Bajwa Dies," *Times of India*, October 21, 2007.

15. Iqbal Malik, P. K. Seth, and Charles H. Southwick, "Population Growth of Free-Ranging Rhesus Monkeys at Tughlaqabad," *American Journal of Primatology* 7 (1984): 311–321; Iqbal Malik, "The Monkeys of Tughlaquabad," *International Primate Protection Newsletter* 11, no. 3 (1984): 3–4, available at: http://www.ippl.org/newsletter/1980s/035_v11_n3_1984–12.pdf; Iqbal Malik and Charles H. Southwick, "Feeding Behavior and Activity Patterns of Rhesus Monkeys (*Macaca mulatta*) at Tughlaquabad, India," in *Ecology and Behavior in Food-Enhanced Primate Groups*, ed. John E. Fa and Charles H. Southwick (New York: Allen R. Liss, 1988), 95–111.

16. Dmitri Alexander Photo, http://www.dmitriphoto.com/index
.php#/GALLERIES/Monkey%20Menace/1.

17. "Himachal High Court Stays Monkey Culling," *Himvani,* January 6, 2011; Sandeep K. Rattan, "Managing Human-Macaque Conflict in Himachal, India," in *Monkeys on the Edge: Ecology and Management of Long-Tailed Macaques and Their Interface with Humans,* ed. Michael D. Gumert, Agustín Fuentes, and Lisa Jones-Engel (Cambridge: Cambridge University Press, 2011), 283–286.

18. Aman Sethi, "Unsettled Lives," *Frontline,* December 3, 2005; Anita Soni, "Tell Us Where to Go," *Tehelka,* July 15, 2006; Anita Soni, "Use Us, Don't Abuse Us Please," *Tehelka,* July 22, 2006.

19. Avishek G. Dastidar, "Simian Trouble," *Hindustan Times,* March 13, 2008; Vasudha Ravichandran, Utkarsh Dwivedi, and Anupriya Karippadath, "Safe Haven for Whom?" *Envision,* Anil Agarwal Green Centre, June 2009, 2–3, www.cseindia.org/userfiles/Envision_Transformers.pdf.

20. Ekwal Imam, H. S. A. Yahya, and Iqbal Malik, "A Successful Mass Translocation of Commensal Rhesus Monkeys *Macaca mulatta* in Vrindaban, India," *Oryx* 36 (2002): 87–93; Ekwal Imam and H. S. A. Yahya, "Management of Monkey Problem in Aligarh Muslim University Campus, Uttar Pradesh," *Zoo's Print Journal* 17 (2002): 685.

21. Harish V. Nair and Avishek G. Dastidar, "HC Approves Monkey Snare," *Hindustan Times,* January 1, 2001; Bindu Shajan Perappadan, "Capital Simians May Bully the Kuno Lions," *Hindu,* August 18, 2004.

22. "CPCSEA & Primate Estate: Part 2," *Primates in Peril* (blog), March 31, 2007, http://primatesinperil.blogspot.com/2007/03/cpcsea-primateestate-part-2.html; "The Vatavaran Primate Estate," *Primates in Peril* (blog), February 8, 2007, http://primatesinperil.blogspot.com/2007/02/vatavaran-primate-estate.html.

23. Malik, "Population Growth," 311–321.

24. Rattan, "Managing Conflict," 284–285.

25. Geeta Seshamani and Kartick Satyanarayan, "The Dancing Bears of India," World Society for the Protection of Animals, occasional report (London, 1997); Neil D'Cruze et al., "Dancing Bears in India: A Sloth Bear Status Report," *Ursus* 22 (2011): 99–105; "The

Life of a Dancing Bear," *International Animal Rescue,* http://www
.internationalanimalrescue.org/projects/13/The+life+of+a+dancing
+bear.html.

26. Meena Radhakrishna, "Civil Society's Uncivil Acts: Dancing
Bear and Starving Kalandar," *Economic and Political Weekly* 42
(2007): 4222–4226.

Chapter 5. The Night Visitor

Headnote: David Pimentel, Rodolfo Zuniga, and Doug Morrison,
"Update on the Environmental and Economic Costs Associated with
Alien-Invasive Species in the United States," *Ecological Economics* 52
(2005): 276.

1. "Rattus rattus," *Global Invasive Species Database,* last modified January 11, 2011, http://www.issg.org/database/species/ecology
.asp?si=19&fr=1&sts=&lang=EN; "Rattus norvegicus," *Global Invasive Species Database,* last modified March 14, 2011, http://www
.issg.org/database/species/ecology.asp?si=159&fr=1&sts=sss; Sullivan, *Rats,* 6.

2. D. H. R. Spennemann, "Distribution of Rat Species (*Rattus*
Spp.) on the Atolls of the Marshall Islands: Past and Present Disper-
sal," *Atoll Research Bulletin 446* (Washington, DC: Smithsonian Institution, 1997); James Silver, "The Introduction and Spread of House
Rats in the United States," *Journal of Mammology* 8 (1927): 58–60.

3. Robert S. Devine, *Alien Invasion: America's Battle with Non-
Native Animals and Plants* (Washington, DC: National Geographic
Society, 1998), 3.

4. Joyce Carol Oates, "Against Nature," in *(Woman) Writer: Oc-
casions and Opportunities* (New York: Dutton, 1988), 68.

5. Centers for Disease Control and Prevention and US Department of Housing and Urban Development, "Disease Vectors
and Pests," *Healthy Housing Reference Manual* (Atlanta: US Department of Health and Human Services, 2006), 2–3; Samuel Anthony
Barnett, *The Story of Rats: Their Impact on Us, and Our Impact on
Them* (Crows Nest, Australia: Allen and Unwin, 2001), 27–44.

6. Ike Matthews, *Full Revelations of a Professional Rat-Catcher,
After 25 Years' Experience* (London: Friendly Societies, 1898),

available at: http://www.gutenberg.org/files/17243/17243-h/17243-h.htm.

7. Sullivan, *Rats*, 11. Robert Corrigan, "Answers from an Urban Rodentologist," *City Room* (blog), *New York Times*, November 28, 2011, http://cityroom.blogs.nytimes.com/2007/11/28/answers-from-the-urban-rodentologist/.

8. Centers for Disease Control, "Disease Vectors," 2–3.

9. Robert Corrigan, "Answers from an Urban Rodentologist, Part 2," *City Room* (blog), *New York Times*, November 29, 2011, http://cityroom.blogs.nytimes.com/2007/11/29/answers-from-the-urban-rodentologist-part-2/.

Chapter 6. Backyard Bruins

Headnote: David R. Foster et al., "Wildlife Dynamics in the Changing New England Landscape," *Journal of Biogeography* 29 (2002): 1342.

1. Jerry Leonard, *Wildlife Watching in the U.S.: The Economic Impacts on National and State Economies in 2006* (Arlington, VA: US Fish and Wildlife Service, 2008), 6.

2. David R. Foster et al., "Wildlife Dynamics in the Changing New England Landscape," *Journal of Biogeography* 29 (2002): 1342.

3. Powell, *Ecology and Behavior;* Pam Belluck, "Study of Black Bears Finds It's Not the Mamas That Should Be Feared the Most," *New York Times*, May 11, 2011.

4. Herrero, *Bear Attacks;* Stephen Herrero et al., "Fatal Attacks by American Black Bear on People: 1900–2009," *Journal of Wildlife Management* 75 (2011): 596–603.

5. Jeremy E. Inglis and Mike L. Wilton, "Seasonal Movement Patterns and Feeding Habits of Large Adult Male Black Bears in Algonquin Provincial Park, Ontario," *Algonquin Eco Watch*, http://www.algonquin-eco-watch.com/blackbear.htm.

6. Belluck, "Not the Mamas"; Herrero, *Bear Attacks*.

7. J. Gilchrist et al., "Nonfatal Dog Bite—Related Injuries Treated in Hospital Emergency Departments—United States, 2001," *Morbidity and Mortality Weekly Report* 52 (2003): 605–610, http://www.cdc.gov/mmwr/preview/mmwrhtml/mm5226a1.htm.

8. Lynn Rogers, "Does Diversionary Feeding Create Nuisance Bears and Jeopardize Public Safety?" *Human-Wildlife Interactions* 5 (2011): 287–295; Valerius Geist, "Wildlife Habituation: Advances in Understanding and Management Application," *Human-Wildlife Interactions* 5, no. 2 (2011): 9–12; Lynn Rogers and S. Mansfield, "Misconceptions About Black Bears: A Response to Geist," *Human-Wildlife Interactions* 5, no. 2 (2011): 173–176.

9. J. J. Beringer, S. G. Siebert, and M. R. Pelton, "Incidence of Road Crossing by Black Bears on Pisgah National Forest, North Carolina," *International Conference on Bear Research and Management* 8 (1990): 85–92; J. Walter McCown et al., "Effect of Traffic Volume on American Black Bears in Central Florida, USA," *Ursus* 20 (2009): 39–46; M. J. Reynolds-Hogland and M. S. Mitchell, "Effects of Roads on Habitat Quality for Bears in the Southern Appalachians: A Long-Term Study," *Journal of Mammalogy* 88 (2007): 1050–1061.

10. M. L. Fies, D. D. Martin, and G. T. Blank, "Movements and Rates of Return of Translocated Black Bears," *Papers of the International Conference on Bear Research and Management* 7 (1987): 369–372; Lynn L. Rogers, "Effects of Translocation Distance on Frequency of Return by Adult Black Bears," *Wildlife Society Bulletin* 14 (1987): 76–80.

11. Powell, *Ecology and Behavior*, 14–16.

12. Scott G. Miller, Richard L. Knight, and Clinton K. Miller, "Wildlife Responses to Pedestrians and Dogs," *Wildlife Society Bulletin*, 29, no. 1 (2001): 124–132.

13. John E. McDonald Jr. and Todd K. Fuller, "Effects of Spring Acorn Availability on Black Bear Diet, Milk Composition, and Cub Survival," *Journal of Mammalogy* 86 (2005): 1022–1028; Dave Taylor, *Black Bears: A Natural History* (Markham, ON: Fitzhenry and Whiteside, 2006), 57–59.

14. Kenneth D. Elowe and Wendell E. Dodge, "Factors Affecting Black Bear Reproductive Success and Cub Survival," *Journal of Wildlife Management* 53 (1989): 962–968; Albert L. LeCount, "Causes of Black Bear Cub Mortality," *International Conference on Bear Research and Management* 7 (1987): 75–82.

15. Masterson, *Living with Bears,* 210.

16. Dan Ring, "Massachusetts Sees Drop in Number of Black Bears

Killed During 2010 Hunting Seasons," *Republican,* February 8, 2011; Keith Bradsher, "Ban Bear Hunts? Trends Converge to Force a Vote," *New York Times,* August 27, 1996.

17. Brunner, *Bears,* 216–217.

Chapter 7. Notes from a Twenty-First-Century Rat Catcher

Headnote: David Pimentel, Rodolfo Zuniga, and Doug Morrison, "Update on the Environmental and Economic Costs Associated with Alien-Invasive Species in the United States," *Ecological Economics* 52 (2005): 275; M. Lynne Corn et al., "Invasive Non-Native Species: Background and Issues for Congress," Congressional Research Service, updated November 25, 2002, http://www.nationalaglawcenter .org/assets/crs/RL30123.pdf.

1. Samuel I. Zeveloff, *Raccoons: A Natural History* (Vancouver: UBC Press, 2002), 91–111.

2. Lopez, *When Raccoons Fall Through Your Ceiling,* 9–10.

3. L. Kristen Page et al., "Backyard Raccoon Latrines and Risk for *Baylisascaris procyonis* Transmission to Humans," *Emerging Infectious Disease* 15 (2009): 1530–1531; Jason E. Perlman et al., "*Baylisascaris procyonis* Neural Larva Migrans in an Infant in New York City," *Journal of Neuroparasitology* 1 (2010): 1–5.

4. Lopez, *When Raccoons Fall Through Your Ceiling,* 92–95.

5. Terrell P. Salmon, Desley A. Whisson, and Rex E. Marsh, *Wildlife Pest Control Around Gardens and Homes,* 2nd ed. (Oakland: University of California Agriculture and Natural Resources, 2006), 67.

6. Ekwal Imam, H. S. A. Yahya, and Iqbal Malik, "A Successful Mass Translocation of Commensal Rhesus Monkeys *Macaca mulatta* in Vrindaban, India," *Oryx* 36 (2002): 87–93.

7. Lopez, *When Raccoons Fall Through Your Ceiling,* 24–25.

8. W. Paul Gorenzel and Terrell P. Salmon, *Bird Hazing Manual: Techniques and Strategies for Dispersing Birds from Spill Sites* (Oakland: University of California Agriculture and Natural Resources, 2008).

9. Eric A. Tillman, John S. Humphrey, and Michael L. Avery, "Use of Vulture Carcasses and Effigies to Reduce Damage to Property and

Agriculture," in *Proceedings of the 20th Vertebrate Pest Conference,* ed. R. M. Timm and R. H. Schmidt (Davis: University of California, Davis, 2002), 123–128.

10. Isolde Raftery, "400 Park Geese Die, for Human Fliers' Sake," *New York Times,* July 12, 2010; Prospect Park Management Advisory Committee, *Canada Goose Management Plan,* November 2010, http://bit.ly/I9EpuK.

11. "Fruit Wildlife Damage," National Agricultural Statistics Service, May 26, 1999, http://usda.mannlib.cornell.edu/MannUsda/viewDocumentInfo.do?documentID=1078; Masumoto, *Epitaph for a Peach,* 200–201.

Chapter 8. The Bees of Brooklyn

Headnote: Roger A. Morse and Nicholas W. Calderone, "The Value of Honey Bees as Pollinators of U.S. Crops in 2000," *Bee Culture* 128 (2000): 1–15; John E. Losey and Mace Vaughan, "The Economic Value of Ecological Services Provided by Insects," *BioScience* 56 (2006): 311–323.

1. *Queen of the Sun,* dir. Taggart Siegel, 83 min., Collective Eye, 2010.

2. E. C. Mussen, *Pest Notes: Bee and Wasp Stings,* University of California Agricultural Natural Resource Publication 7449, September 2011, http://www.ipm.ucdavis.edu/PMG/PESTNOTES/pn7449.html.

3. David W. Roubik and Melvin M. Boreham, "Learning to Live with Africanized Bees," *Interciencia* 15, no. 3 (1990): 146; Winston, *Killer Bees.*

4. Washington State University Extension, "Insect Answers: Protecting Honeybees Against Yellowjackets," *Washington State University Extension Fact Sheet FS017E,* 2010, cru.cahe.wsu.edu/CE Publications/FS017E/FS017E.pdf.

5. Longgood, *Queen Must Die,* 15; Langstroth, *Hive and Honey-Bee,* 53–55.

6. Longgood, *Queen Must Die,* 13; Buchmann, *Letters from the Hive,* 127–128; Seeley, *Honeybee Democracy.*

7. Longgood, *Queen Must Die,* 54.

8. Flottam, *Backyard Beekeeper,* 35–38.

9. Emily S. Rueb, "Around Bee Rescue, Honey and Rancor," *City Room* (blog), *New York Times,* August 30, 2011, http://cityroom .blogs.nytimes.com/2011/08/30/bee-rescue/.

10. Winston, *Killer Bees.*

11. *Added Value,* http://www.added-value.org/; Jill Slater, "A Farm in the Asphalt Heart of Brooklyn," *Seasonal Chef,* October 2005, http://www.seasonalchef.com/farmredhook.htm.

12. Susan Dominus, "The Mystery of the Red Bees of Red Hook," *New York Times,* November 29, 2010.

13. Wilson, *Hive,* 140–150.

14. Dennis van Engelsdorp et al., "'Entombed Pollen': A New Condition in Honey Bee Colonies Associated with Increased Risk of Colony Mortality," *Journal of Invertebrate Pathology* 101 (2009): 147–149; C. A. Mullin et al., "High Levels of Miticides and Agrochemicals in North American Apiaries: Implications for Honey Bee Health," *PLoS ONE* 5 (2010): 9754.

15. Jacobsen, *Fruitless Fall;* Conrad, *Natural Beekeeping,* 226–229.

16. Backwards Bees, www.backwardsbeekeepers.com.

17. US Department of Agriculture–Agricultural Research Service, "What to Do If Attacked by Africanized Honey Bees," http://www .ars.usda.gov/research/docs.htm?docid=11059&page=3.

18. Flottam, *Backyard Beekeeper,* 22.

19. Langstroth, *Hive and Honey-Bee,* xv–xvi; Longgood, *Queen Must Die,* 36–37.

20. Longgood, *Queen Must Die,* 188.

21. US Department of Agriculture–Agricultural Research Service, "What to Do."

22. Langstroth, *Hive and Honey-Bee,* 365–366.

23. Great Pollinator Project, "Bee Watchers: Bee Fact Sheet," http://greatpollinatorproject.org/pollinators/resources.

24. David Bjerklie, "City Centipede: An Urban Legend with Real Legs," *Time,* August 5, 2002; Ira Flatow, "Taking a Walk on New York's Wild Side," *Science Friday, National Public Radio,* April 6, 2012, http://www.npr.org/2012/04/06/150123939/taking-a-walk -on-new-yorks-wild-side; Center for Biodiversity and Conservation,

"Metropolitan Biodiversity, Leaf Litter Invertebrates of Central Park, Summary," http://cbc.amnh.org/leaflitter/summary.html.

25. Erik Olsen, "City Bees Newly Discovered, Yet Here All Along," *City Room* (blog), *New York Times,* November 10, 2011, http://cityroom.blogs.nytimes.com/2011/11/10/bees/.

26. Horn, *Bees in America,* 68–80.

27. Sternfeld, *Walking the High Line.*

28. David and Hammond, *High Line;* Paul Goldberger, "Miracle Above Manhattan," *National Geographic,* April 2011, 122–137; Adam Gopnik, "A Walk on the High Line," *New Yorker,* May 21, 2001, 44–50.

29. John Kieran, *A Natural History of New York* (1959; reprint ed., New York: Fordham University Press, 1982); Rosenzweig and Blackmar, *Park;* Sanderson, *Mannahatta;* Betsy McCully, *City at the Water's Edge: A Natural History of New York* (Piscataway, NJ: Rutgers University Press, 2007).

30. Todd, *Tinkering with Eden,* 135–138; Charles Mitchell, "The Bard's Bird, or the Slings and Arrows of Avicultural Harmony, a Tragicomedy in Five Acts," *Terrain.org,* no. 26, 2010, http://www.terrain.org/articles/26/mitchell.htm.

Chapter 9. Zoopolis

Headnote: Dener Giovanni, "1st National Report on the Traffic of Wild Animals," *Renctas* (2001): 31–32.

1. McKinney, "Urbanization," 256.

2. Steward T. A. Pickett et al., "Beyond Urban Legends: An Emerging Framework of Urban Ecology, as Illustrated by the Baltimore Ecosystem Study," *BioScience* 58 (2008): 139–150.

3. Marina H. L. Duarte, Vinícius D. L. R. Goulart, and Robert J. Young, "Designing Laboratory Marmoset Housing: What Can We Learn from Urban Marmosets?" *Applied Animal Behavior Science* 137, no. 3 (2012): 127–136.

4. "Brazil: Country Specific Information," US Department of State, http://travel.state.gov/travel/cis_pa_tw/cis/cis_1072.html#crime.

5. Lisa W. Foderaro, "Dark Days Behind It, Central Park Pulses at Night," *New York Times,* December 28, 2011.

6. Ann P. Kinzig et al., "The Effects of Human Socioeconomic Status and Cultural Characteristics on Urban Patterns of Biodiversity," *Ecology and Society* 10 (2005), http://www.ecologyandsociety.org/vol10/iss1/art23/.

7. *Pixote*, dir. Hector Babenco, 128 min., Embrafilme, 1981; *City of God*, dir. Fernando Meirelles, 130 min., O2 Filmes, 2002.

8. Simon Romero, "Rio Slum Is 'Pacified' in Advance of Games," *New York Times*, November 13, 2011; John Lee Anderson, "Through Rio's Favelas, Guns Drawn," *News Desk* (blog), *New Yorker*, Oct. 20, 2009, http://www.newyorker.com/online/blogs/newsdesk/2009/10/police-raid-rio-favela.html.

9. Marina H. L. Duarte et al., "Noisy Human Neighbours Affect Where Urban Monkeys Live," *Biological Letters* 7 (2011): 840–842.

10. Duarte, Goulart, and Young, "Designing Laboratory Marmoset Housing," 7.

11. Marina H. L. Duarte and Robert J. Young, "Sleeping Site Selection by Urban Marmosets (*Callithrix penicillata*) Under Conditions of Exceptionally High Predator Density," *International Journal of Primatology* 32 (2010): 329–334.

12. Giovana C. Leite, Marina H. L. Duarte, and Robert J. Young, "Human-Marmoset Interactions in a City Park," *Applied Animal Behaviour Science* 132 (2011): 187–192.

13. Vinicius D. L. R. Goulart, Camilla Texeira, and Robert J. Young, "Analysis of Callouts Made in Relation to Wild Urban Marmosets (*Callithrix penicillata*) and Their Implications for Management," *European Journal of Wildlife Research* 56 (2010): 641–649.

14. Ibid., 647.

15. Duarte and Young, "Sleeping Site Selection," 334.

16. Maria C. M. Kierulff, "Invasive Introduced Golden-Headed Lion Tamarins: A New Threat to Golden Lion Tamarins," *Tamarin Tales* 10 (2010): 5–7.

17. Alexander C. Lees and Diana J. Bell, "A Conservation Paradox for the 21st Century: The European Wild Rabbit *Oryctolagus cuniculus*, an Invasive Alien and an Endangered Native Species," *Mammal Review* 38 (2008): 309.

18. IUCN, "The IUCN Red List of Threatened Species," www.iucnredlist.org; Lou Ann Dietz, "Community Conservation Educa-

tion Project for the Golden Lion Tamarin, Brazil: Building Support for Habitat Conservation," in *Culture: The Missing Element in Conservation and Development,* ed. R. J. Hoage and Katy Moran (Dubuque, IA: Kendall-Hunt, 1988), 85–94; A. B. Rylands et al., "A History of Lion Tamarin Research and Conservation," in Kleiman and Rylands, *Lion Tamarins,* 3–41; Ardith Eudey, "To Procure or Not to Procure," in Norton et al., *Ethics on the Ark,* 146–154.

19. Denise M. Rambaldi, Carlos R. Ruiz-Miranda, and James M. Dietz, "Metapopulation Management of Golden Lion Tamarins," *Tamarin Tales* 10 (2010): 3.

20. M. Cecilia Kierulff et al., "Reintroduction and Translocation as Conservation Tools for Golden Lion Tamarins," in Kleiman and Rylands, *Lion Tamarins,* 271–282.

21. R. W. Sussman, *Primate Ecology and Social Structure,* vol. 2 (Needham Heights, MA: Pearson Custom, 2000).

22. Leonardo C. Oliveira and James M. Dietz, "Predation Risk and the Interspecific Association of Two Brazilian Atlantic Forest Primates in Cabruca Agroforest," *American Journal of Primatology* 73 (2011): 852–860.

23. Leonardo C. Oliveira et al., "Abundance of Jackfruit (*Artocarpus heterophyllus*) Affects Group Characteristics and Use of Space by Golden-Headed Lion Tamarins (*Leontopithecus chrysomelas*) in Cabruca Agro-Forest," *Environmental Management* 48 (2011): 248–262.

24. Leonardo C. Oliveira et al., "Key Tree Species for the Golden-Headed Lion Tamarin and Implications for Shade-Cocoa Management in Southern Bahia, Brazil," *Animal Conservation* 13 (2010): 60–70; A. Waite et al., "Sanctuary in the City: Urban Monkeys Buffered Against Catastrophic Die-Off During ENSO-Related Drought," *EcoHealth* 4 (2007): 278–286.

Epilogue

Headnote: Madhu Venkataramanan, "A Flying Success," *Scienceline,* May 30, 2011, http://scienceline.org/2011/05/a-flying-success/; Helen Babbs, "Urban Birdlife: Encouraging Peregrine Falcons in London," *Ecologist,* August 24, 2010, http://www.theecologist.org/

how_to_make_a_difference/wildlife/573303/urban_birdlife_encour
aging_peregrine_falcons_in_london.html.
1. B. Dalsgaard et al., "Impacts of a Volcanic Eruption on the Forest Bird Community of Montserrat, Lesser Antilles," *Ibis* 149 (2007):
298–312; G. M. Hilton et al., "Rapid Decline of the Volcanically
Threatened Montserrat Oriole, *Biological Conservation* 111 (2003):
79–89.

Select Bibliography

Baskin, Yvonne. *A Plague of Rats and Rubbervines: The Growing Threat of Species Invasions.* Washington, DC: Island Press, 2002.

Brunner, Bernd. *Bears: A Brief History.* New Haven: Yale University Press, 2007.

Buchmann, Stephen L. *Letters from the Hive: An Intimate History of Bees, Honey, and Humankind.* New York: Bantam Books, 2005.

Conrad, Ross. *Natural Beekeeping: Organic Approaches to Modern Apiculture.* White River Junction, VT: Chelsea Green, 2007.

Croke, Vicki. *The Modern Ark: The Story of Zoos, Past, Present and Future.* New York: Scribner, 1997.

David, Joshua, and Robert Hammond. *High Line: The Inside Story of New York City's Park in the Sky.* New York: FSG Originals, 2011.

DeBlieu, Jan. *Meant to Be Wild: The Struggle to Save Endangered Species Through Captive Breeding.* Golden, CO: Fulcrum, 1991.

DeStefano, Stephen. *Coyote at the Kitchen Door: Living with Wildlife in Suburbia.* Cambridge, MA: Harvard University Press, 2010.

de Waal, Frans. *The Ape and the Sushi Master: Cultural Reflections by a Primatologist.* New York: Basic Books, 2001.

Earley, Lawrence S. *Looking for Longleaf: The Fall and Rise of an American Forest.* Chapel Hill: University of North Carolina Press, 2006.

Flottam, Kim. *The Backyard Beekeeper.* Rev. ed. Minneapolis, MN: Quarry Books, 2010.

Fuentes, Augustin, and Linda D. Wolfe, eds. *Primates Face to Face: The Conservation Implications of Human-Nonhuman Primate Interconnections.* Cambridge: Cambridge University Press, 2002.

Gift, Nancy. *A Weed by Any Other Name: The Virtues of a Messy Lawn, or Learning to Love the Plants We Didn't Plant.* Boston: Beacon, 2009.

Hancocks, David. *A Different Nature: The Paradoxical World of Zoos and Their Uncertain Future.* Berkeley: University of California Press, 2002.

Herrero, Stephen. *Bear Attacks: Their Causes and Avoidance.* New York: Nick Lyons Books/Winchester Press, 1985.

Holmes, Hannah. *Suburban Safari: A Year on the Lawn.* New York: Bloomsbury, 2005.

Horn, Tammy. *Bees in America: How the Honey Bee Shaped a Nation.* Lexington: University of Kentucky Press, 2005.

Jacobsen, Rowan. *Fruitless Fall: The Collapse of the Honey Bee and the Coming Agricultural Crisis.* New York: Bloomsbury, 2008.

Kleiman, Devra G., ed. *The Biology and Conservation of the Callitrichidae: A Symposium Held at the Conservation and Research Center, National Zoological Park, Smithsonian Institution, August 18–20, 1975.* Washington, DC: Smithsonian Institution Press, 1977.

Kleiman, Devra G., and Anthony B. Rylands, eds. *Lion Tamarins: Biology and Conservation.* Washington, DC: Smithsonian Institution Press, 2002.

Langstroth, L. L. *Langstroth on the Hive and the Honey-Bee: A Bee Keeper's Manual.* 1853. Project Gutenberg, 2011, http://www.gutenberg.org/files/24583/24583-h/24583-h.htm#Page_53.

Longgood, William F. *The Queen Must Die! And Other Affairs of Bees and Men.* New York: Norton, 1985.

Lopez, Andrea Dawn. *When Raccoons Fall Through Your Ceiling: The Handbook for Coexisting with Wildlife.* Denton: University of North Texas Press, 2002.

Masterson, Linda, and Tom Beck. *Living with Bears: A Practical Guide to Bear Country.* Boulder, CO: Pixyjack Press, 2006.

Masumoto, David Mas. *Epitaph for a Peach: Four Seasons on My Family Farm.* San Francisco: HarperCollins, 1995.

McKinney, Michael L. "Urbanization as a Major Cause of Biotic Homogenization." *Biological Conservation* 127 (2006): 247–260.

Mullan, Bob, and Gary Marvin. *Zoo Culture: The Book About Watching People Watch Animals.* 2nd ed. Urbana: University of Illinois Press, 1999.

Norton, Bryan, et al., eds. *Ethics on the Ark: Zoos, Animal Welfare, and Wildlife Conservation*. Washington, DC: Smithsonian, 1996.

Powell, Roger A., John W. Zimmerman, and David E. Seaman. *Ecology and Behavior of North American Black Bears: Home Ranges, Habitat, and Social Organization*. New York: Chapman and Hall, 1997.

Quammen, David. *The Flight of the Iguana*. New York: Scribner, 1988.

Queen of the Sun. Directed by Taggart Siegel. 83 min. Collective Eye. 2010.

Rosenzweig, Roy, and Elizabeth Blackmar. *The Park and the People: A History of Central Park*. Ithaca, NY: Cornell University Press, 1993.

Salmon, Terrell P., Desley A. Whisson, and Rex E. Marsh. *Wildlife Pest Control Around Gardens and Homes*. 2nd ed. Oakland: University of California Agriculture and Natural Resources, 2006.

Sanderson, Eric. *Mannahatta: A Natural History of New York*. New York: Abrams, 2009.

Seeley, Thomas D. *Honeybee Democracy*. Princeton, NJ: Princeton University Press, 2010.

Sternfeld, Joel. *Walking the High Line*. 2nd ed. London: Steidl, 2009.

Sullivan, Robert. *Rats: Observations on the History and Habitat of the City's Most Unwanted Inhabitants*. New York: Bloomsbury, 2004.

Todd, Kim. *Tinkering with Eden: A Natural History of Exotic Species*. New York: Norton, 2002.

Tudge, Colin. *Last Animals at the Zoo: How Mass Extinction Can Be Stopped*. Washington, DC: Island Press, 1992.

Wilson, Bee. *The Hive: The Story of the Honeybee and Us.* New York: St. Martin's Griffin, 2007.

Winston, Mark L. *Killer Bees: The Africanized Honeybee in the Americas.* Cambridge, MA: Harvard University Press, 1992.

Index

Index

circuses, 134
cities: animals living on margins of,
    37; dual nature of, 9; landscape
    ordinances, 10; percentage of
    humans living in, 20–21; wildlife
    species adopted as symbols by,
    277–278. *See also* urbanization
citizen scientists, 264
climate and climate change, 2, 3
coatis, 302–303, 304
cockroaches, 8
coexistence, of humans with wild-
    life, 81, 113, 134, 142–143, 326;
    competition for food and, 56–57,
    69–72; limits of, 231; meaning of,
    327–328
colony collapse disorder, 256
Columbia (South Carolina), city
    of, 200, 275, 318, 328–329; city
    codes, 12; Riverbanks Zoo, 19
common marmoset, 318
common yellowthroat, 272
composting, 5
Cooper's hawk, 7
copperhead, 202, 243
coral reefs, 2
coreopsis, 267
cows, 96, 111, 124, 130; garbage
    as food for, 104; sacred status in
    India, 104, 128
coyotes, 236
crayfish, 240
creepers, 7
crepe myrtle, 55
Criadouro Científico, 294
crows, 82, 104
Cuban anole, 50

daffodils, 163
deer, 17, 20, 52, 169
deforestation, 309
Delhi (India), city of, 74–76, 325;
    airport, 77–78, 81; garbage in,
    104; monkey population of,
    105; poverty in, 79–81, 103; sanc-
    tuary for monkeys near, 116–121,

124, 125–126; traffic danger in,
    84–85
dengue fever, 318
Denis, Armand, 25–27, 36
disease, zoonotic, 136, 151, 218,
    222, 229. *See also* rabies
distemper, 229, 298
dogwood tree, 55
domestication, 133–135
dormice, 60
Duarte, Marina, 284–290
Dutch elm disease, 47

earthworms, 58–59
ecosystems, 42, 200, 243, 267
ecotourism, 312
elephants, 94, 134
endangered species, 1, 43, 209, 325;
    human contact with, 321–322; as
    invasive species, 307–308; trap-
    ping and relocation of, 310
eucalyptus trees, 289
excluders, for nuisance animals,
    204, 214, 222, 224
extinction, 2, 9, 277

falcons, 134
fig trees, 286, 289
fireflies, 2
fires, 14
Fish and Wildlife Service, US, 208,
    209
Fitzgerald Lake Conservation Area
    (Massachusetts), 193
flies, 100, 103, 136–137, 268
flowers: bees and, 60, 61, 63, 267,
    272; as food for monkeys, 23, 41
flycatchers, 7, 58
flying squirrels, 155
food chain, 72, 174
foxes, 46, 191, 219
free-tailed bat, 204
frogs, 2, 302, 320
Fuller, Dave, 163–168, 180–181,
    190–191; on bear behavior
    toward humans, 171–173; on

Index

Index

bees, 255; social structure and behavior, 246–247; stings of, 241, 246, 257, 258–259
house sparrows, 46, 264, 268, 274
hoverfly, 60
hummingbirds, 7
hyacinth macaw, 296, 299

IBAMA (Brazilian Institute for the Environment and Renewable Natural Resources), 293, 294, 297
iguanas, 22–23, 29
insecticides, 53, 65
insects, 60, 241, 253–254
International Journal of Primatology, 24
International Union for Conservation of Nature (IUCN), 74, 309
interspecies contact, 34–35
invasive species, 5, 47, 310
inventories, 6
invertebrate animals, 9
irises, 18
Irwin, Steve ("Crocodile Hunter"), 35, 202

jackfruit, 315, 317, 319–320
Jamaican anole, 50
Johnson, Liz, 261–263
jumping mice, 208
juncos, 7
juniper, 10

Kalandars, 133–134, 135, 139, 142
"keyholes" (fetid rainwater pools), 8
Kierulff, Cecilia, 310, 311
kites, 96, 104
knapweed, 267
Knight anole, 50

landscape architecture, 55
langurs, 89, 90, 120; garbage as food source for, 104; long tails of, 92; trained, 98–99. *See also* monkeys, in India

Lasioglossum gotham (sweat bee species in New York), 263
laurel oak, 10
lawns, 2, 22, 163; herbicide use on, 6, 12; ornamental vegetation and, 55; size of, 5; unmown, 4; watering and fertilizing of, 14; wilderness boundary and, 60
leafcutter bees, 62
LEED (Leadership in Energy and Environmental Design), 4, 5
legless lizards, 7
Leopold, Aldo, 61, 69
light pollution, 284
lions, 89, 94
live oak, 10
lizards, 7, 29, 50–51, 291
longleaf pine, 14
Lyme disease, 20

macaques. *See* rhesus macaques
macaws, 295, 296, 299
Machado, Cindy, 72
magnolia tree, 55
Malik, Iqbal, 102, 111, 113, 116, 230; on population growth of monkeys, 126; translocation of monkeys and, 125
manatee, 43
Mangabeiras Municipal Park (Brazil), 300–306
mangroves, 30, 32, 42
marmosets. *See* black-tufted marmoset
"mason" bee, 62–63
McKinney, Michael, 9, 274
Metropolitan Biodiversity Program, 261
mice, 8, 210
microclimate, 272
Minnich, Dale, 21, 27, 31, 40, 42
Mississippi kite, 8
Mizejewski, David, 4–5, 327
mockingbirds, 7, 269
monarch butterfly, 8, 268

Index

Index

07 · 15